W9-CJR-316

FOUNDATION
CENTER

Knowledge to build on.

FOUNDATION FUNDAMENTALS

Eighth Edition

Sarah Collins, Editor

FOUNDATION
CENTER
Knowledge to build on.

FUNDRAISING GUIDES

FOUNDATION FUNDAMENTALS

Eighth Edition

Sarah Collins, Editor

Library of Congress Cataloging-in-Publication Data
Foundation fundamentals. Sarah Collins, editor.— 8th ed.
    p. cm.
  Includes bibliographical references.
  ISBN-13: 978-1-59542-156-2 (pbk.)
  1. Endowments—United States—Information services. 2. Research
grants—United States—Information services. I. Foundation Center.
  HV41.9.U5F686 2008
  361.7'632—dc22
                                        2008004530

Table of Contents

List of Figures

Foreword

When the Foundation Center was established in 1956, it could identify only about 5,000 U.S. philanthropic foundations making grants totaling $300 million a year. Fifty years later, we track some 72,000 foundations disbursing more than $41 billion in grants annually. In addition to the dramatic increase in the number of independent, corporate, and community foundations and in their levels of giving, particularly in recent years, we are seeing the emergence of new forms of philanthropy and new kinds of "foundations." Collecting information on philanthropic institutions and charting their giving has become an ever-increasing challenge—and meeting that challenge continues to be the hallmark of the Foundation Center.

The Foundation Center has been a vital force in the evolution of the new philanthropic sector. During its first 51 years, it has grown from a single library with books about foundations, to publisher of *The Foundation Directory* and a whole line of directories and reports on foundations and their giving, to the preeminent resource—online and at sites around the country—for information and knowledge about the dynamic field of organized philanthropy.

During the recent period of exponential growth and diversification of philanthropy, the nonprofit sector has also grown dramatically in size, scope of activity, and importance to the vitality of our civil society, not only in the United States but all over the world. The sector has come to rely on the Center for information, education, and assistance in researching and approaching foundations for support. Indeed, for anyone wanting to learn about the world of organized philanthropy, the Foundation Center is the place to go.

Having recently celebrated our 50th anniversary at a time of exploding media focus on foundations—and therefore increased competition for their funds, as well as interest in becoming a part of this exciting field—the Center is releasing the eighth edition of our flagship guide, *Foundation Fundamentals.* As with prior editions, this one provides an in-depth, systematic orientation to the foundation field and the funding research process. It also describes the many tools, resources, and services available from the Center and from other sources to assist you in your quest for reliable information. We have revised this new edition to focus primarily on web resources to help those of you new to the field to take advantage of cutting-edge technologies in your research.

We hope that you will find this guide of value in your work.

Sara L. Engelhardt, President
The Foundation Center
January 2008

Introduction

The nonprofit sector plays an increasingly essential role in American society. As the delivery of more human services that were formerly conducted by government agencies becomes the responsibility of voluntary agencies, and as attention is drawn to prominent philanthropies and the new wealth generated largely by the boom in technology fields, average citizens are seeking to understand the place of foundations in our world.

During a period when the nonprofit sector, and foundations, in particular, saw unprecedented growth and attention, one fact has remained constant: for more than 25 years, *Foundation Fundamentals* has introduced grantseekers, grantmakers, and other interested parties to the world of organized philanthropy. This new edition builds on the work of its many previous editors. In fact, the Library of Congress lists editions going back to 1980, edited by Carol M. Kurzig, Patricia E. Read, Judith B. Margolin, Mitchell F. Nauffts, Pattie J. Johnson, and Kief Schladweiler. The latter four remain key employees of the Foundation Center, so that I have had the privilege of calling on their expertise as I picked up the mantle to serve as editor of this eighth edition. This edition proceeds organically from the work of those previous editors, expanding as the field of philanthropy itself becomes more complex and also more transparent, and the numbers of both foundations and other nonprofit organizations increase each year.

Upon initiating this revised edition it seemed propitious to re-examine the content and organization of this guide to ensure that it correctly reflects the ways that grantseekers and others perform research in the early 21st century. Very little remains static in our fast-changing world, and this is especially true in the field of information gathering and distribution. The earliest editions of *Foundation Fundamentals* assumed that readers would have traditional print materials accessible (most published by the Center itself) and would also utilize microfiche in order to scrutinize tax returns and annual reports filed by foundations. Since that long-ago time, as new technology has become essential in both the collection and distribution of data, the Center has been quick to adopt it. Recent editions of *Foundation Fundamentals* have bridged a period of transition of information from print to electronic formats, and ultimately to full web-based accessibility. In the span of just the few years since the previous edition of this guide was issued, much has changed in the resources that are widely available to grantseekers.

One of the challenges of presenting advice about research methodology in the electronic age is knowing that more, and perhaps better, tools will become available in fairly short order. And so even as this guide goes to press, new enhancements to *Foundation Directory Online Professional*—the premier database for information on America's foundations—continue apace with many more changes anticipated down the road I hope that this book will provide readers with the underlying principles that are relevant to foundation research even as new and perhaps different tools become available.

The guide is organized in such a way as to answer some of the most pressing questions for grantseekers, grantmakers, students of philanthropy and the nonprofit sector, and other kinds of researchers. You may use the table of contents to zero in on areas of specific interest, focus on particular chapters, or read *Foundation Fundamentals* from cover to cover. Chapter 1 describes the various types of foundations, the regulations that govern their activities, and a brief history of their development. Chapter 2 examines support from private foundations in relation to other forms of private philanthropy and to other sources of support for nonprofits. Chapter 3 looks at who gets foundation grants in the context of nonprofit tax exemption. Chapter 4 delves into the essential strategies that should inform your grantseeking research. Chapter 5 describes specific tools and information available on the web. Chapter 6 depicts in some detail how you can take advantage of *Foundation Directory Online Professional* to conduct grantmaker, grants, and Form 990 searches, illustrated by tips and examples Chapter 7 focuses solely on finding information about corporate giving. Chapter 8 provides information for those who continue to utilize traditional print and CD-ROM formats. In this edition for the first time, in Chapter 9, we've paid special attention to the research needs of individual grantseekers. Finally, Chapter 10 provides well-tested guidance on the topic of compiling and submitting your grant proposal.

The figures, illustrations, and worksheets you will find throughout the guide have been completely updated to reflect the many changes in form and content of information resources for grantseekers and the best funding prospect research practices in use today. Each of the appendices has been updated with the most current information available. Appendix A, an extensive bibliography, includes print and web-based resources, supplementing each chapter with additional recommendations.

Like previous editors of *Foundation Fundamentals*, I have relied on the generously shared expertise of many staff members of the Foundation Center: Steven Lawrence, Larry McGill, and Loren Renz of the Center's research department; Maggie Morth of communications; Mirek Drozdzowski, Renée Westmoreland, Kathye Giesler, and Emmy So of the information technology department; Phyllis Edelson, Jeff Falkenstein, Margie Feczko, Yinebon Iniya, Ruth Kovacs, David Jacobs, Rebecca MacLean, Ben McLaughlin, Jonathan Miller, Matthew Ross, and Sara Wyszomierski of publishing and information services; Alice Garrard, Mitch Nauffts, and Emily Robbins of *Philanthropy News Digest*; Elan DiMiao of planning and evaluation; and JuWon Choi and Inés Sucre of nonprofit services. In addition, Janet Camarena, David Clark, Charlotte Dion, and Barry Gaberman, chair emeritus of the Center's board, were instrumental in reading and commenting on drafts of selected chapters, each of which was improved due to their expertise and candor Appendices represent the work of Jimmy Tom, Erin Harper, Ruth Kovacs, Sara Wyszomierski, Steve Proffitt, and Kief Schladweiler. Also, thanks are due to Christine Innamorato for her creative design and production efforts. I owe a particular debt of gratitude to Sara Engelhardt, president of the Foundation Center, who managed to find the time to revise and update Chapter 1.

Outside the Center special recognition is due to Sherry Seward and Jane Geever. Sherry's work largely informed Chapter 4 on research strategies. Jane continues to help lead the Center's efforts to illuminate the process of proposal writing, and her work has contributed much to the content of Chapter 10.

I have been fortunate to have the wisdom and direction of Judi Margolin throughout this venture. Her good humor and perseverance have added greatly to my enthusiasm for this project, as well as for many others.

Sarah Collins, Editor

What Is a Foundation?

Carnegie Corporation of New York, the Chicago Community Trust, the Duke Endowment, Rockefeller Brothers Fund—what's in a name? The answer is: not much, if you're looking for a grantmaking foundation. These four institutions are among the nation's top grantmaking foundations, but none has the word "foundation" in its name. Conversely, many nonprofit organizations with "foundation" in their name do not make grants.

The difficulty of identifying grantmaking foundations by name alone causes confusion and leads to misunderstanding about the scope and activities of the foundation field. This is where the Foundation Center comes in. The Center enables those looking for grants to identify grantmaking foundations that might be good prospects, and it analyzes growth trends and giving patterns in the field as a whole and among the various types of foundations.

Defining a Foundation

The Foundation Center distinguishes two main types of grantmaking foundations—private and public—based largely on the federal tax regulations that apply to them. The most common distinguishing characteristic of a private foundation is that its funds come from an individual, a family, a corporation, or some combination of related parties. We use the term "public foundation" to refer to a public charity that has grantmaking as a primary purpose. Like other public charities, public foundations generally receive their funding from multiple unrelated donors, which may include private foundations, individuals, and government grants. Further, they must continue to seek funding from diverse sources in order to retain their public charity status.

Historically, most of the government and media scrutiny of foundations has focused on private foundations, which lack the built-in accountability that fundraising from multiple sources gives public foundations. The determination as to whether a charity is private or public is made by the Internal Revenue Service (IRS). Under the Tax Reform Act of 1969, different rules and regulations apply to those nonprofits found by the IRS to be "private foundations."

A nonprofit that has been established under state law must obtain recognition as a charitable organization from the IRS in order for contributions to it to be tax deductible. Section 501 of the Internal Revenue Code covers many types of organizations that are exempt from federal income tax. And Section 501(c)(3) specifically covers tax-exempt organizations that are "organized and operated exclusively for religious, charitable, scientific, testing for public safety, literary, or educational purposes . . ." and thus are eligible to receive contributions that are tax deductible to the donor.

An organization that meets the definition of Section 501(c)(3) is then measured against Section 509(a) of the Internal Revenue Code, which declares that *unless* it meets one of four criteria, it is presumed to be a private foundation. Those considered "not a private foundation" are:

- Organizations described in Section 170(b)(1)(A), which covers churches; schools, colleges, etc.; hospitals, medical research institutes, etc.; supporting organizations to educational institutions; governmental units; and publicly supported organizations (including community foundations);

- Organizations that normally receive more than one-third of their support from gifts, grants, fees, and gross receipts from admissions, sales, etc., *and* normally receive *not more* than one-third of their support from investment income;

- Supporting organizations, which, although not publicly supported, are controlled by and operated in close association with a public charity; or,

- Organizations operated exclusively for testing for public safety.

PRIVATE FOUNDATIONS

Because of their narrow base of support, private foundations are subject to federal laws and regulations intended to assure that they serve the public good. These rules include, among other things, a minimum annual distribution requirement, an excise tax on investment income, limits on the proportion of a for-profit enterprise they may own, and restrictions on grantmaking for certain kinds of recipients and activities.

The calculations required to administer these regulations are fairly complex. For instance, private foundations must make "qualifying distributions" of at least 5 percent of the average market value of their assets in any fiscal year by the end of the following year, a rule often referred to as "the payout requirement." Qualifying distributions include not only grants, direct charitable activities, and assets acquired directly for the active conduct of exempt functions, but also the administrative expenses required to operate those programs; they do not include such costs as those incurred in managing the foundation's investments. The calculation for the payout requirement is likewise complex, being based not only on the average asset value over the prior year, but also on the foundation's payout over the past five years (with any cumulative payout carry-forward being applied to the current year). In addition, certain "set-asides" of funds for future use count toward the payout requirement for that year.

The rules also require that private foundations annually file Form 990-PF with the IRS. These "information returns" are available to the public and can be useful for researching foundations' finances, board members, and grants, when this information is not available elsewhere. The Foundation Center's web site provides free access to Forms 990-PF through its 990 Finder feature.

The IRS differentiates between private foundations and private operating foundations, based on the different regulations that apply to them. The Foundation Center also breaks down the private foundation and private operating foundation designations into "independent" and "corporate," based on whether they or their donors are individuals or corporations. In 2005, the nation's private grantmaking foundations held $506 billion in assets and their grants totaled over $33 billion.

Independent foundations (often called "family foundations") are the most prevalent type of private foundation, comprising nearly 89 percent of those in the Foundation Center's database. Established by an individual or family through gifts or bequests, these foundations are extremely varied in size, style of operating, and grantmaking interests.

Most independent foundations have very small—or no—endowments. Often called "pass-though" foundations, they make grants from periodic gifts into the foundation. Many of today's large foundations began as pass-through foundations and subsequently received a major bequest upon the death of the donor. The number of "born large" foundations has increased during the past couple of decades, as individuals who have made substantial fortunes at a relatively young age endow their foundations early on. While endowed private foundations may exist in perpetuity, the donor or the governing board may decide to "spend out" the assets over a set time period or in connection with a triggering event, such as the death of the donor.

Fewer than 4,000 of the 69,569 independent foundations in the Center's database employ staff. The vast majority of unstaffed foundations report few or no administrative expenses. They are often managed by the donor, the family, and/or the trustees. The larger the foundation and the more complex the giving program, the more likely a private foundation is to employ staff.

Independent foundations' grantmaking activities range from gifts to local charities or educational institutions with which family members are associated to the multi-faceted, issue-driven grant programs—often dubbed "strategic philanthropy"—more likely to be practiced by larger, staffed foundations. They may operate programs locally, regionally, nationally, and/or internationally. Although their principal activity is grantmaking, they may also accomplish their mission through foundation-run programs (termed "direct charitable activities" by the IRS) or even through program-related investments, which is a specific type of grant/loan to a nonprofit.

Operating foundations, like other independent foundations, receive their assets from an individual or a small group of donors. However, most accomplish their charitable purposes largely by operating their own programs, rather than by making grants. The Foundation Center collects basic financial information on all private operating foundations. It creates more extensive profiles on the almost two-thirds that also make grants, which are usually for purposes related to the programs they operate.

Many of today's operating foundations started as independent foundations and increasingly began using their funds to operate charitable programs directly or to invest in "charitable assets," such as a building to be used as a nonprofit training center. When an independent foundation's charitable programs are mainly carried out not through grants but through direct charitable activities, it may apply to the IRS for reclassification as a "private operating foundation." A private operating foundation has different payout requirements and greater deductibility of new donations, allowing it to raise funds to help support its charitable activities.

Corporate foundations (also called company-sponsored foundations) generally receive their assets from a publicly held company rather than an individual or family. Although often closely tied to the company, a corporate foundation and the company that established it are separate legal entities. A corporate foundation often maintains a small corpus relative to its grants program, with the supporting company funding the bulk of its giving through annual gifts to the foundation. The company may augment the foundation's assets in some years to enable it to make grants from its corpus during years in which profits are down, it is expanding company operations, or it decides to cut back on gifts to the foundation for other reasons. This permits the foundation to maintain a reasonably steady grants program, despite business fluctuations.

Like independent foundations, corporate foundations often operate grantmaking programs in such areas as the arts, community development, education, or human services. However, their giving tends to focus on communities in which the parent company has operations, on company employees, or on activities that will raise awareness of the company in target markets, rather than on "strategic philanthropy." For example, many corporate foundations provide scholarships for children of employees and encourage employee involvement in charitable activities through employee matching gifts and programs that support employee volunteering.

Many companies make grants, provide sponsorships, or give in-kind gifts without using the foundation mechanism. Some make contributions both directly and through a non-operating or operating foundation. While corporate foundations and operating foundations must adhere to the private foundation rules, corporate direct giving programs have no IRS classification and are not subject to public disclosure requirements. Nonetheless, the Foundation Center collects information about corporate direct giving programs, when available, because of their significance to the overall fundraising strategies for a great many U.S. nonprofits.

Corporate operating foundations have recently become popular as the means through which pharmaceutical companies distribute significant quantities of their medicines to people who cannot afford them. In-kind donations of products are reported on the Form 990-PF as part of the "total giving" of these foundations. Over the years, corporate foundations have occasionally reported gifts of works of art, land, or other non-cash items. However, these new operating foundations appear to have been set up by pharmaceutical companies for the explicit purpose of donating medicines.

In the past decade, approximately a dozen of these foundations have been established. The value of their combined donations in 2005 came to more than $3.3 billion.

PUBLIC FOUNDATIONS

A public foundation is a public charity that operates a grants program as one of its primary purposes. Because their funds come from multiple sources, public foundations have less arduous legal constraints. Like other public charities, they are required to file Form 990 with the IRS on an annual basis.

The IRS does not have special rules for public foundations, so grantmaking public charities (as they are sometimes called) can be difficult to identify, but a growing number of public charities operate grantmaking programs.

Community foundations are the oldest and best-known group of public foundations. Their origins go back almost a hundred years, when banks and trust companies set up community foundations by pooling the numerous small trusts they managed, thus creating a central source of charitable funds that could be systematically focused on community development and other needs in their local area. It was not until the Tax Reform Act of 1969, however, that federal law clearly set community foundations apart from the more prevalent independent foundation form by declaring them "not a private foundation" and conferring favorable tax status on them, as public charities. Currently more than 800 community trusts or foundations across the United States serve specific geographic areas, whether it be a city, region, or state. A number of these also administer funds intended to benefit other geographic areas, including some outside the United States.

Modern community foundations receive contributions from a great variety of sources, including private foundations. Their endowments may be composed of an assortment of individual funds (which may bear the donors' names), funds restricted to certain program areas (such as public school education), and unrestricted funds that the foundation can use to initiate new efforts or supplement existing ones. Several banks or investment firms normally manage community foundation investments, but most have their own staff to run the grantmaking or direct charitable programs and to attract additional resources to the foundation. Their grantmaking activities are usually overseen by the governing board or by a distribution committee representative of various community interests. Community foundations frequently administer donor-advised funds contributed by individuals who wish to designate their fund's recipients, and some of the newer community foundations are predominantly made up of such funds. Increasingly, living donors play an active role in determining grant recipients for community foundations of all sizes and ages.

Other public foundations encompass a range of grantmakers that raise and dispense funds around a particular community of interest. Community foundations, however, are the only public foundations currently included in the Center's statistical analyses, such as the annual *Foundations Today* series and the online FC Stats, because they are the only type of public foundation for which enough reliable information has been consistently available over time to permit trends to be documented. However, as the Center identifies and adds other types of grantmaking public charities into its database, it will be possible to produce reports on additional categories of public foundations and their work.

Increasingly, public foundations have been established to receive funds and make grants for special populations or for specific subject areas. Many public foundations start as a fund within a community foundation, and they often focus on a special population or area of need in their geographic area. Women's funds, for instance, have been established in communities across the country to raise money and make grants to benefit women and girls. Other public foundations focus their giving on the arts, health, the environment, social change, or any number of issues at a local, regional, national, or international level. Some public foundations receive funding primarily from a racial/ethnic, identity-based, or religious community, but their grantmaking programs may extend beyond this particular community of interest.

Donor-advised funds originated within community foundations as a means to allow donors to establish a relatively small individual fund and to retain the right to direct gifts to eligible recipients. The donor receives a tax deduction for a contribution to a donor-advised fund and, as the name implies, gives up formal control of its investment or distribution. Donor-advised fund services are increasingly being offered by other types of public charities, such as federated giving programs, universities, and other existing charitable institutions. During the 1990s, a number of financial institutions also adopted this model as a means to help their clients manage their philanthropic giving, as well as their investments. Fidelity, Vanguard, and Schwab, among others, established public charities, often called "commercial gift funds," to handle donor-advised funds exclusively. Their assets are in the billions of dollars, and their giving is in the hundreds of millions of dollars.

How Did Foundations Evolve?

Philanthropy dates back to ancient times, but legal provision for the creation, control, and protection of charitable funds (forerunners of U.S. foundations) was first codified in 1601 by England's Statute of Charitable Uses, which granted certain privileges to private citizens or groups of citizens in exchange for support or performance of charitable acts intended to serve the public good. Since then, legal doctrines in the common law countries have generally preserved this status for most types of charitable entities, including foundations, churches, hospitals, and schools, and have afforded them tax exemption, so long as they serve a charitable purpose.

THE ORIGINS AND DEVELOPMENT OF PRIVATE FOUNDATIONS

Most early foundations in the United States were established for the benefit of a particular institution, such as a hospital or school, or to meet a specific social need, such as relief for the poor. Early in the 20th century, a new kind of foundation began to emerge in the United States. Exemplified by Carnegie Corporation of New York (established in 1911) and the Rockefeller Foundation (established in 1913), "general-purpose" foundations are usually endowed independent or family foundations with broad purpose statements that enable them to address major social issues. They may focus their grantmaking on one or more areas for a period of time, but their governing boards have considerable latitude to change their focus as social conditions change. Modern-day general-purpose foundations may be limited by their charters to specific issues or geographic areas, but within those limitations they may periodically review and adapt their grantmaking strategies or programs.

More than ever, today's independent or family foundations are a diverse group of institutions that conduct their charitable work in myriad ways, reflecting the values and goals of their donors, the strategic oversight of their governing boards, and the environments in which they operate. As a consequence, their operating styles are also quite varied. They range from "checkbook" style foundations, which make grants in essentially the same way an individual philanthropist might, to large, staffed foundations operated on the model of the early general-purpose foundations. These larger entities not only make grants but might also conduct substantial operating programs, such as commissions to build knowledge about a particular field or technical assistance programs for their grantees.

Independent foundations began to attract congressional scrutiny soon after the Carnegie and Rockefeller foundations were created. The U.S. Commission on Industrial Relations of the U.S. Congress (called the Walsh Commission for its chairman) launched the first investigation of independent foundations in 1915, looking into charges that wealthy capitalists were using the foundation form to protect their economic power, but no major legislation or restrictions resulted. Two subsequent world wars and the Great Depression produced a relatively quiet period for foundations, as Congress focused on other issues.

The 1950s ushered in a period of growth in the field, spurred by the creation of new wealth and a tax structure favorable to foundation formation. Independent foundations again became the target of congressional criticism. First the Select Committee to Investigate Foundations and Other Organizations (the Cox Committee) in 1952 and then the Special Committee to Investigate Tax-Exempt Foundations and Comparable Organizations (the Reece Committee) in 1954 looked into allegations that the large foundations were promoting "un-American activities" and Communist subversion of the capitalist system. The Cox Committee's *Final Report* found that, ". . . on balance, the record of foundations is good," and the very negative majority report from the Reece Committee hearings was generally discredited. Again, no major restrictive legislation resulted.

An open-ended investigation of foundations initiated in 1961 by Congressman Wright Patman, chairman of the Select Committee on Small Business, and a 1964 study of foundations by the Treasury Department ultimately led to a whole new legal and regulatory framework for foundations in the Tax Reform Act of 1969. This Act created the private foundation designation and included company-sponsored foundations in the rules governing them. It set forth special rules that, among other things, prohibit certain transactions between foundations and "disqualified persons," including their donors and managers, as "self dealing"; restrict foundation ownership and control of private businesses; limit the percentage of an individual's annual income that can be donated to a private foundation as a tax-deductible contribution; regulate foundation giving to individuals, other foundations, and non-exempt organizations; and ban grants or other activities to influence legislation or support political campaigns.

The 1969 Act also required a private foundation to distribute for charitable purposes either all of its "adjusted net income" or a percentage, to be set each year, of the market value of that year's assets, whichever was higher. This "payout requirement" was later set at 5 percent of the average market value of that year's assets, to be paid out by the end of the following year. Finally, the legislation called for foundations to file two annual information returns with the IRS (Form 990-AR and 990-PF), to make the forms available for inspection by the public, and to file copies of the forms with charity authorities in the state where the foundation is incorporated. (Beginning in 1982, foundations have been required to file only one form, a revised Form 990-PF.) Legislation passed in 1998 and finalized in 2000 requires private foundations to provide a "take-home copy" of their current tax return to any individual who makes a request in person or in writing. If a foundation's Form 990-PF is widely available on the Internet, that satisfies the disclosure requirement, so this requirement has become obsolete.

At the time of its passage, the Tax Reform Act of 1969 was assumed to spell the end of private foundation formation. This prediction seemed to be borne out by the sharp decline in foundation birth rate in the 1970s. To the surprise of many, the 1980s brought renewed growth in private foundation establishment rates, a trend that gathered momentum throughout the 1990s and has continued into the 21st century.

With the new surge in foundation formation and explosive growth in foundation resources has come renewed scrutiny of private foundations, along with other nonprofit organizations. Starting in 2004, in response to media stories of possible abusive or unethical practices by individual charities, the U.S. Senate Finance Committee conducted a series of hearings on oversight and reform. In its testimony, the IRS identified several areas of questionable practice, including misuse of donor-advised funds and supporting organizations and widely varying practices for setting executive compensation. These hearings led to the passage of the Pension Protection Act of 2006, which included a number of charitable reform measures for private and community foundations. The Act aimed to provide certain charitable giving incentives while introducing tighter restrictions on supporting organizations and donor-advised funds. The Act also doubled the penalty excise taxes for private foundations with excess business holdings and, for the first time, applied the private foundation excess business holdings rule to donor-advised funds and certain supporting organizations.

In response to calls for self-regulation of the sector and with encouragement from the Senate Finance Committee, in 2004 Independent Sector, an association of grantmaking and grantseeking charities, convened a Panel on the Nonprofit Sector. The Panel engaged hundreds of representatives of nonprofit organizations and foundations in a thorough examination of the sector's governance, transparency, and ethical standards. In 2005, the Panel issued a series of reports to Congress and the nonprofit sector with recommendations on a wide range of issues, such as compensation, financial audits, and abusive tax shelters. The Panel has continued to work on unfinished reform issues, including recommendations for revising Tax Forms 990 and 990-PF. Taken together, the inquiries undertaken by Congress, the IRS, and the sector itself constitute the most comprehensive review of the governance, regulations, and operations of the charitable community in three decades.

A BRIEF HISTORY OF CORPORATE FOUNDATIONS

Corporate contributions to nonprofit organizations date back to the 1870s, when railroad companies began supporting the development of Young Men's Christian Associations (YMCAs) at their divisional and terminal points to provide accommodations for their workers, and until World War I, the YMCA was the only major recipient of corporate contributions. The war prompted a major national fundraising drive aimed at corporations by the American National Red Cross, as well as the YMCA. It also led to the creation of "war chests" in local communities, which evolved into Community Chests following the war, with corporations leading the way in their support. The Revenue Act of 1935 greatly increased the corporate income tax, but it also provided, for the first time, a charitable deduction for corporate contributions.

Although a few corporate foundations existed prior to World War II such as the Bausch & Lomb Foundation and the Chicago Sun-Times Charity Trust, the higher corporate tax rates of the 1950s led to a boom in the creation of new ones. Also in the 1950s, regulation was increased to prevent the use of the foundation mechanism for private enrichment or business purposes.

Formation of corporate foundations slowed considerably in the 1970s, due both to the Tax Reform Act of 1969 and to the state of the economy. But with federal cutbacks in funding for social services, education, and the arts in the early 1980s, the call went out for private sources, notably business, to pick up the slack. In an unsuccessful bid to increase company giving levels during this time, the tax deduction limit for corporate charitable contributions was increased from 5 to 10 percent of a company's pretax earnings. Nonetheless, starting in the 1980s, the number of new corporate foundations has continued to grow.

THE COMMUNITY FOUNDATION MOVEMENT

The community foundation movement dates back to the establishment of the Cleveland Foundation in 1914. The idea of centralizing the governance of numerous separate trusts that were dedicated to charitable purposes in the community was welcomed by local trust offices, and community trusts or foundations were set up across the country, mostly at the initiative of banks and trust companies or chambers of commerce. The movement lost momentum during the Great Depression, but following World War II, it was revived by leaders in the community planning arena as a suitable means of strengthening their cities and regions.

The rate of community foundation formation increased dramatically when the 1969 Tax Reform Act regulations were finally issued in 1976. These clarified the significant new advantages that community foundations had over private foundations, including fewer limitations on their grantmaking, exemption from the excise tax on net income of private foundations, and greater deductibility of gifts as a proportion of donors' pretax income. Soon thereafter, a number of independent foundations began matching-gift, technical assistance, and "pass-through" grant programs to encourage the growth of the movement in communities across the United States (and some, around the world). In the 30 years since 1977, the field has grown from 170 community foundations to 832, a remarkable 389 percent increase.

Recent History

The 20th century saw the development of a foundation field in the United States. It was a century of innovation, witnessing the emergence of the general-purpose foundation, the corporate foundation, and the community foundation and other types of public foundations. A legal and regulatory framework for the field was created, and an infrastructure of organizations and associations to document its dimensions and activities, advocate policy, promote public understanding, and study practices grew up around it. The stock market's exuberance at the end of the century created an unprecedented boom in philanthropy, and at the millennium, it seemed to many that the "Golden Age of Philanthropy" had arrived.

The economic downturn at the start of the 21st century slowed the remarkable growth of the foundation field but in no way staunched either its long-term prospects or its potential for innovation. At the time of the writing of this chapter, in fact, Foundation Center estimates of 2006 inflation-adjusted giving by the nation's more than 71,000 grantmaking foundations surpass the previous record set in 2001. The overall number of foundations has also grown by roughly 10,000 since the beginning of this century. The often-referenced "intergenerational transfer of wealth" suggests that, over the next several decades, many more foundations will be established, and the resources of existing foundations will continue to grow.

More foundations and higher giving levels in no way represent the full impact of the nation's foundation community. A growing grantmaker focus on effectiveness and measurable outcomes and the willingness of some foundations to take on major social challenges will undoubtedly continue to drive the field's agenda. An increasingly global perspective on giving characterizes the priorities of growing numbers of foundations, as global warming, pandemics, and terrorism bring home issues that know no borders. It appears inevitable that U.S. foundations will continue to make unique and vital contributions to communities here and around the world.

Where Foundations Fit in the Total Funding Picture

Patterns of Growth in the Foundation Field

The Foundation Center's analysis of trends since 1975 has examined three principal types of grantmaking foundations: independent, corporate, and community. These types of foundations historically have been the most prolific and consistent in terms of levels of giving. Operating foundations are also included in the Center's trends analysis. Although grantmaking is not the principle activity for most operating foundations, they account for a large share of foundations' total giving. According to the Center's 2007 edition of *Foundation Yearbook*, in 2005 there were 71,095 independent, corporate, community, and grantmaking operating foundations with a total of $550.6 billion in assets.

Independent foundations, which comprise the largest segment of this foundation universe (63,059 or 88.7 percent), increased their giving in 2005. Independent foundations made contributions of $25.2 billion, up $1.9 billion or 8 percent from 2004. The assets of independent foundations increased 7.2 percent to a record $455.6 billion in 2005.

Corporate (or company-sponsored) foundations represent only one of many channels (direct cash and in-kind gifts, donations of staff time and expertise, etc.) that corporations use to make charitable contributions. However, corporate foundation giving is significant, comprising 11.0 percent of total foundation grant dollars awarded in 2005. That year, corporate foundations paid out nearly $4 billion in grants and contributions, up $566 million or 16.5 percent from 2004. (These figures exclude giving by company-sponsored operating foundations.) Assets are not usually indicative of corporate foundation annual giving because companies frequently make annual gifts—based on profits—to their foundations for grantmaking purposes. Still, assets of corporate foundations increased 6.9 percent between 2004 and 2005, from $16.6 billion to $17.8 billion.

Community foundations represent a relatively small, but extremely vital, component of the foundation universe (707 or 1 percent of foundations in 2005). The number of community foundations in the Center's foundations database has grown by 71 percent, from 413, since 1995. Asset values of community foundations in 2005 increased 15 percent, from $38.8 billion in 2004 to $44.6 billion. In 2005, community foundations distributed $3.2 billion in grants, up by $301 million or 10.3 percent from 2004.

Operating foundations use their resources primarily for providing a direct service, rather than for grantmaking. In 2005, the number of grantmaking operating foundations increased 7.1 percent from the prior year to 4,722. The value of operating foundation grantmaking increased 84.4 percent to nearly $4 billion, surpassing for the first time the value of community foundation grantmaking and almost equaling corporate foundation grantmaking. This dramatic growth in giving by operating foundations was driven primarily by approximately a dozen pharmaceutical manufacturers who established foundations to provide medication to individuals in need. Contributions of product—in this case medication—are counted as part of a foundation's total giving.

Figure 2-1. Aggregate Fiscal Data by Foundation Type, 2005

Foundation Type	Number of Foundations	%	Assets	%	Gifts Received	%	Qualifying Distributions[1]	%	Total Giving[2]	%	PRIs/Loans[3]	%
Independent	63,059	88.7	$455,570,231	82.7	$17,365,562	55.2	$27,522,803	68.0	$25,199,394	69.2	$184,813	84.8
Corporate	2,607	3.7	17,795,181	3.2	4,008,064	12.7	4,167,673	10.3	3,995,705	11.0	9,446	4.3
Community	707	1.0	44,583,970	8.1	5,586,604	17.8	3,314,681	8.2	3,217,048	8.8	11,913	5.5
Operating	4,722	6.6	32,602,668	5.9	4,504,664	14.3	5,468,367	13.5	3,990,487	11.0	11,674	5.4
Total	71,095	100.0	$550,552,049	100.0	$31,464,894	100.0	$40,473,524	100.0	$36,402,633	100.0	$217,846	100.0

Source: The Foundation Center, *Foundation Yearbook*, 2007. Due to rounding, figures may not add up.

[1] Qualifying distributions are the expenditures used in calculating the required 5 percent payout for private foundations; includes total giving, as well as reasonable administrative expenses, set-asides, PRIs, operating program expenses, and the amount paid to acquire assets used directly for charitable purposes.

[2] Includes grants, scholarships, and employee matching gifts; excludes set-asides, loans, PRIs, and program expenses.

[3] Program-Related Investments (PRIs) include low- or no-interest loans and charitable investments for projects clearly related to the foundations' grantmaking interests. These disbursements count toward qualifying distributions.

Figure 2-2. Fiscal Data of Grantmaking Foundations by Region and State, 2005

Region	Number of Foundations	%	Assets	%	Gifts Received	%	Qualifying Distributions[2]	%	Total Giving[3]	%
NORTHEAST	**21,510**	**30.3**	**$161,407,686**	**29.3**	**$ 9,893,972**	**31.4**	**$13,923,179**	**34.4**	**$12,768,631**	**35.1**
New England	**6,048**	**8.5**	**26,377,839**	**4.8**	**1,802,232**	**5.7**	**2,145,385**	**5.3**	**1,921,451**	**5.3**
Connecticut	1,405	2.0	6,551,609	1.2	603,114	1.9	676,468	1.7	640,987	1.8
Maine	289	0.4	1,540,397	0.3	67,222	0.2	105,834	0.3	91,875	0.3
Massachusetts	3,026	4.3	14,414,868	2.6	905,428	2.9	1,112,891	2.7	969,445	2.7
New Hampshire	302	0.4	1,191,069	0.2	50,940	0.2	77,337	0.2	61,889	0.2
Rhode Island	798	1.1	2,220,587	0.4	129,174	0.4	145,732	0.4	135,743	0.4
Vermont	228	0.3	459,310	0.1	46,354	0.1	27,122	0.1	21,513	0.1
Middle Atlantic	**15,462**	**21.7**	**135,029,847**	**24.5**	**8,091,739**	**25.7**	**11,777,793**	**29.1**	**10,847,180**	**29.8**
New Jersey	2,550	3.6	19,600,828	3.6	2,870,420	9.1	3,348,255	8.3	3,254,747	8.9
New York	9,016	12.7	91,430,190	16.6	4,081,632	13.0	6,413,113	15.8	5,683,005	15.6
Pennsylvania	3,896	5.5	23,998,829	4.4	1,139,687	3.6	2,016,426	5.0	1,909,427	5.2
MIDWEST	**17,415**	**24.5**	**116,588,187**	**21.2**	**5,957,046**	**18.9**	**8,373,383**	**20.7**	**7,676,744**	**21.1**
East North Central	**12,403**	**17.4**	**87,593,777**	**15.9**	**3,725,314**	**11.8**	**5,944,126**	**14.7**	**5,424,492**	**14.9**
Illinois	3,902	5.5	23,657,024	4.3	992,249	3.2	1,490,030	3.7	1,397,701	3.8
Indiana	1,141	1.6	15,818,467	2.9	527,931	1.7	1,018,887	2.5	964,942	2.7
Michigan	2,061	2.9	24,852,573	4.5	809,218	2.6	1,708,081	4.2	1,457,773	4.0
Ohio	3,172	4.5	15,908,227	2.9	915,674	2.9	1,136,339	2.8	1,047,748	2.9
Wisconsin	2,127	3.0	7,357,486	1.3	480,243	1.5	590,789	1.5	556,327	1.5
West North Central	**5,012**	**7.0**	**28,994,410**	**5.3**	**2,231,732**	**7.1**	**2,429,257**	**6.0**	**2,252,253**	**6.2**
Iowa	808	1.1	2,670,474	0.5	212,235	0.7	215,868	0.5	204,939	0.6
Kansas	695	1.0	2,125,897	0.4	90,399	0.3	139,678	0.3	131,995	0.4
Minnesota	1,354	1.9	11,902,594	2.2	582,469	1.9	826,927	2.0	740,374	2.0
Missouri	1,320	1.9	8,944,218	1.6	703,630	2.2	945,173	2.3	883,823	2.4
Nebraska	634	0.9	2,798,500	0.5	597,747	1.9	267,766	0.7	257,764	0.7
North Dakota	80	0.1	193,113	0.0	16,295	0.1	8,828	0.0	9,798	0.0
South Dakota	121	0.2	359,615	0.1	28,957	0.1	25,015	0.1	23,560	0.1
SOUTH	**19,570**	**27.5**	**121,983,584**	**22.2**	**8,457,716**	**26.9**	**9,061,410**	**22.4**	**8,134,945**	**22.3**
South Atlantic	**12,379**	**17.4**	**69,315,912**	**12.6**	**4,396,097**	**14.0**	**5,414,601**	**13.4**	**4,835,698**	**13.3**
Delaware	544	0.8	3,864,798	0.7	456,443	1.5	561,707	1.4	546,906	1.5
District of Columbia	402	0.6	5,178,972	0.9	338,020	1.1	448,881	1.1	364,210	1.0
Florida	3,739	5.3	16,939,674	3.1	937,663	3.0	1,157,550	2.9	1,057,769	2.9
Georgia	1,354	1.9	9,918,675	1.8	745,757	2.4	801,480	2.0	718,009	2.0
Maryland	1,531	2.2	11,939,957	2.2	566,604	1.8	860,597	2.1	734,764	2.0
North Carolina	2,803	3.9	11,739,430	2.1	724,646	2.3	931,435	2.3	886,961	2.4
South Carolina	414	0.6	1,690,189	0.3	86,420	0.3	121,302	0.3	109,276	0.3
Virginia	1,354	1.9	7,016,308	1.3	394,357	1.3	467,456	1.2	357,421	1.0
West Virginia	238	0.3	1,027,909	0.2	146,177	0.5	64,194	0.2	60,383	0.2
East South Central	**2,076**	**2.9**	**9,335,674**	**1.7**	**569,891**	**1.8**	**709,281**	**1.8**	**666,367**	**1.8**
Alabama	672	0.9	2,042,792	0.4	103,326	0.3	139,624	0.3	134,197	0.4
Kentucky	434	0.6	1,687,846	0.3	81,157	0.3	112,487	0.3	106,477	0.3
Mississippi	237	0.3	986,813	0.2	47,809	0.2	76,428	0.2	67,527	0.2
Tennessee	733	1.0	4,618,223	0.8	337,599	1.1	380,741	0.9	358,166	1.0
West South Central	**5,115**	**7.2**	**43,331,998**	**7.9**	**3,491,729**	**11.1**	**2,937,529**	**7.3**	**2,632,880**	**7.2**
Arkansas	282	0.4	2,629,877	0.5	668,464	2.1	440,149	1.1	421,890	1.2
Louisiana	444	0.6	2,473,714	0.4	117,904	0.4	131,350	0.3	118,360	0.3
Oklahoma	616	0.9	8,471,739	1.5	1,087,428	3.5	420,614	1.0	339,936	0.9
Texas	3,773	5.3	29,756,668	5.4	1,617,933	5.1	1,945,416	4.8	1,752,694	4.8
WEST	**12,581**	**17.7**	**150,528,553**	**27.3**	**7,148,448**	**22.7**	**9,107,595**	**22.5**	**7,817,877**	**21.5**
Mountain	**3,522**	**5.0**	**21,852,983**	**4.0**	**1,632,220**	**5.2**	**1,359,477**	**3.4**	**1,216,405**	**3.3**
Arizona	689	1.0	3,806,946	0.7	798,941	2.5	213,415	0.5	193,454	0.5
Colorado	1,148	1.6	8,031,521	1.5	354,166	1.1	504,986	1.2	437,134	1.2
Idaho	189	0.3	1,084,813	0.2	30,617	0.1	62,197	0.2	59,558	0.2
Montana	207	0.3	442,782	0.1	23,265	0.1	29,291	0.1	26,061	0.1
Nevada	435	0.6	3,958,607	0.7	187,884	0.6	247,716	0.6	229,234	0.6
New Mexico	227	0.3	1,230,045	0.2	50,486	0.2	85,114	0.2	64,810	0.2
Utah	449	0.6	2,064,558	0.4	110,520	0.4	144,393	0.4	139,885	0.4
Wyoming	178	0.3	1,233,711	0.2	76,341	0.2	72,366	0.2	66,269	0.2
Pacific	**9,059**	**12.7**	**128,675,570**	**23.4**	**5,516,228**	**17.5**	**7,748,118**	**19.1**	**6,601,472**	**18.1**
Alaska	70	0.1	681,304	0.1	22,848	0.1	37,205	0.1	33,288	0.1
California	6,606	9.3	83,759,417	15.2	4,452,955	14.2	5,264,889	13.0	4,404,772	12.1
Hawaii	301	0.4	1,599,290	0.3	69,845	0.2	91,000	0.2	80,715	0.2
Oregon	739	1.0	4,296,391	0.8	206,991	0.7	286,128	0.7	265,965	0.7
Washington	1,343	1.9	38,339,167	7.0	763,588	2.4	2,068,890	5.1	1,816,732	5.0
CARIBBEAN[4]	**17**	**0.0**	**41,387**	**0.0**	**7,194**	**0.0**	**5,626**	**0.0**	**4,027**	**0.0**
Puerto Rico	6	0.0	32,499	0.0	4,497	0.0	3,098	0.0	1,525	0.0
Virgin Islands	11	0.0	8,889	0.0	2,697	0.0	2,528	0.0	2,502	0.0
SOUTH PACIFIC[4]	**2**	**0.0**	**2,651**	**0.0**	**518**	**0.0**	**98**	**0.0**	**98**	**0.0**
American Samoa	2	0.0	2,651	0.0	518	0.0	98	0.0	98	0.0
Total	**71,095**	**100.0**	**$550,552,049**	**100.0**	**$31,464,894**	**100.0**	**$40,471,290**	**100.0**	**$36,402,322**	**100.0**

Source: The Foundation Center, *Foundation Yearbook*, 2007. Dollars in thousands. Due to rounding, figures may not add up.

[1] Geographic regions as defined by the U.S. Census Bureau.

[2] Qualifying distributions are the expenditures used in calculating the required payout; includes total giving, as well as reasonable administrative expenses, set-asides, PRIs, operating program expenses, and amount paid to acquire assets used directly for charitable purposes.

[3] Includes grants, scholarships, and employee matching gifts; excludes set-asides, loans, PRIs, and program expenses. For some operating foundations, program expenses are included.

[4] Private foundations in Puerto Rico, the Virgin Islands and American Samoa are not required to file Form 990-PF. Only a few voluntary reporters are represented.

Where Foundations Are Located

Foundations, whether independent, corporate, community, or operating are located in every state and the District of Columbia, as well as in Puerto Rico, the Virgin Islands, and American Samoa. However, the major concentration has historically been in the Northeast. In 2005, New York foundations alone accounted for nearly 17 percent of all foundation assets, while foundations in New England and the Middle Atlantic states combined controlled 29.3 percent of assets (see Figure 2-2).

The unequal distribution of foundation assets across the country is rooted in economic and industrial development patterns as well as in the personal preferences of the donors. This is offset to some extent by the funding policies of large national foundations, which give substantial amounts outside the states in which they are located. Moreover, since 1975, changing demographic patterns and relatively rapid economic and industrial growth in the West and South have stimulated a higher rate of growth in the number of foundations and foundation assets in those areas (see Figure 2-3). Western foundations, for example, have more than tripled their share of assets since 1975, up from 8.6 percent to 27.3 percent in 2005, and increased their portion of grants from 8.8 percent to 21.5 percent over the same period. California now ranks second to New York in foundation assets; it controls 15.2 percent of assets (compared with New York's 16.6 percent) and provides 12.1 percent of grant dollars (compared with New York's 15.6 percent). At the same time, Washington State held 7 percent of foundation assets

Figure 2-3. Foundation Assets by Region, 1975 and 2005

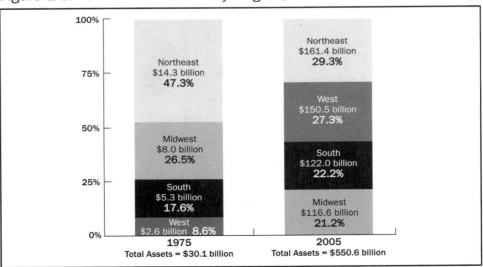

Source: The Foundation Center, *Foundation Yearbook*, 2007. Figures based on unadjusted dollars. "Total Assets" figure includes assets of foundations based in the Caribbean and South Pacific, which accounted for 0.0 percent of total foundation assets in 1975 and 2005.

and provided 5 percent of giving in 2005, up from 0.8 percent of assets and giving in 1975. The establishment of a single exceptionally large foundation accounted for nearly all of this growth.

Foundation assets of Southern states grew from 17.6 percent in 1975 to 22.2 percent in 2005 and grants from 16.9 percent to 22.3 percent. Foundation growth in this area reflects the economic growth of the region. Several established foundations received important additions to their endowments; large new foundations were formed; a few leading foundations relocated to the South; and corporate foundation activity increased.

Key Sources of Revenue for Nonprofits

While the distinctions among different types of foundations, the legal framework within which they exist, the evolution of foundations as philanthropic vehicles, and the scope of the foundation universe in terms of assets and giving are necessary building blocks for the funding research process, it is crucial for grantseekers to be able to distinguish between grants from foundations and other types of revenue that nonprofit organizations may receive. *The Nonprofit Almanac 2008*, published by the Urban Institute Press, presents detailed facts and figures about the independent sector. According to this reference work, earned income, such as fees for services, accounts for most revenue for nonprofits.

EARNED INCOME

Private payments for dues and services accounted for 70.3 percent of the total annual revenue for reporting public charities in 2005 according to *The Nonprofit Almanac 2008* (see Figure 2-4). While some large nonprofits,

Figure 2-4. Nonprofit Sector: Sources of Revenue, 2005

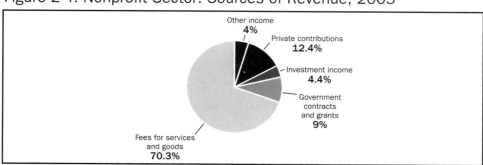

Source: *The Nonprofit Almanac, 2008.* National Center for Charitable Statistics at the Urban Institute

like universities, hospitals, and social service agencies, have always relied heavily on fees for services, more and more smaller nonprofits have turned to income-producing ventures and new dues and fee structures to help cover their operating costs. For some nonprofit organizations, this has meant simply establishing a fee structure for goods and services that they had previously supplied free of charge. Others have looked to capitalize on their existing resources by renting out unused office or meeting space; leasing computer time, services, or equipment; or offering consulting or information services to businesses and clients who can afford to pay. Still others have adopted a more ambitious approach to raising funds through profitable ventures such as gift shops, publications, travel services, and the like. Several books on earned income strategies can be found in Appendix A.

PRIVATE GIVING

The Nonprofit Almanac 2008 reports that private contributions accounted for 12.4 percent of the total annual revenue for the independent sector in 2005. This compares with the previously cited 70.3 percent of revenues from private payments for dues and services and 9 percent from government contracts and grants (see Figure 2-4). However, the average proportion of revenue received from private contributions varied widely among areas of nonprofit endeavor.

According to estimates in the most recent edition of *Giving USA*, published by the Giving USA Foundation, philanthropic contributions in 2006 totaled $295.02 billion (see Figure 2-5). The largest portion of these contributions—$245.80 billion or 83.4 percent—came from individual donors through gifts or bequests. Independent and community foundations accounted for

Figure 2-5. Giving 2006: $295.02 Billion—Sources of Contributions

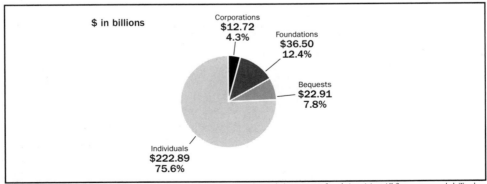

Source: *Giving USA*, Glenview, IL: Giving USA Foundation, 2007. Corporate data includes corporate foundation giving. All figures are rounded. Total may not be 100%.

$36.50 billion or 12.4 percent of this total, while corporations, through their foundations or direct giving activities, were responsible for $12.72 billion or 4.3 percent of total estimated private giving.

Individual Donors and Bequests

Giving by individuals, historically the largest source of private giving, has increased over the past three decades, reaching $222.89 billion in 2006, according to *Giving USA*. As can be seen in Figure 2-5, these gifts by individuals accounted for 75.6 percent of all private giving in 2006. Giving by individuals in 2006 represents an increase of 4.4 percent over *Giving USA's* revised 2005 estimate of $213.47 billion. The 2006 estimate of $222.89 billion is 2 percent of personal income.

Bequests accounted for 7.8 percent, or $22.91 billion, of all private giving in 2006. Because a few large bequests can skew the figures, bequest giving appears erratic when viewed from year to year. Since 2000, between 200 and 330 donor estates with gross estate value of $20 million or more have accounted for 44 to 64 percent per year of the total itemized charitable bequests.

Individual contributions range from a few pennies to millions of dollars and from used appliances and clothing to priceless art collections. Many individuals also contribute another priceless resource—their time—although volunteer time is not consistently reported by all nonprofits in terms of its monetary value.

The list of techniques used by nonprofit organizations to raise money from individual donors is long and varied. It includes increasingly popular online and direct-mail appeals, door-to-door solicitation, membership programs, special fundraising events, and deferred giving programs. A good many guides and handbooks detailing these approaches have been published, and a number of them are listed in Appendix A.

Independent and Community Foundations

Independent and community foundation giving as a proportion of total private philanthropic giving grew during the 1960s from 6.4 percent in 1960 to 9 percent in 1970. During the 1970s the proportion of giving coming from independent and community foundations declined to a low of 5.2 percent in 1979. With a soaring stock market causing increases in foundation assets in the 1980s, independent and community foundation giving as a share of private contributions moved back up to 6.7 percent in 1989 and continued to rise in the 1990s as new foundations were created and existing ones received new assets. The 12.4 percent share captured in 2006 was the highest percentage level for independent and community foundations reported in *Giving USA*.

Corporate Giving

The *Giving USA* estimates for corporate foundation grants and their direct giving activities puts these contributions to the nonprofit sector at $12.72 billion in 2006. Of that amount, $3.4 billion is estimated to have been distributed by corporate foundations, which are believed to be responsible for roughly one-quarter of total corporate giving. While corporate foundation giving can be documented through the Forms 990-PF that all private foundations must file with the IRS, corporate direct giving numbers, even historically, are based on estimates because no formal reporting is required and because corporate direct giving takes so many different forms. Studies of company donations show that as much as one third of the value claimed by companies as tax-deductible contributions are in the form of in-kind or noncash gifts.

FAMILY FOUNDATIONS

The Foundation Center has identified more than 36,700 independent foundations with measurable donor or donor-family involvement. These "family foundations" represent more than half of all independent foundations and account for similar shares of giving and assets of independent foundations.

Family foundations are not legally distinct from other independent foundations, requiring the Center to identify them using several objective and subjective criteria. These criteria include independent foundations with "family" or "families" in their name, a living donor whose surname matches the foundation name, or at least two trustee surnames that match a living or deceased donor's name, along with any independent foundations that self-identify as family foundations on annual Foundation Center surveys.

Larger family foundations included in the Foundation Center's 2005 grants sample were more likely to provide funding for education, health, the environment and animals, religion, and science and technology than independent foundations overall. By types of support, family foundations directed very similar shares of giving for general support and capital projects compared to independent foundations overall.

According to *Giving USA*, corporate giving represented between 5 and 6 percent of philanthropic giving throughout the 1990s, after a five-year period from 1984 through 1988 with between 6 and 7 percent share. Corporate giving first outstripped independent and community foundation giving, according to *Giving USA* estimates, in 1983. The mid-1980s were initially hailed as a turning point in corporate philanthropy, with predictions that it would continue to gain in relation to independent and community foundation giving. However, this new equilibrium did not last long. In fact, in the late 1980s, the Foundation Center noted a growing gap between grants paid out by corporate foundations and new gifts into these foundations, indicating that companies were eroding their foundation asset base to maintain giving levels. This pattern reversed for several years in the prosperous mid- and late 1990s, when corporations put more into their foundations than they paid out. However, while corporate gifts into their foundations have remained high in the first years of the new century, they have not kept pace with increases in giving. Another recent development was the establishment of operating foundations by pharmaceutical manufacturers for the purpose of distributing medications to patients with financial hardships. Together, these "pharmaceutical foundations" provided $3.2 billion of in-kind support in 2005.

Information on resources for corporate grantseeking will be found in Chapter 7 and in Appendix A.

Government Funding

Government funding is the third most important source of income for America's nonprofits. Government contracts, reimbursements, and grants accounted for 9 percent of the total annual revenue for the independent sector in 2005 according to *The Nonprofit Alamanc 2008*, reflecting a widespread pattern of partnership between government and the nonprofit sector in carrying out public purposes.

Most grantseeking nonprofits will want to become familiar with the activities and funding programs of the federal, state, and local government agencies with responsibility for their service areas. If your organization is seeking funding from federal government sources, Grants.gov is a web site you might want to visit. Grants.gov, a partnership of 11 agencies, led by the U.S. Department of Health and Human Services, provides a single location for information on, and the ability to apply for, more than $400 billion in annual grants from 26 federal grantmaking agencies and more than 1,000 individual programs.

You can search grant opportunities by keyword, funding opportunity number, *Catalog of Federal Domestic Assistance* number, funding activity category (such as agriculture, education, health, housing, and more), by governmental agency, and other criteria. You can also register to receive automatic e-mail notifications of new grant opportunities as they are posted to the site. Grants.gov also features the ability to download a grant application package, and then view and complete it offline—giving you the flexibility to complete grant applications quickly and save them easily for future reference.

In contrast to the wealth of information on federal government programs, information about funding by state and local governments is not always readily available. Most state and large municipal governments issue some type of guidebook or manual listing the addresses of departments and agencies along with brief descriptions of their program responsibilities. Sometimes the offices of state senators and congressional representatives may guide you to appropriate sources of local funding information. You'll want to check with your local public library for the specific resources available in your area.

Information on other guides and handbooks about government funding is included in Appendix A.

Summary

As detailed in this chapter, foundations may be important sources of support for organizations, but their grants represent a relatively small proportion of the total philanthropic dollars received by nonprofit organizations. Earned income vastly overshadows the entire field of philanthropy in accounting for nonprofit revenue, while government funding sources are also important. While the most successful nonprofit organizations develop strategic fundraising plans that encompass a range of income sources, this guide focuses on strategies for securing information on funding from foundations, corporations, or grantmaking public charities. In future chapters, we provide step-by-step assistance in identifying those grantmakers that will be most likely to fund your project, program, or organization. Next, we will examine who gets foundation grants.

Who Gets Foundation Grants?

The overwhelming majority of foundation grants are awarded to nonprofit organizations that qualify for "public charity" status under Section 501(c)(3) of the Internal Revenue Code. An organization may qualify for this tax-exempt status if it is organized and operated exclusively for charitable, religious, educational, scientific, or literary purposes; monitors public safety; fosters national or international amateur sports competition (but only if its activities do not involve the provision of athletic facilities or equipment); or is active in the prevention of cruelty to children or animals. These tax-exempt organizations must also certify to the IRS that no part of their income will benefit private shareholders or individuals and that they will not, as a substantial part of their activities, attempt to influence legislation or participate in political campaigns for or against any candidate for public office.

Under federal law, foundations are permitted to make grants to individuals and organizations that do *not* qualify for public charity status, *if* they follow a set of very specific rules covering "expenditure responsibility." Essentially, the rules for expenditure responsibility involve submitting a number of financial and fiduciary reports certifying that the funds were spent solely for the charitable purposes spelled out in the grant agreement, and that no part of the funds was spent to influence legislation. As opposed to provisions regulating support for nonprofit organizations, those governing grants to individuals require advance approval of the program by the IRS and prohibit giving to "disqualified persons"—a broad category covering contributors to the foundation and their relatives, foundation managers, and certain public officials. Although some 5,000 foundations have, nonetheless, instituted giving programs that support individuals directly, they represent a small segment of the foundation universe. (Another 1,500 grantmaking public charities are included in the *Foundation Grants to Individuals Online* database.)

Nonprofit Organizations

Foundations award grants to a wide variety of nonprofit organizations. The majority confine their giving to nonprofits that provide services in the foundation's home community. Others restrict their grants to specific types of institutions or organizations active in a particular subject area, such as medical research, higher education, or youth services. Still others limit their giving to specific purposes, such as capital campaigns, providing seed money, or bolstering endowments. The research strategies outlined in the chapters that follow are designed to help nonprofit grantseekers identify funders that are likely to fund organizations like theirs.

HOW TO FORM A NONPROFIT CORPORATION

Virtually every grantmaker you identify through your research will want to know that your organization is recognized as a 501(c)(3) organization by the IRS, and most will ask to see a copy of your IRS exemption letter. Depending on the particular state in which your organization is located, the foundation may also wish to see that you've received the appropriate state certification for tax-exempt charitable organizations. If your organization has not yet received tax-exempt status, you'll want to read the IRS booklet *Tax-Exempt Status for Your Organization* (IRS Publication 557), which includes the actual application forms for Section 501(c)(3) organizations as well as for most other tax-exempt organizations. The publication can be viewed and downloaded in PDF format from the IRS web site (www.irs.gov/pub/irs-pdf/p557.pdf). Copies of the booklet can also be obtained by calling the tax information number (800-TAX-FORM).

A corporation is a legal entity that allows a group of people to combine their money, expertise, time, and effort for certain activities, which can be for-profit (e.g., has the ability to issue stock and pay dividends) or nonprofit (cannot issue stock or pay dividends). Although most for-profit corporations can be formed for "any lawful purpose," state statutes usually require nonprofit corporations to be established to accomplish some specific purpose to benefit the public or a community. As previously stated, only those nonprofit corporations formed for religious, charitable, scientific, educational, or literary purposes of benefit to the public are eligible for tax-exempt status under Section 501(c)(3) of the Internal Revenue Code.

Once a nonprofit organization has been incorporated in one of the 50 states or the District of Columbia and has obtained a federal Employer Identification Number (EIN), it can then apply for tax exemption from the IRS. The nonprofit organization may also have to file for separate exemption under the state's revenue regulations. Thereafter, the nonprofit must report income receipts and disbursements annually to the IRS and to the state revenue department. Also, it will usually have to renew its registration with the appropriate state agency on an annual basis.

Figure 3-1 outlines the basic steps involved in forming and operating a nonprofit corporation. Since the process of incorporating as a tax-exempt nonprofit organization is regulated under federal, state, and sometimes local law, it is advisable to consult an attorney, preferably one with nonprofit experience, to guide you through the process. There are also a number of handbooks that explain the application procedures and examine the legal ramifications and issues involved in structuring your organization. Many of these are listed in the bibliography in Appendix A and can be examined free of charge at Foundation Center libraries. Other resources for establishing a nonprofit organization can be found through the Foundation Center's web site in the Get Started area.

BENEFICIARIES OF FOUNDATION SUPPORT

The nonprofits that benefit from foundation grants are many and varied. As can be seen in Figure 3-2, education was the most popular subject category for grant dollars in 2005 (24 percent), followed by health (21 percent), human services (15 percent), arts and culture (13 percent), and public affairs/society benefit (11 percent). These five areas also received the most grants, but in slightly different percentages, with human services receiving the largest number of grants (26 percent), followed by education (20 percent), arts and culture (14 percent), health (13 percent), and public affairs/society benefit (12 percent).

A look at beneficiaries by major field types of recipients (see Figure 3-3) shows that educational institutions, with 32 percent of the grant dollars distributed in 2005, were far and away the most likely nonprofits to receive foundation funding. Colleges and universities received most of these grants with 17.9 percent. Human service agencies, with 10.5 percent of the 2005 grant amounts, and public/general health organizations, with 9 percent, came in second and third, respectively. The distribution of grants by field-specific recipient type has remained fairly consistent since 1992. The major types of

Figure 3-1. How to Form and Operate a 501(c)(3) Nonprofit Corporation

	Steps	Applicable Form	Results
State's Corporation Division	Contact your state's corporate filing office and let them know of your interest in forming a 501(c)(3) organization.	They will send packet with a sample or fill-in-the blank Articles of Incorporation, nonprofit corporation laws, a filing fee schedule, and forms and instructions for checking the availability of your proposed organization's name.	You have obtained an overview of all that you will need to get started.
Organization Name	Reserve the name of your organization (optional) for a small fee.	Check your packet for applicable form. File the application for reservation of name with the appropriate agency in your state.	Reserves your name so that no other organization can, for a limited period of time, incorporate under that same name in your state.
Articles of Incorporation	Prepare Articles of Incorporation. It should include purposes and any other clauses that are required by your state not-for-profit law.	This form should also be in your packet. File Articles of Incorporation with your Secretary of State.	The State recognizes your organization as an incorporated nonprofit organization (i.e., one conducting nonprofit activities for charitable, educational, religious, scientific, literary, cultural, or other purposes).
Federal Employer Identification Number	File with the Internal Revenue Service (IRS) as a nonprofit, even if you do not have employees.	IRS Form SS-4	Your organization will be assigned an Employer ID Number (EIN) so the IRS can track your reports and IRS Form 1023 tax exempt application (see below).
Federal Tax Exemption	After the corporate filing office returns a copy of your filed Articles, you should submit your federal 501(c)(3) tax exemption application to the IRS.	Complete IRS Form 8718 and IRS Package 1023. For information on filling out these forms read IRS Publication 557 (you can obtain all of these items for free by calling 800-TAX- FORM, or you can download them from the IRS web site at www.irs.gov).	Your organization is recognized by the IRS as exempt from paying income tax on most revenues related to your charitable functions. In general, donations made to your organization are tax deductible only if you are a 501(c)(3) organization.
State Registration and Reporting	Contact the Secretary of State (Corporate Division) and Attorney General (Charities Division)	Registration forms and fiscal annual reports; fee will vary with size of your organization's operating budget.	Your organization is officially registered as a charity to solicit funds, do business, or own property in your state. You may have to apply for a separate exemption under your state's regulations.
Reporting to the IRS	Organizations with gross revenues over $100,000 report annually to the IRS. Organizations with gross revenues under $100,000 report annually to the IRS. (Certain types of organizations with gross annual receipts of less than $25,000 are not required to file.)	IRS Form 990 IRS Form 990 EZ	Provides the IRS with a report of your organization's income and disbursements.

Nonprofit Connection, 50 Broadway, Suite 1800, New York, N.Y. 10004   nonprofitconnection.org

Figure 3-2. Grants by Major Subject Categories, 2005

Social Sciences 1%
Religion 3%
Science & Technology 3%
International Affairs 4%
Education 24%
Environment & Animals 6%
Public Affairs/ Society Benefit[1] 11%
Health 21%
Arts & Culture 13%
Human Services 15%

Percent of Grant Dollars

Science & Technology 2%
International Affairs 3%
Social Sciences 1%
Religion 3%
Human Services 26%
Environment & Animals 6%
Public Affairs/ Society Benefit[1] 12%
Education 20%
Health 13%
Arts & Culture 14%

Percent of Number of Grants

Source: The Foundation Center, *Foundation Giving Trends,* 2007. Based on a sample of 1,154 larger foundations.
[1]Includes Civil Rights and Social Action, Community Improvement and Development, Philanthropy and Voluntarism, and Public Affairs.

Figure 3-3. Major Field-Specific Recipient Types, 2005

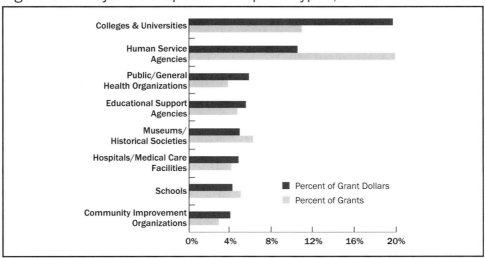

Colleges & Universities
Human Service Agencies
Public/General Health Organizations
Educational Support Agencies
Museums/ Historical Societies
Hospitals/Medical Care Facilities
Schools
Community Improvement Organizations

■ Percent of Grant Dollars
▨ Percent of Grants

0%   4%   8%   12%   16%   20%

Source: The Foundation Center, *Foundation Giving Trends,* 2007. Based on a sample of 1,154 larger foundations. Recipient types representing more than 4 percent of grant dollars.

support provided to nonprofit organizations in 2005 were program support, general/operating support, capital support, research grants, and student aid. While there were differences between the percentage of grant dollars received and the number of grants received by category, the distributions were generally consistent (see Figure 3-4).

FISCAL RESPONSIBILITY

Organizations that do not have tax-exempt status can still participate in the grantseeking process. However, doing so may be challenging. You may receive funds, for example, by affiliating with an existing organization that already is eligible to receive foundation grants and is willing to assume fiscal responsibility for your project, usually on a contract basis. Since grants would then be made directly to the sponsoring organization, your organization and the sponsor should have in advance a clear written agreement about the management of funds received and what fees (if any) may be subtracted by the fiscal sponsor. Since there is no master list of organizations willing to act as sponsors, you will need to investigate those with purposes similar to your own. More detail about fiscal sponsorship and other types of affiliation is provided in Chapter 9.

Profit-Making Organizations

While foundations generally cannot award grants to profit-making groups, they are permitted under the Tax Reform Act of 1969 to make grants to organizations that are not tax exempt, or have not yet received their

Figure 3-4. Major Types of Support, 2005

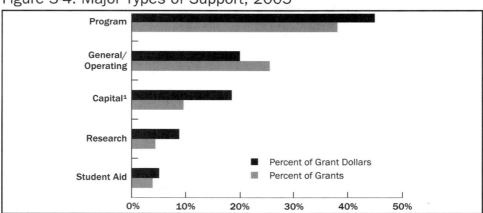

Source: The Foundation Center, *Foundation Giving Trends,* 2007. Based on a sample of 1,154 larger foundations.
[1] Includes endowment funds.

LOANS/PROGRAM-RELATED INVESTMENTS

In addition to grants, some foundations make loans to nonprofits, usually in the form of program-related investments (PRIs). A PRI, broadly defined, is an investment by a foundation to support a charitable project or activity involving the potential return of capital within an established time frame. Unlike grants, PRIs must be repaid— generally with interest—and are governed by strict regulations that mandate greater administrative attention than conventional grants. In addition, the foundation must prove to the IRS that PRI funds are spent only for the designated charitable purpose and that the loan recipient could not have secured funding through traditional financial channels. Despite these restrictions, a number of foundations report an interest in, or have a history of, making program-related investments.

According to a study conducted by the Foundation Center in 2003, there were approximately 255 active PRI funders in the United States. From 2000 through 2001, a sample of 135 leading PRI funders made 667 charitable loans and investments exceeding $421 million. More than 85 percent of these funders were independent foundations, and they accounted for 79 percent of all PRI dollars and 83 percent of PRIs. The same number of community foundations made PRIs as did corporate foundations, but the corporate foundations gave more dollars in the form of PRIs.

Although PRI funders represented all asset sizes, they tended to be among larger U.S. foundations. Fifty-seven percent of PRI funders held assets of $50 million or more, and they accounted for 80.3 percent of new charitable loans and investments.

Still, among the very largest U.S. foundations, many do not have PRI programs. For example, only seven of the 43 U.S. foundations with assets of $1 billion or more reported PRI transactions of $10,000 or more in 2000-2001. This finding suggests that asset size is not the principal determinant for making PRIs. Even foundations with significant resources, and therefore greater capacity to manage loans and charitable investments, have not opted to do so.

Although PRI financing remains closely associated with community development and housing, the practice of making, and using, no- or low-interest charitable loans and investments has spread to nearly all fields. In 2000-2001, more than three fifths of PRIs and of PRI dollars financed projects and organizations in fields other than development and housing, especially education, the environment, arts and culture, human services, health, and church support.

For more information about PRIs, see the Center's publication *The PRI Directory: Charitable Loans and Other Program-Related Investments by Foundations* (2003). A new edition will be issued in 2008.

exemption, for projects that are clearly charitable in nature, so long as the funders exercise "expenditure responsibility." Most foundations do not have the staff to provide the necessary oversight for expenditure responsibility and, therefore, are unlikely to fund profit-making ventures or other organizations that do not have tax-exempt status.

Those seeking funding to start their own for-profit businesses will find information at their local office of the Small Business Administration (sba.gov), their local Chamber of Commerce, business libraries at colleges or universities, and/or the business sections of large public libraries. Foundations do not provide funding for starting private for-profit businesses.

Individuals

As noted previously, under the provisions of the Tax Reform Act of 1969, private foundations may make grants to individuals for "travel, study or similar purposes" if the foundations obtain, in advance, approval from the IRS of their selection criteria and procedures. These procedures must ensure an objective selection process and usually involve extensive follow-up reports that demonstrate adequate performance and appropriate expenditures of the grant funds by the individual receiving the grant. Although foundations may make grants to individuals, only a small percentage do.

Individuals seeking foundation grants should first look at the programs described in *Foundation Grants to Individuals* (issued as both an online database and print directory by the Foundation Center). Both resources contain descriptions of 6,500 grantmakers of all sizes that currently operate grant programs for individuals. Most of these programs have significant geographic and other limitations.

There are, as well, a wide variety of funding sources other than foundations that make grants to individuals. Individual grantseekers should consult general reference books, such as *The Annual Register of Grant Support*, *The Grants Register*, *Awards, Honors and Prizes*, and others that describe grant programs run by government agencies, corporations, associations, and nonprofit groups in such diverse fields as sports, religion, medicine, and the performing arts. The Foundation Center maintains a designated area for individual grantseekers on its web site (foundationcenter.org/getstarted/individuals) with a wide selection of tutorials and links to related FAQs and reference guides.

STUDENTS AND ARTISTS

Many individual grantseekers are either prospective students or practicing artists. Students seeking financial aid for their education should be sure to consult with the financial aid office at the school they plan to attend. Approximately 80 percent of the 6,500 grantmakers in the Center's *Foundation Grants to Individuals Online* and *Foundation Grants to Individuals* book fund programs for educational assistance, including scholarships, fellowships, and loans. There are a number of guides and directories that describe grant programs operated by local and state governments, corporations, labor unions, educational institutions, and a variety of trade associations and nonprofit agencies. Many high school and public libraries maintain, and make available free of charge, collections of funding information resources for students. Chapter 9 provides strategic advice and information on several web sites that may prove helpful as well in the quest for funding.

Individual artists should conduct subject searches using *Foundation Grants to Individuals Online* or look for arts-related headings in the subject index of the print publication *Foundation Grants to Individuals* for potential funders. Fiscal sponsorship is another possibility for artists.

FISCAL SPONSORS

Individuals seeking funds for research or special projects not related to their education may wish to do what organizations without tax-exempt status often do: affiliate with a nonprofit organization that can act as a sponsor for a foundation grant. The typical fee a fiscal sponsor imposes is approximately 5–10 percent. Universities, hospitals, churches, schools, arts organizations, and theaters are just a few of the many types of nonprofits that receive and administer foundation grants for work done by individuals. The challenge to individual grantseekers is to identify those organizations with which they or their project have something in common. For more information about fiscal sponsorship, see Chapter 9 or refer to the Foundation Center's FAQs on this topic (foundationcenter.org/getstarted/faqs/section_5c.html). The FAQ will link to the Guide to Fiscal Sponsorship and Affiliation (foundationcenter.org/getstarted/individuals/fiscalsponsorship/). An important book on the subject is *Fiscal Sponsorship: Six Ways to Do It Right*, 2nd edition, by Gregory L. Colvin.

Summary

Nonprofit organizations with tax-exempt status as public charities under Section 501(c)(3) of the Internal Revenue Code are the most common recipients of foundation grants. The types of nonprofit organizations, the types of support they receive, and the subjects these grants cover vary widely. Individuals and nonexempt organizations can receive grants from foundations and other nonprofits; however, these individuals and groups must perform more research and be more creative in their approach to fundraising. Seeking fiscal sponsorship from a qualifying nonprofit is one such approach.

Nonprofits, as well as other organizations and individuals seeking grants, must plan their research strategies and learn about the resources available to help identify potential funders. In the next two chapters we outline a research strategy and introduce you to the vast array of resources available today in the field of fundraising research.

Planning Your Funding Research Strategy

In this chapter we review the principles of effective foundation research and examine the factors to consider in devising and shaping your list of prospective funding sources. We'll also briefly touch on the types of resources available to create your prospect list, but provide much more detail about each of those tools in Chapter 5. The focus of this chapter is on the steps you should take in evaluating the best prospects for your organization so that the end result of your work will be a targeted list of likely supporters.

The Importance of Doing Your Homework

The key to success is doing your homework. While identifying potential funders requires serious, time-consuming research, most grantseekers determine that it is well worth the effort. The objective of your funding research is to find funders that have the same interests and values as your organization. Foundation trustees and staff generally care deeply about the problems of society and struggle to determine the most effective strategies they can use to produce the greatest impact with their funding dollars. When they describe their programs on their web sites or in their printed guidelines, or when they announce new areas of interest, it is the result of careful planning and consideration. As a grantseeker it is your responsibility to review thoroughly all the available information about a funder to determine if your organization's programs are a potential match with the funder's stated interests. And in order to be a competitive grantseeker, you will need to set aside time to research each prospective funder.

As you conduct your research, be realistic in your expectations. Foundations and corporations cannot meet all, or even most, of your needs. In fact, the vast majority of the money given to nonprofits is actually donated by individuals. As already noted, foundations and corporations currently provide about 16 percent of all philanthropic dollars, but their grants can make up an important part of your support.

Before You Begin—Questions About You and Your Grant Project

Successful fundraising depends on making the right match between your organization and appropriate funders. And both parties must have common interests and motivations for that relationship to work. Determining your options for funding from foundations and corporations requires a thorough examination of where these common interests converge. It is a mistake to produce dozens of copies of the same proposal and then send them to an unscreened list of funders that has been quickly retrieved from some source or other. This approach will yield nothing positive; and even worse, those funders will know that your organization is not adopting effective practices that are generally accepted in the field.

Before you begin the research process it is a good idea to review your organization's attributes and clearly define its programs and financial needs so that you can match those requirements to funders' potential interests and their capacity to give. Your objective here is to think of your organization's work in ways that funders will connect to. In *The Foundation Center's Guide to Proposal Writing* we suggest that you ask yourself the following questions:

- *What is your organization's mission?* Know your organization's guiding principals and fundamental goals. For example, let's assume you represent an organization whose mission is "to strengthen the lives of diverse communities by assisting individuals in attaining their goals for self-sufficiency." Think about the important concepts here— "strengthen the lives of diverse communities" and "attaining their goals for self-sufficiency"—and how these key phrases might connect to funders with similar missions or stated programmatic interests.

- *Is your organization tax exempt?* As noted earlier, most foundation funding is given to tax-exempt nonprofit organizations that are formally recognized by the state where they are incorporated and by the Internal Revenue Service. Funders will need evidence of this status, and will ask for a copy of your organization's Letter of Determination from the IRS. If this is not the legal status of your group, your research strategy may well be different than that of nonprofit organizations that are formally structured. You may need a fiscal sponsor or some other plan to secure funding. Refer to Chapter 9.

- ***Can you describe the audiences served by your organization's programs?*** Does your organization serve the general population, or does it address the needs of one or more specific racial, ethnic, age, gender, or other group, such as Asians, Latinos, immigrants, people with disabilities, women, or youth? An important aspect of making a match with funders' interests is serving audiences they care about.

- ***Where does your organization operate its programs?*** You should be able to describe the geographic scope of your activities, such as in what town, city, county, or state you perform your services. Does your program have a national or international focus, or are there specific countries in which your organization operates? A key tenet of fundraising is that most giving is local. Many funders limit their giving to recipients in particular geographic regions.

- ***Do you have a clear picture of the purpose of the program or project for which you are seeking support?*** It is generally a good idea to have at least a detailed outline of your project or a preliminary proposal in hand before you begin your foundation and corporate funding research. What you have written about your organization's unique characteristics, and the specific details of your project, will equip you with the facts and terminology you need to find funders with similar interests.

- ***What are the distinctive features of your project/organization?*** Are you collaborating with, or do you have an affiliation with another organization? Do your services generate income? Are you creating a model program that other organizations can replicate? Does your organization provide direct services, or are you an advocacy or research group? Your organization or project may have other features that distinguish its activities. In each example here, there are some funders that may look more favorably on an organization that meets one or more of these criteria.

- ***Has your organization previously received foundation funding?*** Getting the first foundation grant is usually challenging because there are no relationships established yet. If your organization is in that position, set modest foundation fundraising goals at the outset. If you have received foundation grants in the past, you should make time to speak with existing foundation donors for leads to others.

- ***Do you know the total dollar amount needed from foundations for your organization or project?*** When you create an outline for your proposal, you will be deciding whether you are seeking general support for your organization or support for a specific project. If you are seeking project support, you must create a budget to determine the amount of money you will need for a specific time frame. Then, through your research you will determine how much of the funding you need is likely to come from one or more foundations and corporations versus other sources.

- ***What is the grant amount you are seeking?*** Before you start your research it can be helpful to consider the general size of the grants you are seeking. This, in turn, will help you gauge the number of funders you will need to fully fund your project. For example, if your project budget is $80,000, are you seeking four grants of $20,000 each, or two grants of $40,000 each? Your organization's annual budget and the size of the project budget, as well as the giving capacity of various funders and their typical grant ranges, will help determine the answer to this question.

- ***Is in-kind support more appropriate than a cash grant?*** For some purposes, it may be helpful to explore the possibility of in-kind donations rather than a cash grant. Many corporations provide product donations, executives on loan, employee volunteer programs, and other types of in-kind support rather than, or in addition to, cash contributions. These can prove to be very beneficial to a nonprofit, and can also lead the way to actual grants at a later time.

The Research Process

Once you have analyzed and pinpointed your organization's funding needs, you can begin to develop a strategy for identifying potential funders. This stage requires serious, time-consuming research, and a certain willingness to engage in "detective" work. If you can identify the person(s) in your organization most likely to enjoy this type of sleuthing—and who are patient and exacting—the research effort will not seem onerous.

Although there are a variety of approaches for uncovering appropriate funding sources, they all boil down to three basic steps:

1. Develop a broad list of prospects—that is, cast a wide net to identify foundations and/or corporate grantmakers that have shown an interest in funding projects or some aspect of programs similar to your own, based on subject, geography, or type and/or size of support they typically provide.

2. Evaluate your list of prospects to eliminate those grantmakers that have giving restrictions making them unable or unlikely to fund projects in your subject field or geographic area, those that do not provide the type or amount of support you need, or those that indicate that they are not appropriate prospects at this time. This necessary winnowing will help you to prioritize the top prospects among your potential supporters.

3. Refine your prospect list by using a variety of sources to investigate thoroughly the funders remaining on your list and determine which ones are most likely to consider your proposal favorably. These resources will help you to determine if there is a good fit.

STEP 1: DEVELOPING A PRELIMINARY LIST OF PROSPECTS

In this first step of the research process, you are looking for funders who meet, at least, these two important criteria:

- Stated program interests that match your organization's needs or with a demonstrated pattern of giving in your field of interest; and

- Giving in the geographic area in which your organization operates, or with no restrictions indicated as to where they give.

Like the individuals and corporations who established them, foundations and corporate giving programs differ dramatically from each other in their giving interests. Try to be inclusive at this first stage for your research. If preliminary investigation makes you think that a specific foundation or corporate donor should be on the list, go ahead and include it. Let further research you conduct on that funder tell you otherwise.

These resources will help you compile your prospect list. Most are accessible online:

- Foundation and corporate databases and directories

- IRS Forms 990-PF

- Grantmaker web sites, guidelines, annual reports, and other publications

- News sources

We will learn more about these in Chapter 5.

Figure 4-1. Prospect Worksheet

PROSPECT WORKSHEET

Date:

Basic Information

Name of Grantmaker	
Address	
Contact Person	

Financial Data

Total Assets	
Total Grants Paid	
Grant Ranges	
Period of Funding	

Is Grantmaker a Good Match?	Grantmaker	Your Organization
Subject Focus (list in order of importance)	1.	1.
	2.	2.
	3.	3.
Geographic Focus		
Type(s) of Support		
Population(s) Served		
Type(s) of Recipients		
Typical Grant Size		
People (Officers, Donors, Trustees, Staff)		

Application Information

Grantmaker has printed guidelines/application forms?	
Initial Approach (letter of inquiry, formal proposal)	
Deadline(s)	
Board Meeting Date(s)	

Sources of Above Information

☐ 990-PF/990 — Year:	
☐ Annual Report — Year:	☐ Requested ☐ Received
☐ Databases/Directories	
☐ Grantmaker web site	

Notes:

Follow-up:

Keeping track of your research progress on each potential funder is essential; keeping careful notes will save time and increase your efficiency. The Prospect Worksheet (see Figure 4-1) we've provided is the format the Foundation Center staff recommends to grantseekers to enable them to focus on funders whose priorities most closely match their projects. During the initial phase of your research, you should concentrate on certain basic facts about the funders you uncover. While you may want to develop your own prospect worksheet, at a minimum it should include the following elements: the grantmaker's name and location; the subject and geographic focus of its grantmaking activities; any stated restrictions or limitations it places on its grants; the size and type of grant it typically awards; and its preferred application procedures, if any.

It is always a good strategy to assume that you will conduct several different searches. While initially you may have the inclination to locate just those funders that match your exact interests, this is not always the best approach. This strategy may yield good results, but you may be excluding other funders that have not supported the precise program you are seeking to fund, even though they may be interested in your organization, nonetheless. Because of the speed and flexibility of database searching, grantseekers can adjust their searches to narrower or broader criteria very easily. So it's not a good idea to limit yourself to just one search strategy.

AVAILABILITY OF RESOURCES

In accordance with its mission of strengthening the nonprofit sector by advancing knowledge about U.S. philanthropy, the Foundation Center provides free public access to funding resources at five library/learning centers (in New York, Atlanta, Cleveland, San Francisco, and Washington, DC) and more than 350 Cooperating Collections throughout the U.S. Visitors to the five Center-operated sites have access to the Center's databases (*Foundation Directory Online* and *FC Search)*, its content-rich web site, and a vast collection of fundraising and philanthropic materials. The Cooperating Collections also provide free access to *Foundation Directory Online* or *FC Search*, the Center's web site, and a core group of other Center publications. The balance of fundraising materials available is unique to each site and often reflects the regional focus of the collection. The Center provides free and fee-based training on topics related to grantseeking, proposal writing and budgeting, and nonprofit management at its library/learning centers, Cooperating Collections throughout the country, and in the "virtual" classroom at its web site.

If your organization is devising a project that is unique, one that has never been attempted before, or is working in an emerging field, it is not likely that you will find subject terms that are an exact match. Thinking more broadly, then, and searching on terms that relate to the audiences you serve that will benefit from the new program, may be the best approach. For example, you might search for funders that support the environment (broad term) rather than just climate change (narrower term for an emerging field).

STEP 2: EVALUATING YOUR PROSPECT LIST—QUESTIONS ABOUT POTENTIAL FUNDERS

In this next stage of your research you will be evaluating the grantmakers on your prospect list by gathering important information on those funders whose guidelines or funding patterns most closely match your organization's funding needs. As you research this initial list of prospects, you will be looking for answers to the following questions put forth in *The Foundation Center's Guide to Proposal Writing*:

- *Does the funder accept applications?* You may find it surprising that some do not. You'll want to determine this early in the research process so you don't waste your time. However, even when the funder says it does not accept applications and/or gives only to pre-selected organizations, you should not completely disregard it as a prospect, *if* your research indicates that it has the potential to be a very good fit. Check to see if anyone on your board of directors, staff, or volunteers knows someone connected to the foundation and/or begin to cultivate the prospective funder by sending a letter introducing your organization. This type of long-term cultivation may prove fruitful.

- *Has the grantmaker demonstrated a real commitment to funding in your subject field?* Check to see that the funder's stated mission, program descriptions, and/or recently awarded grants indicate that there is a match with your organization's funding needs. Sometimes you may come across one or more grants by a particular foundation in your subject area, but they may be the exception to the rule. They may be grants awarded for reasons other than a true commitment to that field, such as a special relationship between a board member and the recipient. Other foundations have historic and continuing relationships with particular organizations, perhaps due to a specified interest of the donor, which may cause them to agree to fund activities outside of their current giving guidelines.

- ***Does it seem likely that the funder will make grants to organizations in your geographic location?*** Although it isn't necessary for a funder to have awarded grants in your state or city, prior giving in your geographic area is a good indication that a funder may be interested in your project. Check the funder's guidelines for specific geographic limitations, and be on the lookout for local or regional giving patterns or concentrated giving in rural or urban areas that might exclude your project.

- ***What are the financial conditions that may affect the foundation's ability to give?*** In general, a foundation's prior level of giving is a good indication of its capacity to give in the future, since foundations must pay out 5 percent of their assets each year. However, this amount can increase if the funder has recently received a large contribution, possibly from the donor. Also, foundations, like any institution, are affected by economic conditions. In a strong economic environment a foundation's assets will often increase, and in a slow economy assets will often decline, reducing the amount of funding that is available to nonprofit grantseekers.

- ***Does the funder give to the same nonprofit groups every year, or have they committed their resources many years into the future?*** Some foundations fund the same organizations each year and have few grant dollars left to support new grantees' projects. Refer to a funder's list of grants for the past two to three years to discern patterns like this that would limit your chances of funding. Other funders make multi-year grant commitments that can limit the amount of funds they have available for new projects. Grants lists should indicate such long-term funding commitments as well.

- ***Does the amount of money you are requesting fit within the funder's typical grant range?*** You are looking for patterns in the foundation's past giving. If your research shows that a grantmaker's largest grant over the past few years is $25,000, you should not ask for $40,000. At the same time you should be looking for more subtle distinctions, such as the giving range in the particular subject area for which you seek funding. Also remember that some funders may give first-time grantees smaller grants until they have an established relationship with your organization.

- ***Does the funder have a policy prohibiting grants for the type(s) of support you are requesting?*** Some foundations will not make grants for the general support of your organization. Others will not provide funds for endowments, building projects, or equipment. Determine whether the funder is willing to consider the type of support you need.

- ***Does the funder usually make grants to cover the full cost of a project or does it favor projects where other funders will participate?*** Unless you are seeking funding for a very small project, it is unlikely that a first-time donor will fund an entire project. Most funders assume that grantseekers will be approaching multiple funders for their project, asking each to contribute a portion of the needed funds.

- ***Does the funder put limits on the length of time it is willing to support a project?*** Some foundations favor one-time grants, while others will continue their support over a number of years. However, it is rare to find a grantmaker that will commit funding to an organization for an indefinite period of time.

- ***What types of organizations does the funder tend to support?*** As part of your research, check to see if the funder favors large, well-established groups such as universities and museums, or supports smaller, community-based groups. Some funders will support a wide range of organizational types, while others will not. Lists of past recipients can provide good insight into this matter, whereas it may not be stated in a funder's printed guidelines.

- ***Does the funder have application deadlines?*** Note carefully any information you uncover regarding deadlines and board meeting dates so that you can submit your proposal at the appropriate time. Some funders have application deadlines, while others review proposals on a continuing basis.

- ***Do you or does anyone on your board or staff know someone connected with the funder?*** You will want to gather background information on the funder's current trustees and staff. In doing so you may find some connections between your organization and a potential funder that will make it easier to approach the funder. While knowing someone who is affiliated with a prospective funder usually is not enough to secure a grant, it does tend to facilitate the process.

STEP 3: REFINING YOUR PROSPECT LIST

The importance of answering all of the above questions to the best of your ability and doing a thorough job in your research cannot be overstated. Since the initial research you performed probably focused on fields of interest and geographic focus, looking closely at a prospect's willingness to provide the type of support your organization needs is critical. Appendix D contains a complete list of types of support with definitions.

Although it is difficult to generalize, larger foundations are usually more likely to provide more sizeable grants—often for special projects—because they have a professional staff with expertise in their subject area(s), whereas smaller foundations are typically volunteer- or family-run enterprises where grants decisions may be made as infrequently as once or twice a year. Smaller foundations usually do not have subject specialists, so they may well provide general operating funds to the local charities in the communities they care about and on a longer-term basis than larger foundations.

For greater success, you'll want to approach multiple grantmakers at one time with *targeted* (not "one-size-fits-all") grant requests. As you winnow and prioritize your list, you may be tempted to focus all your efforts on one or two "ideal" funders. You should resist this temptation. As long as the funder's guidelines and the other information you uncover do not rule out your organization as a potential grantee, you should keep it on your list. A funder may not have stated the exact specifications of your program as a particular area of interest, but your program may still fit within its broader funding goals. It's also very possible that your organization has different, but concurrent, needs and you may be researching prospects for a variety of projects at once. Under these circumstances, you will be wise to devise different priority lists, so that the most likely funders become your primary list, while others that may require research at a later date, or longer-term cultivation, can be relegated temporarily to a secondary list.

For those funders that remain on your primary list, those that match your organization's interests most closely and have the ability to provide the greatest financial support will rise to the top. But don't forget about the others that have made it through your preliminary screening. For example, smaller funders can play a significant role in your overall funding strategies. Remember, this year's small grants may turn into future years' larger grants, and both large and small funders have the ability to become long-term supporters. Also, funders may turn you down this year because your project is not an exact fit with their interests. These same funders, however, could be impressed by your organization's work and may look more favorably at your next request. It is not unusual for fundraisers to be researching more than one list at the same time: prospects for different types of support, or for concurrent projects, for example. You also may have determined that some funders will require longer-term cultivation, so research on those grantmakers will span an extended period of time.

Pulling It All Together

The final phase of your research will focus on those prospects that seem most likely to consider your proposal favorably. During this phase you will be gathering information on the funder's current financial status, its preferred application procedures, and its most recent grantmaking activities. Primary resources, including a foundation's Form 990-PF, web site, and/or printed materials, such as annual reports and guideline brochures, are the essential sources at this stage.

AND DON'T OVERLOOK ...

During this intense phase of your research, you may decide that the applicability of your program to a funder can only be answered by a preliminary telephone call or e-mail to the foundation you have in mind. If this is the case, be fully prepared with hard facts about your project, a brief description of your organization's mission and programs, and the amount of funding you are seeking. With a brief and to-the-point conversation or e-mail correspondence, you are hoping to learn that your project is a potential good fit with the foundation's interests, and that you'll be invited to submit a letter of inquiry or even a full proposal. More advice about initial approaches to foundations can be found in Chapter 10.

It may seem obvious, but don't overlook the background information available in your own organization's fundraising files. All too often, new development staff begin work unaware that clues to good funding prospects may already have been documented by their predecessors; unfortunately, the reverse can also occur—you may find few or only sketchy records about research or contacts that had already been initiated. Whatever the case, your research strategy may well begin by pulling together from a variety of sources the details of your organization's past funding history. The reason for this is that previous supporters are a likely source of grants in the future or, on the other hand, may have stipulated that they would not welcome additional solicitations until a certain amount of time has elapsed. So more often than one would imagine, your research strategy will begin by delving into the records you are able to find in the files of your own development office. And that leads to the following essential advice.

Record What You Do

You must keep careful records of your findings during the research
process and especially once you have made contact with a potential funder.
It helps to think of the first activity as "data gathering" and the second as
"record keeping."

DATA GATHERING

Throughout the research process you should gather as many pertinent facts
about each of your funding prospects as possible. Develop careful files, either
in hard copy or electronically. Each record on a potential funder should
include the information in the Prospect Worksheet shown in Figure 4-1.
These records should be updated on a regular basis to provide a dynamic,
consolidated base of funding information for your organization. Developing
such a system helps to compensate for one of the biggest problems nonprofits
face—the lack of continuity in fundraising efforts due to staff turnover.

It is important to document your research at every step along the way. As
you gather facts about a funder, note the source and date of the information
so that later on, if you come across conflicting information, you can quickly
determine which is more current. While such attention to detail at the outset
may seem needlessly time-consuming, careful data gathering is guaranteed to
save you and your organization time and money in the long run.

RECORD KEEPING

You need to keep track of each and every contact between representatives
of your organization and a staff or board member at a funding institution.
Your files should include copies of your letters of inquiry, formal proposals,
and supporting documents, as well as reports, press releases, and invitations
to events. Print out copies of any e-mail correspondence between you and a
funding representative. In addition, you should keep careful notes regarding
informational and follow-up phone calls, and your written summaries of
interviews and site visits. Each record should include the date and the initials
of the individual who made the contact. Figure 4-2 is a sample all-purpose
form for keeping track of contacts with potential funders. It can also serve as
a "tickler" or reminder to let you know when the next steps need to be taken.
There are a number of resources on commercially available record-keeping
software programs at our web site in the FAQ "Where can I find information
on fundraising and accounting software packages for my nonprofit

Figure 4-2. Record of Funding Contact

Grantmaker (name and address): _____

_____

Principal Contact (name and title): _____

_____

Telephone Calls _____

Date(s): _____

Time(s): _____

Call made by: _____

Spoke to: _____

Comments: _____

_____

MEETINGS	Date: Time: Outcome:	
PROPOSALS	Date submitted: Format: Signed by:	For project: Amount requested: Board meeting date(s):
TICKLER	Deadline: To do: Follow up:	By whom: By whom:
DECISION Yes/No: Notification date: Reason for rejection:		**NEXT STEP** Resubmit: Cultivation: Special activities: Send report:
Notes:		

organization?" (foundationcenter.org/getstarted/faqs/html/software). You can also develop your own system using any versatile data management software package, such as Microsoft Access. The Notepad feature of *FC Search* and the tagging option in *Foundation Directory Online Professional* enable subscribers to create a very basic prospect tracking and tickler system as well.

Summary

Doing your homework is your key to uncovering grant opportunities. Know your own program and develop a clear idea of what you are trying to accomplish. Formulate a plan and calculate what it will cost to carry out your grant project. Then you are ready to compile a broad list of prospects that are interested in your subject field, give in your geographic area, and/or offer the types and amounts of support your organization needs. The list of prospects you compile will need to be refined, and the grantmakers clearly not interested in your program or geographic location eliminated. After all of this is accomplished, you can begin in-depth research on the remaining funders, using several resources to determine the fit. While this is going on, you will need to keep accurate records of your efforts (and continue to do so even after you have submitted a proposal). The next chapter describes in more detail key online resources for performing funding research. After that, we'll provide suggestions about various search strategies.

Online Resources for Funding Research

A wide range of resources is available to help you identify sources of support for your organization or project. Before you can plan effective search strategies you need to become familiar with these resources, their content, features, and how they differ from one another. The types and number of tools you use will depend upon several variables, including the particular grant project you have in mind.

In this chapter we'll concentrate primarily on the resources that are accessible on the Internet (in Chapter 8 we'll cover other tools in print or CD-ROM format) with tips on how to use them. The resources described here can be consulted at the five Center libraries, and most are also available at more than 350 Cooperating Collections (see Appendix F). Although you may want to subscribe to some of the databases or purchase the tools described in this guide as additions to your organization's library, we recommend that, initially, grantseekers invest their time rather than their money. Visit one of our libraries or Cooperating Collections and try out the resources relating to your area of interest before making a decision as to which databases will prove most useful.

Electronically available resources that describe the grantmaking universe usually fall into one of five categories: (1) general grantmaker databases; (2) databases of grants awarded in the recent past; (3) specialized funding databases, such as those that focus on corporate philanthropy; (4) original or primary materials generated or published by grantmakers, including information at their web sites and tax returns filed annually by foundations with the IRS; and (5) secondary resources such as newspaper or journal articles.

The Foundation Center's Database

The Foundation Center first implemented its computerized database in 1972. Since that time the database has grown in size, scope, and quality. Its records provide detailed information on more than one million grants and over 90,000 currently active grantmakers, including background data on the grantmaker; its purpose and programs; application procedures; the names of its trustees, officers, and donors; its current financial data; and more.

Information stored in the Center's database is drawn primarily from one of three sources: (1) information provided by grantmakers, including responses to questionnaires, online update forms, electronically transmitted grants lists, grantmaker-issued reports, application guidelines, financial statements, and informational brochures; (2) annual IRS information returns—Forms 990-PF, filed by private foundations, and Forms 990, filed by grantmaking public charities, both of which the Center receives from the IRS; and (3) grantmaker web sites and other Internet-based resources. Center staff verify and update the data from the latter two sources. The Center then makes the verified information available through several media: online databases (including *Foundation Directory Online, Foundation Grants to Individuals Online, Corporate Giving Online*, Foundation Finder, and 990 Finder); CD-ROMs (*FC Search: The Foundation Center's Database on CD-ROM* and various state directories in CD-ROM format); printed directories; and other publications.

CAVEAT EMPTOR

The following advice is pertinent to *both* online and print publications because you will want to pay attention to the quality of the information in each resource as well as its relevance to your funding search. It is especially important to:

- determine the reputation of the publisher or database compiler, since different resources have varying degrees of reliability;

- note the date the book was published or when the database was last updated and whether or not it contains the most current information available;

- read the introduction and any instructions on how to use the resource, paying particular attention to how the information was acquired and what editorial standards and verification procedures, if any, were used in obtaining it; and

- familiarize yourself with the format, indexes, special features, and the kinds of information about potential funding sources contained in the database or print publication.

Taking the time to evaluate resources for their accuracy and thoroughness prior to using them will save you countless hours that might otherwise be wasted.

FOUNDATION FINDER AND 990 FINDER

The easiest to use of all the online search options are Foundation Finder and 990 Finder—quick look-up tools accessible from the main screen of the Foundation Center's web site. With basic information on more than 90,000 grantmakers in the U.S.—including private foundations, community foundations, grantmaking public charities, and corporate giving programs—Foundation Finder (Figure 5-1) is handy for securing up-to-date information, and it is searchable by grantmaker name (or partial name), grantmaker city, state, zip code, and Employer Identification Number (EIN). The contents of the record in Foundation Finder include: complete address, contact person, type of foundation, brief fiscal data, EIN, and a link to the most recent Forms 990. Using Foundation Finder is a convenient way to verify that your basic information about a funder is still correct. 990 Finder is a tool that provides quick access to Forms 990 (filed by organizations) and 990-PF (filed by foundations). There is no charge to use either Foundation Finder or 990 Finder.

Figure 5-1. Foundation Finder

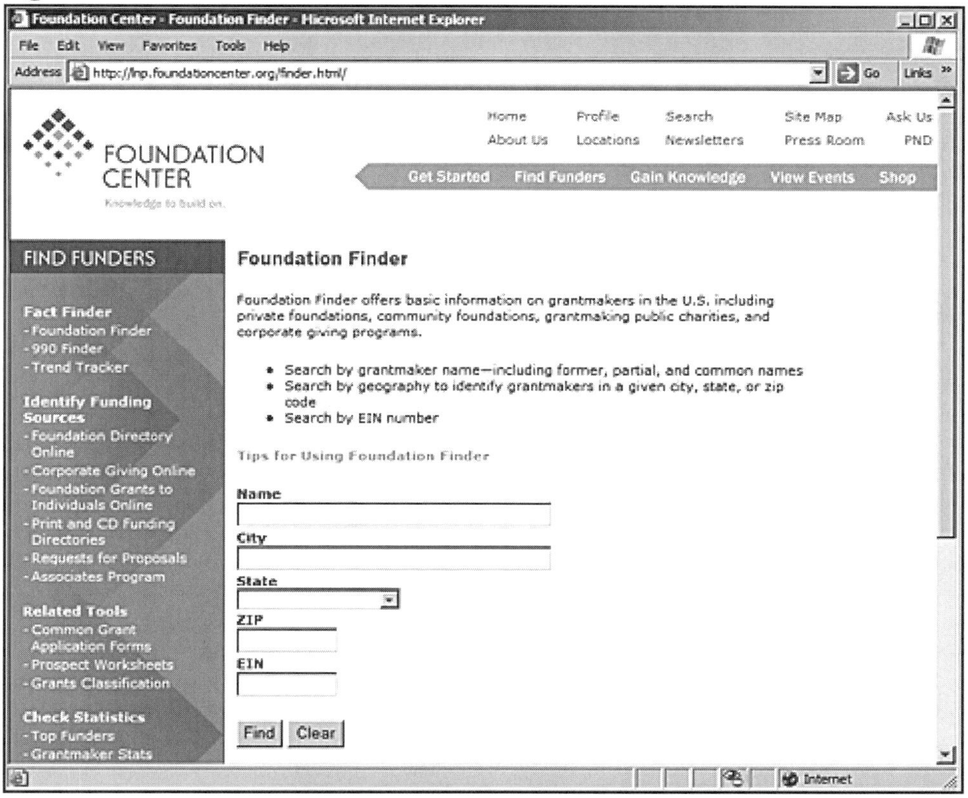

Figure 5-2. Comparison Chart of Subscription Plans for *Foundation Directory Online*

FOUNDATION CENTER
Knowledge to build on.

Plan Features	Basic	Plus	Premium	Platinum	Professional
Complete profiles of the top 10,000 U.S. foundations including trustees, officers, and donors	✓	✓	✓	✓	✓
Daily philanthropy news and RFPs	✓	✓	✓	✓	✓
Multiple search options including keyword search and Boolean operators	✓	✓	✓	✓	✓
Descriptions of more than 1.1 million recent grants		✓	✓	✓	✓
Complete profiles of the top 20,000 U.S. foundations including trustees, officers, and donors			✓	✓	✓
Over 92,000 detailed profiles of all current U.S. grantmakers including trustees, officers, and donors				✓	✓
Profiles of more than 10,500 grantmaking public charities and nearly 1,400 corporate giving programs				✓	✓
Our *Corporate Giving Online* database with links to more than 4,200 corporate foundations and giving programs					✓
"Search 990s" database with ability to search across our complete universe of IRS 990s					✓
Recent news and publications, RFPs, job postings, and key staff affiliations for specific grantmakers					✓
Full-color grant distribution charts analyzing giving trends for specific grantmakers					✓
Update alerts on new and high-growth grantmakers and changes to grantmaker profiles					✓

FOUNDATION DIRECTORY ONLINE

Since its introduction in 1999, *Foundation Directory Online* (fconline. foundationcenter.org), the Center's web-based database, has become the most popular way for Center audiences to search the grantmaking universe for potential funders. *Foundation Directory Online* is a subscription-based service that allows searches across multiple fields, in addition to keyword searching, to return targeted lists of funding prospects. Subscribers can use *Foundation Directory Online* at home or at work to gain immediate access to information on thousands of grantmakers and their giving interests. It is also available for free public use at the Foundation Center's five library/learning centers and more than 350 Cooperating Collections across the nation. New data (updated information on existing foundations as well as on new foundations) is added weekly and enhanced features are introduced on an ongoing and regular basis to further facilitate funding research.

Subscriptions to *Foundation Directory Online* are offered at monthly and yearly rates, and there are discounts available for multiple-user needs. See Figure 5-2 for a comparison of the subscription options for *Foundation Directory Online.* The highest subscription level, *Foundation Directory Online Professional,* contains four separate databases devoted to *Grantmakers, Companies, Grants,* and *990s.* In order to illustrate the greatest number of features, we'll focus on the Professional level of *Foundation Directory Online* (see Figure 5-3) in this and subsequent chapters of the guide. If you visit a Center library or a Cooperating Collection, it is the Professional level of the database that you will be using.

Grantmakers Database

A good initial strategy is to begin with *Foundation Directory Online Professional's* Search Grantmakers database (see Figure 5-4) where you will be examining funder profiles. A successful search result will include a list of foundations and/or corporate giving programs that have a demonstrated interest in your subject area *and* your geographic location, as well as some of the other commonalities described in the prior chapter. You can then research each funder on the list by first reviewing its profile.

Companies Database

The fundraising strategies of many nonprofit organizations include seeking support from corporations. Corporations may provide support to nonprofits in a variety of ways. Some corporations give only through a private foundation, while others give only through direct giving programs. Still others use both vehicles to support nonprofits in their communities. Using the Search Companies database of *Foundation Directory Online Professional* (Figure 5-5) leads the researcher to information on more than 3,600 corporations, with links to profiles about their foundations and other corporate giving programs. Information about these corporate givers is also available in the Grantmakers database, but selecting the Companies database allows you to search corporate-specific data, and link to the 10-K form filed by publicly held companies.

Figure 5-3. Main Screen—*Foundation Directory Online Professional*

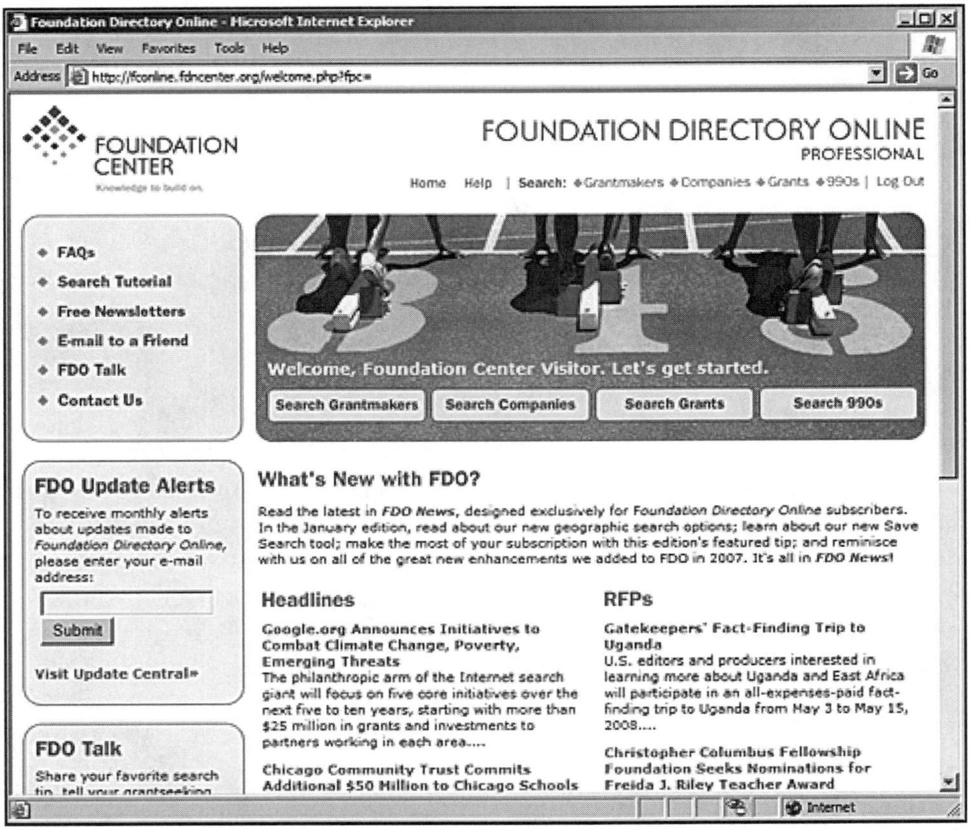

Grants Database

Grants databases (see Figure 5-6) help you identify funders with a demonstrated interest in your subject or geographic area by listing and indexing the actual grants they have awarded. Studying listings of grants a foundation has recently awarded will give you a better understanding of its giving priorities in terms of the types of programs and organizations it funds, the amount of money it awards for specific programs, the geographic area in which it concentrates its grantmaking activities, the population groups it serves through its grants, and the types of support it typically offers.

Figure 5-4. Search Grantmakers—*Foundation Directory Online Professional*

The Foundation Center currently compiles detailed data on reported grants of $10,000 and more awarded by the 1,000 largest foundations (measured by total giving in that year). Because giving by any one foundation may rise or fall from year to year, this group of 1,000 may not be the same every year, although approximately 700 grantmakers usually qualify year after year. For the past several years, grants by the top 15 foundations in each state have also been included and indexed for the database. In this database you will also find selected grants from foundations that report to the Center electronically and from some smaller foundations; these are added when information is available as a way to more completely portray the funding activity of the grantmaker universe. The Center's database currently contains more than one million grant records. Some 200,000 new records are added to the database every year.

Figure 5-5. Search Companies—*Foundation Directory Online Professional*

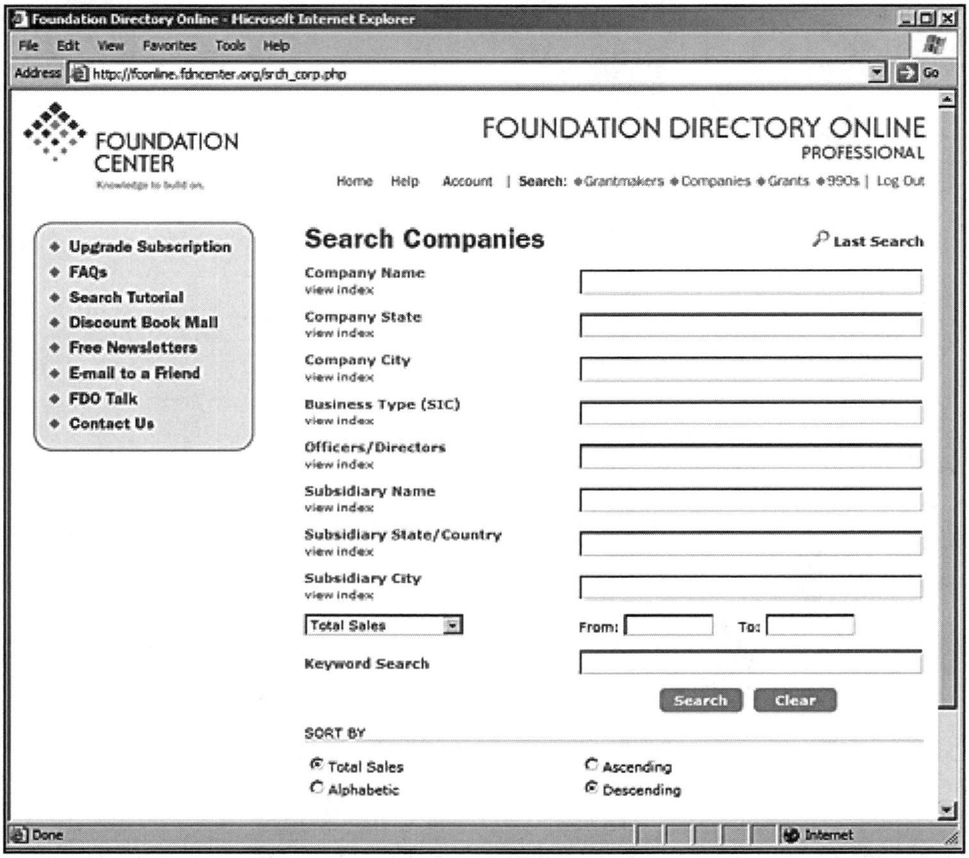

GRANTS CLASSIFICATION—NTEE

The Center introduced a classification system based on the National Taxonomy of Exempt Entities (NTEE) in 1972. The NTEE is a comprehensive coding scheme developed by the National Center for Charitable Statistics that established a unified standard for classifying nonprofit organizations while permitting a multi-dimensional structure for analyzing grants. The Center's classification system provides a concise and consistent hierarchical method with which to classify and index grants and the nonprofit organizations receiving foundation funding. With this system, hundreds of specific terms can be researched with consistent results, and grant dollars can be tallied to determine distribution patterns. For more information about NTEE and the Center's Grants Classification System, see Appendix C.

Figure 5-6. Search Grants—*Foundation Directory Online Professional*

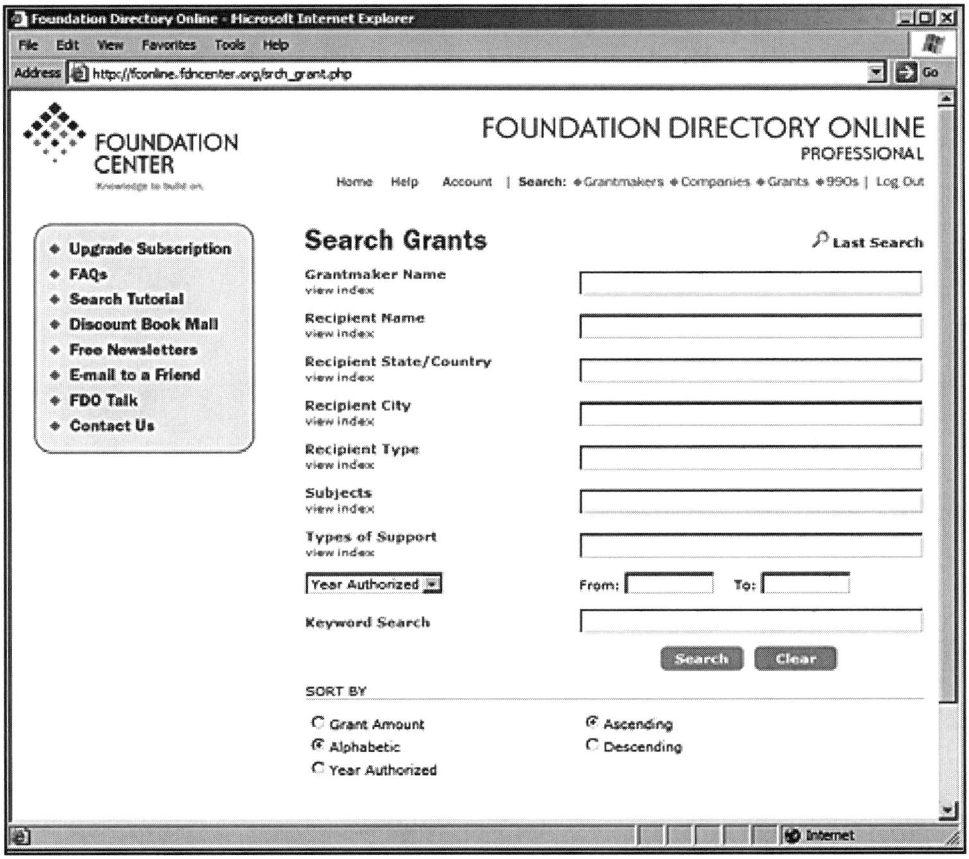

990s Database

Among other information, a foundation's 990-PF contains a complete list of grants for each year. A search of the 990s Database scans all of the 990-PF and 990 documents for the specific terms that you input, and so can reveal more information on mission statements, names of organizations or people who run foundations and recipient organizations, as well as uncovering smaller grants and/or grants awarded by smaller foundations that are not indexed in the Center's Grants Database. Figure 5-7 shows the search screen for this database. Most grantseekers search 990s as an adjunct to traditional subject searches. Although 990-PFs can be read individually using other search mechanisms, this search option in *Foundation Directory Online Professional* is distinctive and powerful.

More details on searching the four databases that comprise *Foundation Directory Online Professional* along with tips and strategies for the grantseeker can be found in Chapters 6 and 7.

Figure 5-7. Search 990s—*Foundation Directory Online Professional*

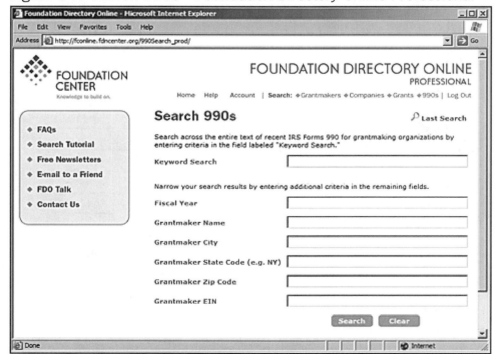

Additional Online Funding Research Tools

FOUNDATION INFORMATION RETURNS: THE FORM 990-PF

As noted, the Form 990-PF is one of the best and most comprehensive sources of information on private foundations. Private foundations are required to file this tax form annually with the Internal Revenue Service (IRS). Federal law requires that these documents, unlike personal or corporate tax returns, be made available to the public by both the IRS and by the foundations themselves. This means that for all private foundations, regardless of size, basic facts about their operations and grants are a matter of public record. Unlike other tax-exempt organizations, private foundations are also required to make the names and addresses of their donors available to the public.

Many types of researchers use IRS Forms 990 and 990-PF to uncover information that's included in these documents. For example, scholarly articles, dissertations, and research reports about the nonprofit field are often based on data from these forms. Congressional investigators and journalists look to these documents in preparing factual reports and analyses. Investment counselors and other financial professionals can find information about a grantmaker's investments here. Job seekers and others look at forms filed by specific foundations and nonprofits to find information on staffing patterns and to ascertain salary information for key executives. Grantmakers themselves peruse the Forms 990-PF to compare staffing, salary, and program information for other foundations of a similar size to their own. They can also determine what grants other foundations are making in a particular field when seeking potential funding partners. And of course, staff at the Foundation Center refer to these forms for key information on foundations, especially newer or smaller ones.

Forms 990-PF supply key information as well as a complete list of grants awarded in a particular year. For many smaller foundations this information return is the *only* complete record of their operations and grantmaking activities. (Be aware that the 990-PFs for larger foundations may be hundreds of pages in length, and so might not be the most efficient tool for funding research, especially since larger grantmakers are likely to publish annual reports and/or maintain web sites.) See Figure 5-8 for a diagram of the Form 990-PF indicating where some of the most important information will be found, including contact information, assets, list of officers, application information, listings of grants paid, and of future planned or committed grants.

Figure 5-8. Form 990-PF

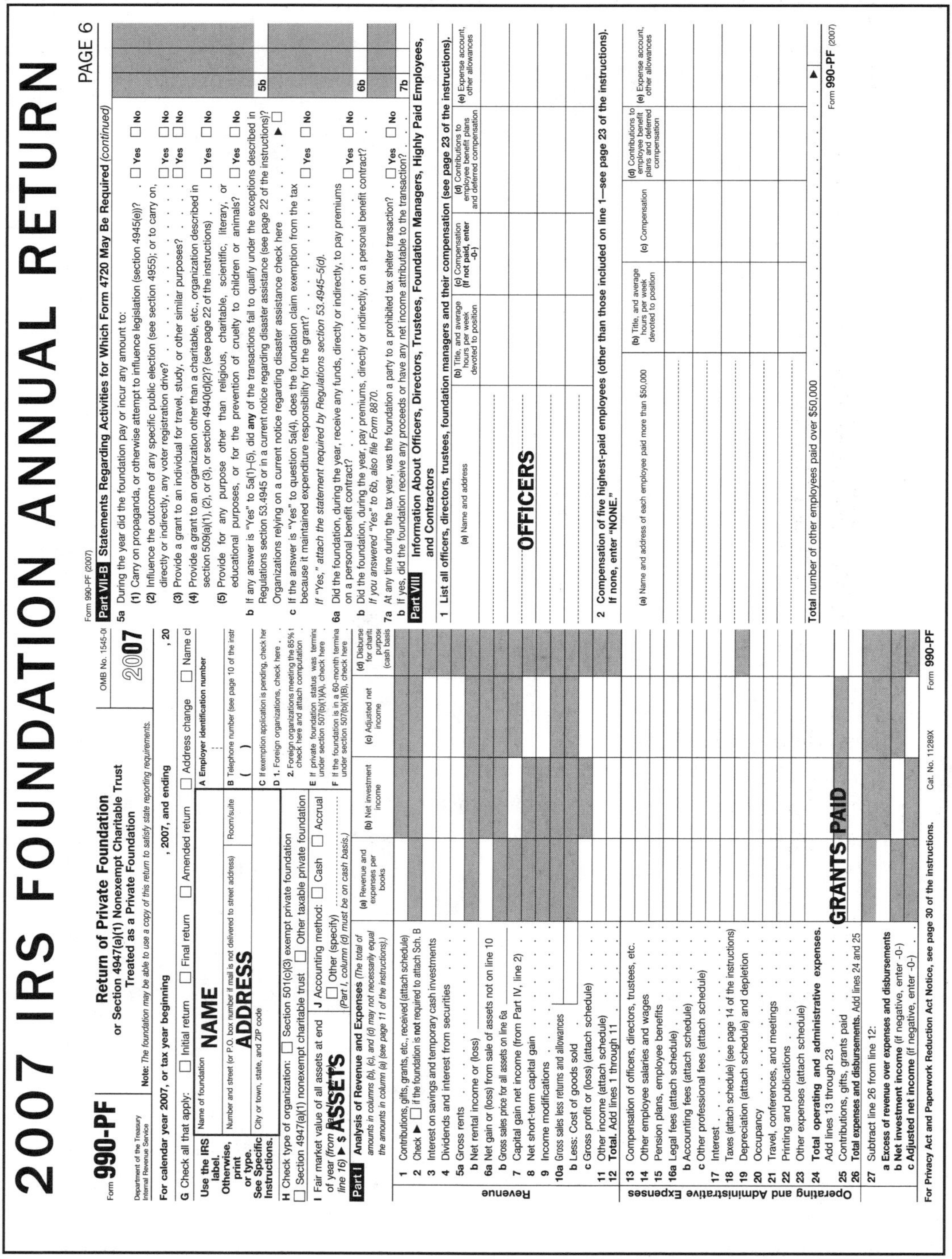

Figure 5-8. continued

PAGE 10

Form 990-PF (2007)

Part XIV Private Operating Foundations (see page 27 of the instructions and Part VII-A, question 9)

1a If the foundation has received a ruling or determination letter that it is a private operating foundation, and the ruling is effective for 2007, enter the date of the ruling . . . . . ▶

b Check box to indicate whether the foundation is a private operating foundation described in section ☐ 4942(j)(3) or ☐ 4942(j)(5)

	Tax year		Prior 3 years		
	(a) 2007	(b) 2006	(c) 2005	(d) 2004	(e) Total
2a Enter the lesser of the adjusted net income from Part I or the minimum investment return from Part X for each year listed					
b 85% of line 2a					
c Qualifying distributions from Part XII, line 4 for each year listed . . .					
d Amounts included in line 2c not used directly for active conduct of exempt activities					
e Qualifying distributions made directly for active conduct of exempt activities. Subtract line 2d from line 2c . .					
3 Complete 3a, b, or c for the alternative test relied upon:					
a "Assets" alternative test—enter:					
(1) Value of all assets					
(2) Value of assets qualifying under section 4942(j)(3)(B)(i)					
b "Endowment" alternative test—enter ⅔ of minimum investment return shown in Part X, line 6 for each year listed . .					
c "Support" alternative test—enter:					
(1) Total support other than gross investment income (interest, dividends, rents, payments on securities loans (section 512(a)(5)), or royalties)					
(2) Support from general public and 5 or more exempt organizations as provided in section 4942(j)(3)(B)(iii) . .					
(3) Largest amount of support from an exempt organization . . .					
(4) Gross investment income . .					

Part XV Supplementary Information (Complete this part only if the foundation had $5,000 or more in assets at any time during the year—see page 28 of the instructions.)

1 Information Regarding Foundation Managers:

a List any managers of the foundation who have contributed more than 2% of the total contributions received by the foundation before the close of any tax year (but only if they have contributed more than $5,000). (See section 507(d)(2).)

b List any managers of the foundation who own 10% or more of the stock of a corporation (or an equally large portion of the ownership of a partnership or other entity) of which the foundation has a 10% or greater interest.

2 Information Regarding Contribution, Grant, Gift, Loan, Scholarship, etc., Programs:

Check here ▶ ☐ If the foundation only makes contributions to preselected charitable organizations and does not accept unsolicited requests for funds. If the foundation makes gifts, grants, etc. (see page 28 of the instructions) to individuals or organizations under other conditions, complete items 2a, b, c, and d.

a The name, address, and telephone number of the person to whom applications should be addressed:

b The form in which applications should be submitted and information and materials they should include:

APPLICATION
INFORMATION

c Any submission deadlines:

d Any restrictions or limitations on awards, such as by geographical areas, charitable fields, kinds of institutions, or other factors:

Form **990-PF** (2007)

PAGE 11

Form 990-PF (2007)

Part XV Supplementary Information (continued)

3 Grants and Contributions Paid During the Year or Approved for Future Payment

Recipient		If recipient is an individual, show any relationship to any foundation manager or substantial contributor	Foundation status of recipient	Purpose of grant or contribution	Amount
Name and address (home or business)					
a Paid during the year					

GRANTS PAID

Total . . . . ▶ 3a

b Approved for future payment

FUTURE GRANTS

Total . . . . ▶ 3b

Form **990-PF** (2007)

Since community foundations generally are classified as public charities and not as private foundations, they are not required to file a Form 990-PF with the IRS. Like other public charities, they file Form 990. Most community foundations also issue separate annual reports, have web sites, or otherwise make available information about their activities. Keep in mind that many community foundations are actively engaged in soliciting funds as well as in grantmaking. Hence, it is in their self-interest to make their activities broadly known.

Where to Obtain IRS Form 990-PF Information Returns

Most grantseekers use the Internet to access 990s. 990 Finder (foundationcenter.org/findfunders/990finder) provides access to more than 440,000 of these documents in Adobe PDF format. (Multiple years are provided when available.) Forms 990-PF are updated at the Center's web site with new returns approximately every four to six weeks. There is no need to register to use this tool. See Figure 5-9.

Figure 5-9. 990 Finder

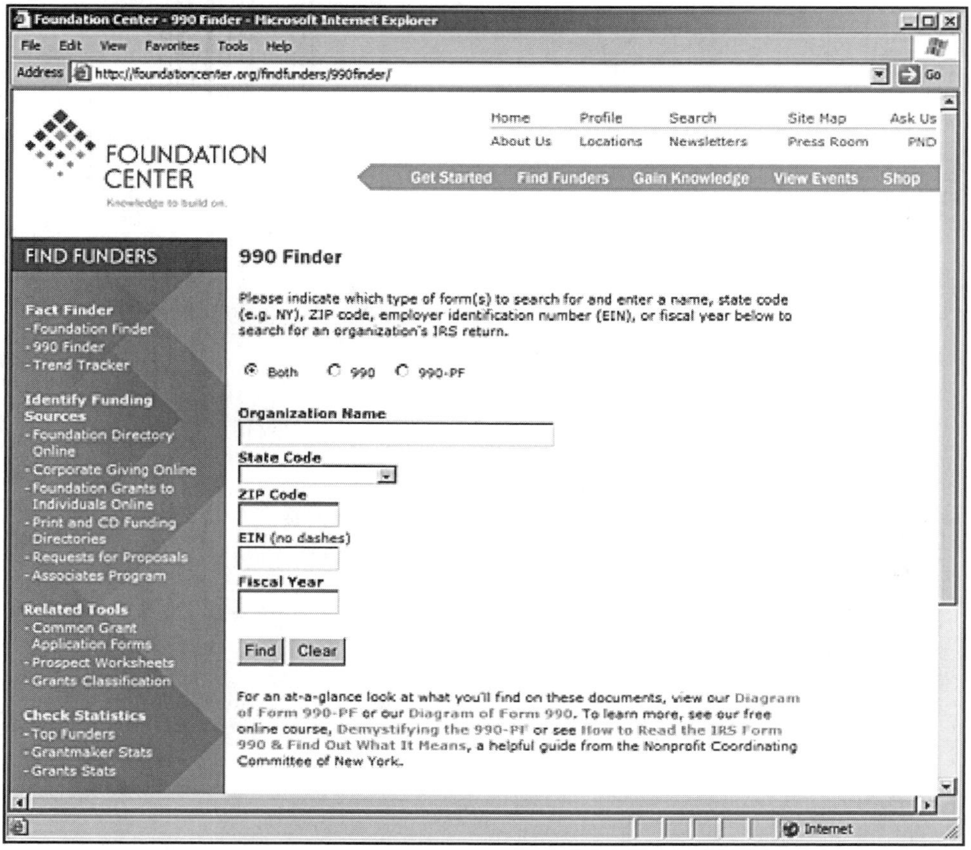

In addition to the Foundation Center's 990 Finder, GuideStar and Economic Research Institute provide ready links to the forms.

GuideStar (guidestar.org), an online database of information on the activities and finances of nearly one million nonprofit organizations, run by Philanthropic Research Inc., makes nonprofit tax returns—Forms 990-PF and 990—accessible at its web site. To use GuideStar at the basic level of service, registration is required.

Economic Research Institute's web site (eri-nonprofit-salaries.com/ index.cfm?FuseAction=NPO.Search) has a search tool to find nonprofit information, including links to Forms 990. This company provides compensation, benefits, and human resource research for private and public organizations in the form of published reports and software database products.

If none of these options yield a Form 990 that you are seeking, you may try to ascertain if a state attorney general's office (naag.org/ag/full_ag_table.php) has copies of Form 990-PF or state tax returns available for public persual. For instance, if the organization you are looking for is located in California, the State Attorney General's office of California (caag.state.ca.us/charities) posts California charity and foundation tax returns (Forms CT-2, 990, 990-EZ, and 990-PF) on its web site.

HOW SOON WILL A FOUNDATION'S FORM 990-PF BE AVAILABLE?

Grantseekers often ask how long it takes for new Form 990-PF information to appear in Center databases and publications. The following timeline may help to explain the most likely scenario: Foundations are required to file their 990-PF within four and a half months from the time their fiscal year closes. Since approximately 70–75 percent of foundations have a January 1–December 31 fiscal year, this means that the filing deadline for most foundations is May 15 of the following year. However, foundations can request a six-month extension from the IRS. Many foundations do this, and the IRS grants the extension in almost all cases. If an extension is granted, the 990-PF is not due to be submitted to the IRS until November. It then takes the IRS several months to process, prepare, and scan the 990-PFs into a digitized format and to send them to the Foundation Center. The practical impact of this typical scenario is that grantseekers will not be able to view the 2007 activities of most foundations until sometime in 2009. For more information, see the FAQ at our web site: "What is the lag time between the close of a foundation's fiscal year and the date its tax return is available in a Foundation Center library or on its web site?" (foundationcenter.org/getstarted/faqs/html/lag_time.html).

GRANTMAKER WEB SITES

It is important that you review all the information that is relevant to your organization's potential solicitation of a funder, and the information on a foundation's web site is likely to provide the most *current* description available. Remember, this is one of the few primary sources other than the grantmaker's 990-PF or annual report. And it is often the best place to read about a foundation's interests in its own words. Upwards of 10,000 grantmakers (including *all* types of funders in the Center's database) currently have a presence on the Internet. The most useful foundation web sites include content that can help you determine if your nonprofit's programs are a good fit with a funder's priorities. Typical grantmaker web site contents include a brief history of the foundation, program descriptions, recent grants lists, and application guidelines. Some also contain electronic versions of the foundation's annual reports. A few foundations provide these publications and other information *only* on the web, and this may be a growing trend. The breadth of information on grantmaker web sites can vary significantly from one foundation to another. Although the quantity of information available often correlates with a funder's size, sometimes you will come across a small foundation with a very comprehensive web site, and the reverse may be true as well.

The Foundation Center helps grantseekers identify which foundations and corporate giving programs have web sites. At the Center's own web site you can search Foundation Finder, which has links to the home pages of funders that have web sites. *Foundation Directory Online* provides ready access to grantmaker web sites by a link in the foundation's profile. Foundation Center print directories also list the web addresses of available grantmaker web sites.

THE FOUNDATION CENTER'S WEB SITE

The Internet has rapidly become *the* essential tool for almost any type of research endeavor. The scope and quantity of new web resources mushrooms daily. The web is an important tool for the grantseeker because it can provide access to both primary and secondary resources from a very wide range of sources. Because of the proliferation of web-based information, the challenge for grantseekers is to locate the most reputable sites and learn how to navigate efficiently through their most important features.

The Center's web site (foundationcenter.org) is particularly useful to the grantseeker because it is an authoritative and information-rich source of up-to-date information on private philanthropy in the United States. The ever-changing content is designed to assist both novice and experienced grantseekers, grantmakers, researchers, members of the media, and the general public. Because of this depth of information, currently it can be somewhat challenging to the first-time visitor. To facilitate navigation through the site, it is divided into five main areas: Get Started, Find Funders, Gain Knowledge, View Events, and Shop (see Figure 5-10). Each area is organized to create a logical path for users. There is also a site map for ease of navigation.

Figure 5-10. Foundation Center's Web Site

Some of the most frequently visited areas of the Center's web site include:

- 150 searchable FAQs, with well-researched answers to questions on a range of topics, from proposal writing, to the do's and don'ts of starting a nonprofit organization, to the funding research process itself;

- Foundation Finder and 990 Finder (described on page 53)—both free, quick look-up tools;

- Proposal Writing Short Course (in English, French, Mandarin, Portuguese, Russian, and Spanish);

- Common Grant Application Forms and Prospect Worksheets;

- Information about our five library/learning centers—in Atlanta, Cleveland, New York, San Francisco, and Washington, DC—where you can learn more about Foundation Center programs, and philanthropy in general, in your part of the country. It's easy to sign up for the free weekly e-mail newsletter from the library nearest you;

- Our network of 350+ Cooperating Collections that puts the Center's database, a core collection of Foundation Center publications and supplementary materials, along with expertise on how to use them, within convenient driving distance for most residents of the continental United States;

- Online calendars and registration forms for our in-person training or e-classes;

- Other areas where you can find the most recently available statistics on foundations and grants; access the Center's "Ask Us" service; and subscribe to online database products.

Additional Research Sources

Secondary sources of use to grantseekers include information produced by some source other than grantmakers themselves. Newspaper and periodical articles are the most-often-referred-to secondary sources. Increasingly, you may see articles about individual grantmakers or foundations in general in local and national newspapers and on the Internet. You'll note that while a few foundations seem to receive a great deal of press coverage, most are never mentioned. The Foundation Center maintains several resources to help identify and access relevant print and electronic articles that are available free to the public at the Center's web site. These include Catalog of Nonprofit Literature (CNL), PubHub, and *Philanthropy News Digest* (PND).

The Catalog of Nonprofit Literature (cnl.foundationcenter.org), a searchable database of the literature of philanthropy, incorporates the unique contents of the Foundation Center's five libraries and provides the ability to mine the Center's rich collection of books, articles, and electronic publications related to the field of philanthropy and the nonprofit sector. This research tool is updated daily and helps you keep abreast of the published information on philanthropy, the foundation world, corporate giving, voluntarism, and more. During the research phase on a specific funder, it's a good idea to check CNL to see if recent articles can provide more information. The Catalog contains more than 26,000 bibliographic citations, most with informative abstracts, and many with links to full texts. CNL can be searched (see Figure 5-11) simultaneously by subject, author, title, publisher, journal

Figure 5-11. Catalog of Nonprofit Literature

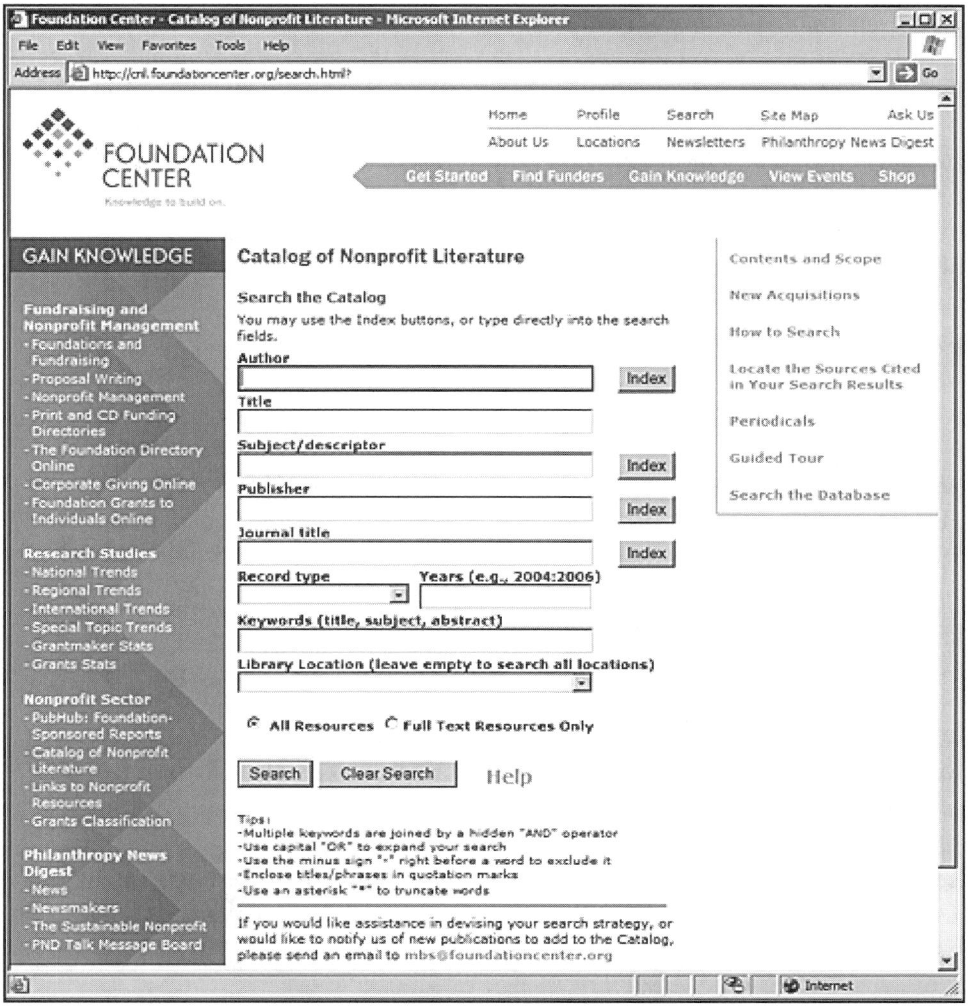

title, record type, year of publication, keyword, and library location. The "New Acquisitions" feature contains the latest additions to the database organized by subject category. The CNL blog (cnl-librarian.blogspot.com) provides a forum for sharing information related to new publications of interest to the field.

PubHub (foundationcenter.org/gainknowledge/pubhub) is a searchable repository of annotated links to reports and issue briefs covering the full scope of philanthropic activity in the United States. PubHub was created to showcase and make more accessible the knowledge generated or supported by foundations. This initiative is a working collaboration between the Foundation Center and the Indiana University-Purdue University Indianapolis Library to develop a permanent digital repository for the long-term preservation of these publications. You can search PubHub by keyword or browse by subject, publication year, and/or organization. Publications are added on a daily basis, and you can register to receive an e-mail alert when a new entry is posted in your area of interest. Many grantseekers also look to PubHub for quick access to foundation annual reports.

Philanthropy News Digest (PND) is the Center's long-running digest of philanthropy-related news (Figure 5-12). The many features of PND make it an essential part of your grantseeking research repertoire. PND offers a window on the changing nonprofit world—a daily magazine with an extensive line-up of ever-changing content in addition to abstracts of philanthropy-related news gleaned from major media outlets, funder press releases, and many other sources. Articles most likely to be summarized in PND include notices of large grants, profiles of grantmakers, trends in philanthropy, and obituaries of philanthropists. Each news abstract summarizes the content of the original article and provides links to organizations mentioned in the article as well as a citation and link to the original source. Because the PND archive is searchable by keyword, it's also a useful tool for uncovering recent articles and information about specific grantmakers and/or your particular area of interest.

For information on grant opportunities for both nonprofits and individuals, refer to the requests for proposals in PND (foundationcenter.org/pnd/rfp). Requests for proposals (RFPs) are an increasingly popular vehicle for private, corporate, and government funding sources to notify the public of funds available. Listings in the RFP area of PND are categorized in 30 different fields of interest, and can be searched by keyword or browsed by subject area. Both PND and the RFP Bulletin are available as free weekly e-mail subscription newsletters and as daily alert services.

Philanthropic Studies Index

Another resource that helps you locate secondary sources about foundations and fundraising is the Philanthropic Studies Index, compiled and maintained by the Special Collections Department of the Indiana University-Purdue University Indianapolis University Library. The Index is a reference to literature, primarily academic journals and research reports, on nonprofit organizations and issues concerning the nonprofit sector. The bulk of citations currently indexed are from academic journals dating from 1940 to the present. Dissertations and working papers are also included. It is available on the Internet (cheever.ulib.iupui.edu/psipublicsearch) and can be searched in a variety of ways, including by author, title, subject, source, or citation

Figure 5-12. *Philanthropy News Digest*

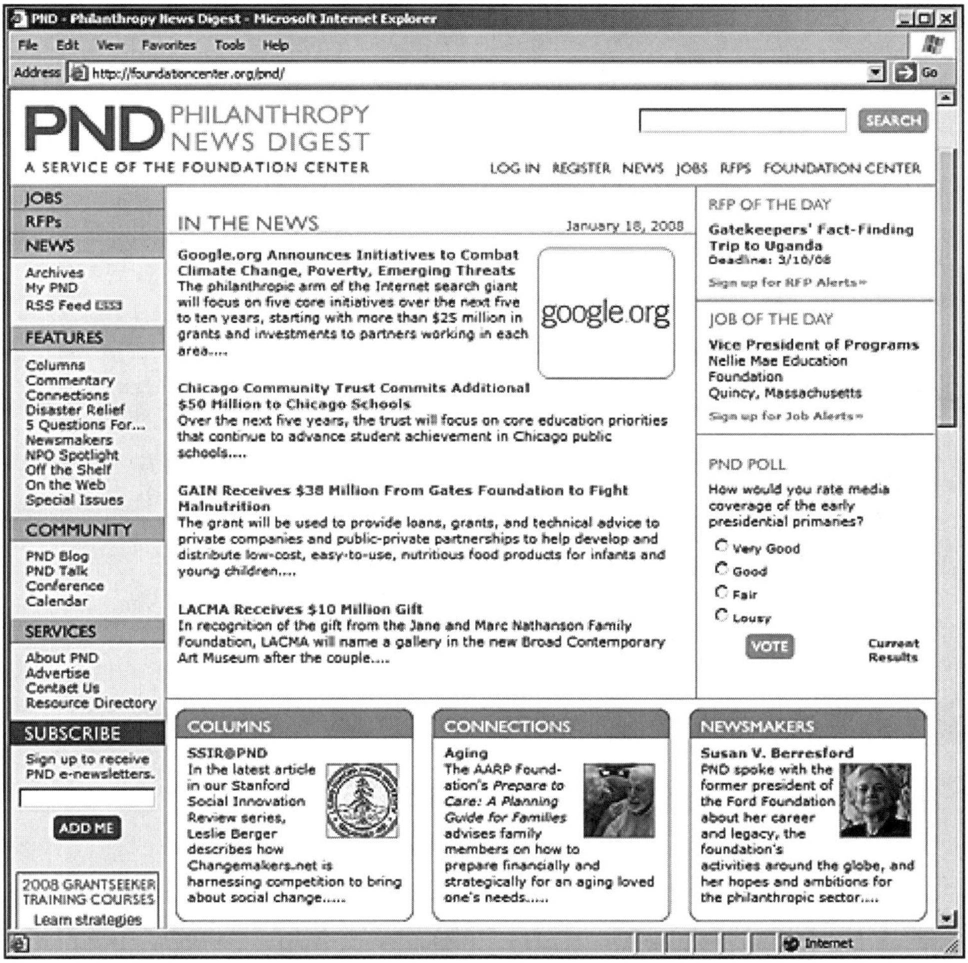

date. While the Index does not include abstracts, it is a useful resource for scholars and others interested in philanthropy.

ONLINE PERIODICALS

One of the most popular publications for grantseekers (and also for grantmakers) is the *Chronicle of Philanthropy* (philanthropy.com), published biweekly in print and on the web. This news source covers philanthropy and the nonprofit world, including articles on foundations and other grantmakers, coverage of recently issued annual reports, and announcements of recently awarded grants. In addition to using it as a source to keep current on the foundation field, subscribers to the print version can acquire a password to search back issues online and the "Guide to Grants" feature by keywords. This can be helpful, for example, in uncovering a recent article on a specific foundation, or a list of grants in a specific subject area. Other notable periodicals that are available online (some requiring payment of a subscription fee) include *Nonprofit Quarterly*, *NonProfit Times*, and *Stanford Social Innovation Review*. See Appendix A for the web addresses of these and other relevant periodicals. By scanning these news sources regularly (or signing up for the e-newsletter versions), along with the local newspapers and business journals in your community, and any newsletters produced by local grantmakers or grantmaker associations, you can add potential funders to your prospect list.

Other Online Tools

ONLINE SEMINARS AND WORKSHOPS

Webinars and podcasts are becoming increasingly common in the nonprofit sector. They offer grantseekers and others the opportunity to attend and participate in panel discussions, seminars, training workshops, and other types of live events from remote locations. The Foundation Center has begun to develop video or audio versions of many of its live programs and is making them available on its web site. See the Events Archive to access these online presentations (foundationcenter.org/events/archive).

LISTSERVS AND MESSAGE BOARDS

Listservs and message boards have greatly advanced the ability of grantseekers to share information and advice about prospecting, and other strategies with colleagues. The Foundation Center maintains an active message board in the *Philanthropy News Digest* directory of its site. PND Talk (members4.boardhost.com/PNDtalk) is a very lively forum where both new and experienced members of the nonprofit community—development professionals, consultants, individual grantseekers, and others—share insights, puzzle over issues, and seek and receive advice from other interested users. FDO Talk (members4.boardhost.com/FDOExpress) is a message board where subscribers can post messages and queries to other subscribers.

BLOGS

Blogs are a growing phenomenon on the Internet, and they provide items of interest and information for the nonprofit sector as they do in most other areas of interest. Blogs in the fundraising field are just being established and many may be transitory in nature. Some of the most interesting include "Philanthropy 2173" (philanthropy.blogspot.com), "Opinion Blog" of *Stanford Social Innovation Review* (ssireview.org/opinion), "Tactical Philanthropy" (tacticalphilanthropy.com) and the Center's own "PhilanTopic"(pndblog.typepad.com/pndblog).

Summary

There are many sources of information available online in a variety of formats to help you find out about the interests, policies, procedures, and funding guidelines of U.S. grantmakers. You will want to become familiar with as many of them as possible to enable you to sift through the mass of available information in order to compile your own prospect list and to narrow that list to the most appropriate potential funders. In this chapter, we've focused primarily on online resources, while print and CD-ROM tools will be discussed in Chapter 8. The next chapter is devoted to techniques used in online searching to compile and refine your prospect list.

The Savvy Searcher

In the previous chapter we examined the scope and variety of resources designed to enable grantseekers to conduct their online foundation funding research. In this chapter we will focus on a powerful search tool: *Foundation Directory Online Professional*. This is the Foundation Center's "next-generation" service that provides subscribers and visitors to our libraries and Cooperating Collections with access to timely, comprehensive information on grantmakers and their grants. Included is our database of more than 90,000 foundations, corporate giving programs (with sponsoring company information), and grantmaking public charities, as well as approximately one million recently awarded grants. This online tool has four databases—*Grantmakers*, *Companies*, *Grants*, and *990s*. In this chapter, we'll concentrate on searching grantmakers, grants, and 990s, while we'll explore the companies database in the next chapter. In all of the examples cited throughout this chapter, we'll assume use of the highest level of the database, *Foundation Directory Online Professional*, which can be utilized at the five Center libraries, and at most of the more than 350 Cooperating Collections (see Appendix F).

Search Grantmakers

Most searches begin with the Search Grantmakers database because it is quite straightforward to generate a preliminary prospect list using the main indexed fields included on the search screen. The Foundation Center's staff analyzes and indexes a great deal of data related to grantmakers in order to make targeted searching possible. Grantmakers are assigned any of more than 1,000 terms that will identify their giving interests. This is essential information for determining whether a particular funder might have an interest in the programs of your nonprofit organization. And because *Foundation Directory Online* allows for flexible searching as well as use of the keyword search feature, you'll find it easy to construct various search strategies to uncover good leads for your projects. There are multiple ways to approach searching, and it's a good idea to be comfortable with a number of them. Each attempt may bring up a slightly different results list, but that should come as no surprise. Our best advice for grantseekers initially is to try your searches in a variety of ways, casting as wide a net as possible, and then, upon further investigation, begin to refine your list to a targeted group of the most likely funders.

THE GRANTMAKER PROFILE—HOW IT CAN HELP YOU LEARN ABOUT A FUNDER'S INTERESTS

While the content of a grantmaker's profile depends largely upon the size and nature of its grantmaking programs and the availability of information on the funder, most grantmaker profiles include any combination of the following elements (although for some very small foundations detailed data may not be available): the grantmaker's name, address, and telephone number; separate application address(es) and contact person(s); fax number and e-mail and/or web addresses; fields of interest reflected in the grantmaker's giving program(s); geographic parameters, including geographic focus, county,

---

SUPPLEMENTAL FEATURES

The Grantmaker Profile window in *Foundation Directory Online Professional* has supplemental information when it is available. The **Grants** tab provides three options for learning more about the grants of a particular funder: *Search*, *List*, or *Charts*. The *Search* screen allows you to refine the list of grants made by this grantmaker. Behind the *Charts* tab you'll find a graphic presentation of this funder's grants activity by subject, recipient type, type of support, population group, recipient location (U.S. or international), and state. Some of the profiles of larger funders show tabs for **News, Jobs,** and **RFPs,** and **Publications,** where there are links to foundation publications in PubHub and Catalog of Nonprofit Literature, both resources at the Center's web site. The **People** tab provides information, when available, on the leadership and decision makers at the foundation, including titles and affiliations. These supplemental features may prove very helpful when you are doing in-depth research on prospects that you intend to approach.

and metropolitan statistical areas when available; type(s) of support; names of donors, officers, and trustees; financial information, including fiscal year-end date, total assets, gifts received, expenditures, amount and number of grants paid, and separate information on amount and number of employee matching gifts, grants to individuals, or loans; IRS Employer Identification Number (EIN); links to the foundation's most recent Forms 990-PF; type of grantmaker; background information; purpose and activities; specific limitations on grantmaker giving by geographic area, subject focus, or types of support; publications and printed material available from the grantmaker; application information, including preferred initial approach, the number of copies of proposals required, deadline(s), board meeting date(s), and final notification date(s); number of full- and half-time professional and support staff; and (for about 16 percent of profiles—typically larger foundations) a selected listing of recently awarded grants designed to provide an overview of a grantmaker's giving interests. Some records also have additional descriptors. Since having the most current information is essential to grantseeking, *Foundation Directory Online Professional* provides a notation at the bottom of each grantmaker record that indicates the date when the record was last updated.

Figure 6-1 shows a partial record from the Grantmakers Database.

GRANTMAKER SEARCH OPTIONS

The Grantmakers Database of *Foundation Directory Online* offers indexed searchable fields and non-indexed fields, including a Keyword search field. The indexed fields allow you to search on the following criteria: Grantmaker Name, Grantmaker State, County, City, or Metropolitan Statistical Area, Fields of Interest, Types of Support, Geographic Focus, Trustees, Officers and Donors, and Type of Grantmaker. Additional fields provide more search options, such as Grantmaker Zip Code, Total Assets, Total Giving, and Establishment Year (see Figure 6-2).

Most preliminary searches focus on the Fields of Interest, Geographic parameters, and Types of Support. Let's discuss each of these briefly.

Fields of Interest: In developing your initial list, it's often wise to think broadly about the Field of Interest terms you select. For example, "Museums" is an indexed term, but adding two other indexed terms, "Visual arts" or "Arts" will expand the search parameters. Similarly, a search to find funders for a program about child nutrition for a day care center might include terms such as "Day care," "Children," or "Nutrition." A fundraiser who seeks grants for a program in Costa Rica will be wise to look also at "Latin America" in the Field of Interest category. If you don't readily locate Field of Interest terms that match your nonprofit's activities, you can use the Keyword field. Details about that type of searching will be found later in this chapter.

Geographic Parameters: Since funders tend to "give where they live," giving interests for grantmakers most likely will be the city, county, state, or region in which the grantmaker is located. Corporate givers tend to make contributions where they have employees, operations, and/or plants. A simple approach is to search for funders in the city and state where your agency

Figure 6-1. Partial Grantmaker Profile—*Foundation Directory Online Professional*

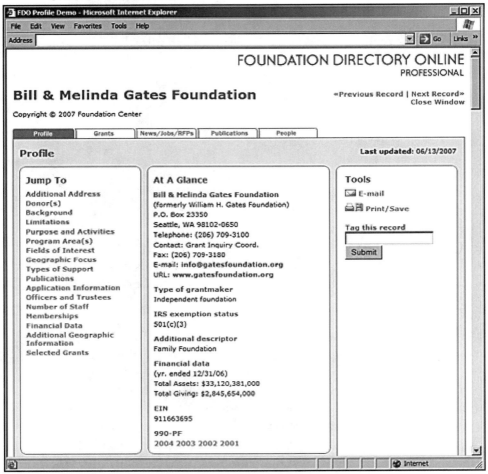

is located in order to find grantmakers that are in close proximity. The Geographic Focus field affords another method for identifying prospects, because it lists the 50 states, the District of Columbia, and U.S. territories in which the grantmaker has a record of or indicates it is interested in giving, whether the grantmaker is based there or not. Keep in mind that just because a grantmaker is incorporated in one state, this does not automatically mean that it will only give grants to recipients in that state. And it's not uncommon for funders to maintain an interest in the states in which they were originally

Figure 6-2. Search Grantmakers Search Screen—
Foundation Directory Online Professional

incorporated or the state their donor(s) come from, even if the grantmaker has moved to a different state. For example, retirees who move to Florida and establish a foundation in that state may retain an interest in their original home communities and continue to give to organizations in that state.

In addition to the names of all 50 states, the District of Columbia and U.S. territories, the Geographic Focus field has generic terms that can be helpful— "National," "International," and "National; international." Grantmakers with "National" as their geographic focus are interested in funding projects in many (or all) states. Grantmakers with "International" as their geographic focus give to organizations located outside the U.S. Grantmakers with "National; international" as their geographic focus give to both U.S.-based organizations and those outside the U.S. When using the Geographic Focus field, it's almost always wise to combine the term "National" with that of your state (using the Boolean operator OR between the terms), since this will retrieve those funders whose programs extend to any location in the U.S. If your program is located outside the U.S., select "International" for this search field and combine it with a country name from the Fields of Interest index. See Figure 6-3 for an example of the use of several geographic fields in a search for funders interested in programs that serve children in Massachusetts.

Types of Support: The concept of types of support can be confusing for first-time grantseekers, especially when distinguished from fields of interest. Types of support refer to the form that a particular grantmaker's giving takes. You'll find that grantmakers tend to limit their giving to a few types of support. Although many grantmakers provide general operating support (and indeed, this is often the most desirable form of support for smaller nonprofits), some grantmakers prefer project support, or endowment funds, or capital campaigns. *Foundation Directory Online* provides the ability to search 45 different types of support. In the planning stages that precede a search for funding sources, you should clarify the specific type(s) of support your organization needs. For definitions of the types of support used in Foundation Center databases and directories, see Appendix D.

TIP: Because Geographic Focus information is available for only about 75 percent of grantmakers, it is a good idea to conduct at least two searches, one using Grantmaker State/Grantmaker City, Zip Code, or Metropolitan Statistical Area, and the other using Geographic Focus, and then compare your results. See which funders appear on both lists, and which on one or the other.

ADVANCED SEARCH STRATEGIES

The three basic search approaches outlined above are the most often used, but more experienced grantseekers will want to utilize other search fields and advanced techniques in order to optimize their use of the data. The following will illustrate some of the more effective strategies for grantmaker research.

Boolean Operators

The use of Boolean operators—OR, AND, NOT, and NEAR—lets you combine multiple search criteria in various ways, broadening or narrowing search results based on indexed entries and/or the keywords that you select. Boolean searching is a powerful tool, providing great flexibility in designing complex search strategies.

If we review Figure 6-3, we'll see Boolean operators at work. Our search finds records that meet our criteria in the Grantmaker State, Field of Interest, and Geographic Focus fields. Those three fields are combined with the AND operator. But within the Grantmaker State and Geographic Focus fields, the OR operator is working. With the addition of two Types of Support— "General/operating support" combined by OR with Technical Assistance— we can create a rather specific search that reflects our current organizational funding needs (Figure 6-4).

Type of Grantmaker

For certain fundraising efforts you may want to focus on a particular type of funder. There are currently six options in the Type of Grantmaker field: community foundation, corporate giving program, company-sponsored foundation, independent foundation, operating foundation, and public

> **TIP:** The AND operator between search terms narrows a search, retrieving only records containing both terms, while the OR operator broadens the search, retrieving records containing either or both terms. The NOT operator limits a search, excluding records with terms you enter to the right of the NOT operator. The NEAR operator limits a search to records that include one or more terms in proximity to one another. The proximity—how near one term is in relation to the other—is one that you determine. *Foundation Directory Online*'s search engine automatically inserts the AND Boolean operator between search fields. But OR is automatically inserted between terms within indexed fields.

charity. When grantseekers wish to concentrate only on corporate givers, it is best to select both "Company-sponsored foundation" and "Corporate giving program" from the indexed terms.

Trustees, Officers, and Donors

Seasoned fundraisers will tell you that, essentially, grantseeking is all about people. In your search for funding you may want to find out if a particular

Figure 6-3. Use of Two Geographic Search Fields—
Foundation Directory Online Professional

individual is affiliated in some way with a foundation or a grantmaking public charity. This may be because you know that individual or because his/her name has been associated with a particular cause, or because someone on your board may have mentioned that this individual has a foundation. For this type of search, use the Trustees, Officers, and Donors search field. This field contains more than 400,000 personal and corporate names, arranged under appropriate letters of the alphabet. You'll note that some banks, company names, and other organization names are listed when they serve as donors or trustees of a foundation.

Figure 6-4. Use of Boolean Operators—*Foundation Directory Online Professional*

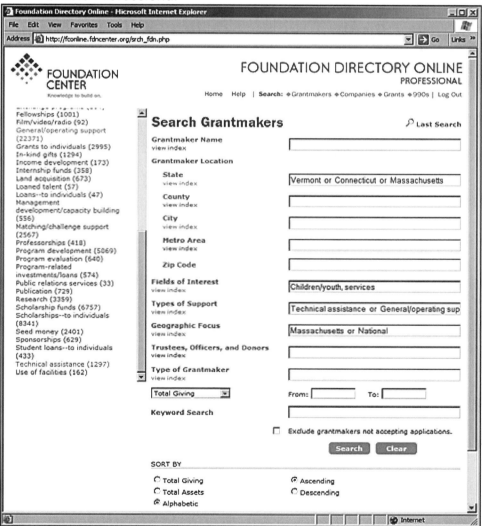

RANGE FIELDS

You may want to target your search by looking only at foundations of a certain size or those that were established recently. The range search fields—Total Giving, Total Assets, and Establishment Year—enable the user to specify a particular range in order to narrow a search by entering upper and lower range parameters.

Total Giving

Grantseekers often add Total Giving or Total Assets criteria to a search in order to focus on larger, or smaller, funders. Bear in mind that Total Giving refers to the entire grants program of a foundation (not the total giving in your subject area), and therefore it is the total of all awards paid by a foundation during the year of record, whether in the form of grants to organizations or to individuals or employee-matching gifts. It is the sum of several categories of funding, but it does not include administrative expenses, set-asides, funds expended for foundation-administered programs, or loans or program-related investments.

Total Assets

It's useful to know the size of a funder in order to know what to expect. You will find that funders with larger assets are more likely to have a professional staff, a telephone number to contact, and a web site. They may award larger grants and have more frequent board meetings at which grant decisions are made. Smaller funders may be entirely volunteer-run, make grant decisions only once or twice a year, support local causes on an ongoing basis, and possibly not accept applications, since it's unlikely that they have staff available to read proposals. The Total Assets figure represents the value of the grantmaker's assets for the year of record. Assets will generally be shown at market value (M).

TIP: To search on these criteria as "greater than" or "less than," use only the upper or lower range limits by typing into only one of the range boxes. To set a lower parameter (greater than) only, type a numerical value into the first box. To set an upper parameter (less than) only, type the numerical value into the second box. The search results will always include the amount typed in as a range parameter. You do not need to use either the dollar sign or commas in the Total Giving or Total Assets search.

The Total Assets search feature has another use that is popular with some grantseekers. You can easily create a representative list of the largest foundations in your state (bearing in mind that different reporting years may apply for the funders on your list). Begin by inputting $100,000,000 in the first box, and then select your state from the index list (or use the two-letter postal code). If you would like to expand the list, change the amount entered into the first box downward, to $75,000,000, and so on. In this way, you can create a custom list of the largest grantmakers in your state. Figure 6-5 shows the results list of a search using Total Assets to find the largest foundations in Colorado.

Grantmaker Establishment Year

This field allows you to narrow your searches to grantmakers established during specific time periods. Grantseekers often use this feature to look for newer foundations, in the hope that an early approach to a recently established foundation may offer a competitive edge. If funders are new, however, it is also likely that there will be less information available on them. And of course, you will not have the advantage of multiple years' worth of grants for comparison in order to identify trends in giving.

EXCLUDING GRANTMAKERS THAT DO NOT ACCEPT APPLICATIONS

Most of the larger, staffed foundations accept applications from grantseeking nonprofits, but many others, particularly smaller, unstaffed foundations, do not. There can be several reasons why a funder does not accept applications, including legal constraints or lack of sufficient staff to review proposals.

The Foundation Center's staff uses a variety of sources to determine whether or not a grantmaker accepts applications. Some foundations indicate their policy regarding applications by way of a check box designated for this purpose on the IRS Form 990-PF. Other grantmakers communicate this information to the Center directly, or outline their policies in printed materials or on their web sites.

To exclude grantmakers that do not accept applications from your search results, click the check box located directly above the Search button on the Search Grantmakers screen.

TIP: Filtering your search results might significantly reduce the number of grantmaker records retrieved. While this approach might be an effective first step in developing a prospect list, that doesn't necessarily mean that grantseekers should disregard all funders that do not accept proposals outright, especially if a grantmaker's interests closely match your organization's needs. Although grantseekers are discouraged from submitting funding requests to grantmakers that do not accept applications, it might be possible to cultivate relationships with these grantmakers in other ways, so as to ultimately "get on their list."

Figure 6-5. Use of Total Assets Search to Find Largest Grantmakers by State—*Foundation Directory Online Professional*

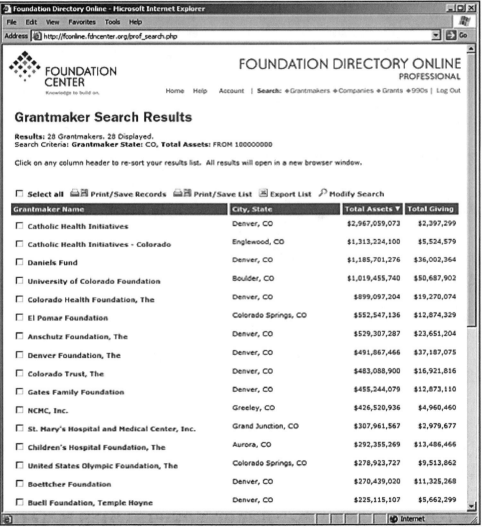

Keyword Searching

Keyword searching is an option that should almost always be considered to enhance your search results. There are many reasons to use the Keyword Search field, which simultaneously scans *all* data elements in the grantmaker profile. For example, if a term in the Field of Interest field is very broad, such as "Arts," the use of the Keyword Search field can help to target the search to your specific interest, such as "Fiber art" or "Ceramics"—terms that are not in the Field of Interest taxonomy.

Use this field, also, if you do not know what term(s) in the taxonomy relate to your subject area. In this case, you begin by inputting into the Keyword Search field the terms that readily describe your nonprofit's endeavors. Such a search will usually yield preliminary search results. Examine these, taking note of the field of interest terms that the Center's staff has applied to the grantmakers in your list. For example, "civil society" is not an indexed term. By searching on "civil society" in the Keyword Search field, you'll be able to determine that the authorized term is "International democracy & civil society development." You can then elect to use the authorized terms in your future searches.

Grantseekers also use the Keyword Search field when terms are newly emerging or not yet formalized, such as "gender equality," "brownfields," or "sustainable development." Keyword Search criteria can be used in combination with any number of indexed search criteria. Because all data elements are searched by the Keyword Search, occasionally you will get false "hits." For example, if in a search for conservation funders the term "water" is used in the Keyword Search, the results will include a few funders whose addresses are on Water Street!

TIP: *Foundation Directory Online*'s Keyword Search field will only return records containing all the words you typed, in the exact order in which you typed them. If you do not wish the words you enter to be interpreted as a phrase, include a Boolean operator such as AND, OR or NOT between each word. For example, typing "giving limited to CA" will retrieve only records that contain that precise phrase, whereas typing "giving" AND "limited" AND "CA" in the Keyword field will return many more hits.

As noted in a prior chapter, grantmakers' web sites can be excellent sources of information about their giving practices and guidelines. In order to find grantmakers that are active in your subject field and that also have web sites, you can type "URL:" in the Keyword Search box, and then add the appropriate terms from the Field of Interest index.

The Keyword search field also provides the ability to use the NEAR operator. As we mentioned above, the searcher will determine the relative number of words that can separate two terms. Some experimentation will inform the process. As an example, try a search using "women" <near/5> "health." This search will find those funder profiles where the two terms (in either order) are within 5 words of each other, anywhere in the record, including the name of the organization. Figure 6-6 shows this search with the use of OR, AND, and NEAR.

Wildcard Searching

To further expand search results and increase your list of prospective funders, the more experienced searcher might want to use wildcards. These are powerful tools for searching for variations on words. The two wildcard characters you can use in a search are the asterisk (*) and the question mark (?). Wildcards can be used in all search fields on the Grantmaker Search Screen except for Grantmaker State, but they are most often used in the Keyword search field.

The asterisk (*) wildcard finds words with variations on several letters at the beginning or end of a word. For example, if you type "art*" in the Keyword search field, you'll retrieve records containing the words art, arts, artist, artists, artistic, etc. On the other hand, using the question mark (?) finds words with variations on a single letter anywhere in a word. So if you type "wom?n" in the Keyword Search field, your search statement matches both woman and women.

An example of the use of both the asterisk and the question mark is the search for "wom?n*" in the Grantmaker Name field. This will return a list of grantmakers with woman, woman's, women, or women's in their names. Figure 6-7 illustrates this technique, with the use of additional search fields.

Search Grants

Grantmaker interests generally are indicated in two ways: by the grantmaker's own description of its purpose and activities and by the giving priorities reflected in the grants it actually awards. Although funders' program interests may change over time, in general the best indication of what a grantmaker will support is often what it has supported in the recent past, and that is one reason the Grants database is a key tool for fundraising research. The

Figure 6-6. Use of Boolean OR, AND, and NEAR Operators— *Foundation Directory Online Professional*

structure and functionality of the Grants database in *Foundation Directory Online Professional* is quite similar to the Grantmaker database, but the field choices are somewhat different.

THE GRANT RECORD—HOW IT CAN HELP YOU LEARN ABOUT A FUNDER'S GIVING PATTERNS

The Foundation Center's staff analyzes and indexes a great deal of data related to grants in order to make targeted searching possible. Grants are assigned any of more than 1,000 terms identifying the purpose of the grant. See Figure 6-8 for an example of a typical grant record.

Figure 6-7. Use of Wildcards in Grantmaker Name Field—
Foundation Directory Online Professional

While the content of a grant record varies based on the availability of information from the Form 990-PF, foundation annual reports, and grants lists provided by the foundation, most grant records include: recipient name and location; a link to the recipient's web site, if available; type of recipient; grantmaker name and location; grantmaker geographic focus; grant amount; year authorized; duration (if applicable); type(s) of support; subject(s); a brief description of the purpose for which the grant was made; the recipient Employer Identification Number (EIN); and links to the recipient's most recent Forms 990. Grant records also include a "Grantmaker" tab linking to the corresponding grantmaker profile in the Grantmakers database.

Figure 6-8. Example of a Grant Record—*Foundation Directory Online Professional*

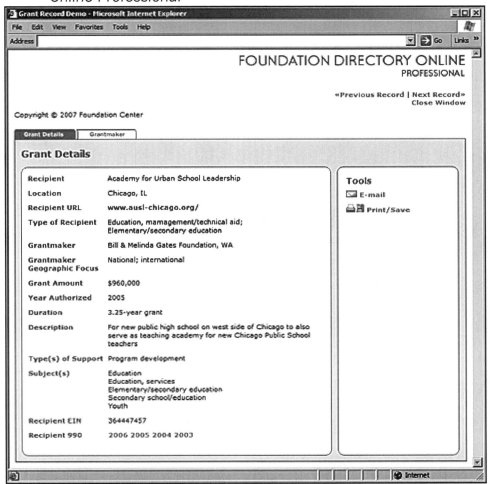

GRANTS SEARCH OPTIONS

Foundation Directory Online Professional's grants file has indexed searchable fields and non-indexed fields, including a Keyword search field. The indexed fields allow you to search on the following criteria: Grantmaker Name, Recipient Name, Recipient State/Country, Recipient City, Recipient Type, Subjects, and Types of Support. Figure 6-9 shows the search screen of the Grants database.

As with the Grantmakers database, a common strategy for searching the Grants database is to look for grants that have been awarded in your field of interest (subject), in the geographic area where your nonprofit is located or operates, and/or for the type of support that you are currently seeking.

Figure 6-9. Search Grants Search Screen—*Foundation Directory Online Professional*

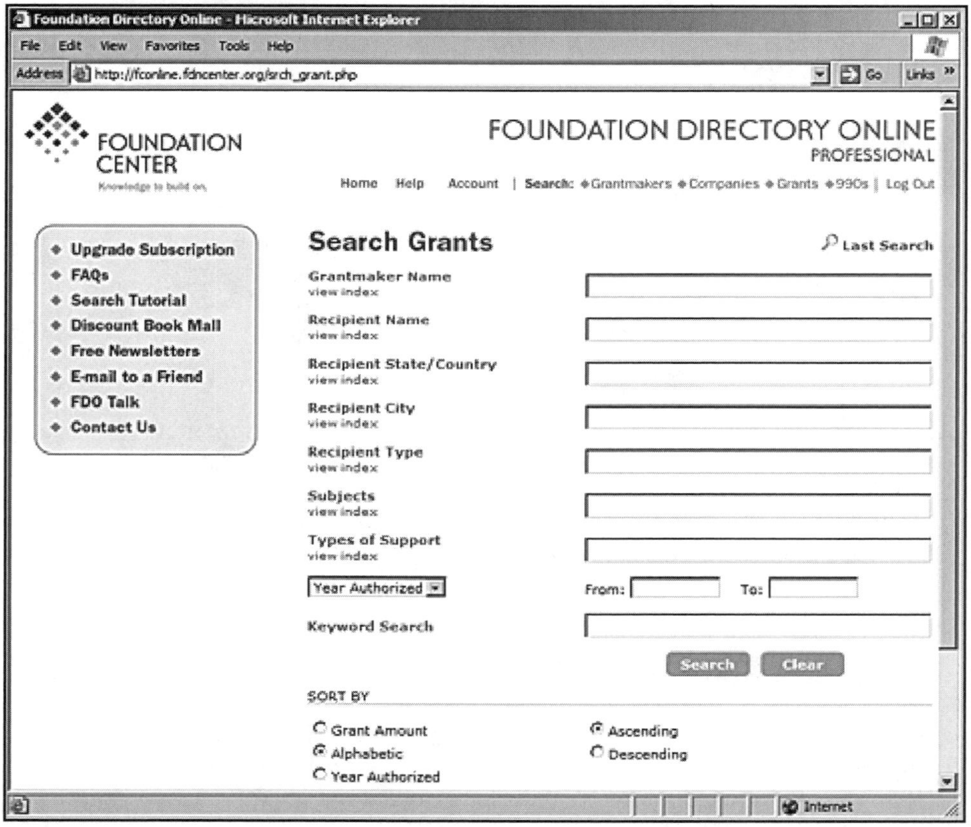

Subjects: Both the Subjects field and the Recipient Type field are the key to finding grants listings in your field of interest. The Recipient Type field shows very specific types of organizations, such as "Animals/wildlife, bird preserves" or "Military/veterans' associations." It is worth taking the time to find the term(s) in this index that most closely match your organization's work.

Geographic Parameters: Using the Recipient State/Country, Recipient Zip Code, Metropolitan Statistical Area, and/or the Recipient City fields is a quick and easy way to look at grants that have been given in your geographic area. The Recipient State/Country field contains all 50 states, the District of Columbia, and U.S. territories as well as more than 150 countries around the world. If you are searching for funding that will support an organization or activities in a specific country, by all means perform a preliminary search by naming that country in the Recipient State/Country field.

Types of Support: The Types of Support indexes in the Grantmaker and Grants databases are similar but not identical. Some terms related to corporate giving and grants to individuals only appear in the Grantmaker database, while some 20 Types of Support terms are only used in the Grants database. The complete list with definitions is in Appendix D.

ADVANCED SEARCH STRATEGIES

Use Boolean operators in the Grants database as you would in the Grantmaker database: AND, OR, NOT or NEAR inserted between terms in a field.

TIP: There are several reasons to conduct a search using the name of a specific recipient. One may be to locate the grants that your own organization has received in the recent past. If you are new to your role as a fundraiser for your organization you may need to reconstruct the funding history of your nonprofit because former staff may not have maintained detailed files. If your organization has received grants in the past few years of $10,000 or more from one of the largest 1,000 foundations, you will find a record in the Grants database. Or you may wish to see who is funding an organization you know of that does similar work to your own. The logic in this case is that funders that are already interested in your field may become amenable to supporting your agency's work as well (assuming that other criteria such as geographic focus and type of support limitations are a match).

RANGE FIELDS

The numerical criteria entry boxes for Year Authorized and Grant Amount provide two fields into which upper and lower range parameters can be entered. The Year Authorized field is used when you want to narrow your search to grants from a particular year or range of years. This is often helpful to locate the most recent grants or to limit the size of a search results list.

Use the Grant Amount search criterion to narrow your search to grants of a specific size or range. This is often useful when your search on a subject retrieves a large number of hits. In designing a grant project for your nonprofit, you'll be determining the amount of support you need—whether it might come from a single funder or from several funders. Focusing on a range that approximates the grant amounts you are seeking will eliminate funders whose typical grant amount is substantially higher or lower than your needs. While there is no precise corollary between the total assets of a foundation and the size of the grants that it awards, it is usually true that larger foundations tend to give larger grants. See Figure 6-10 for the results of a search for grants between $25,000 and $45,000 for arts centers in Florida.

Keyword Searching

As in the Grantmaker database, the Keyword Search field in the Grants database offers many advantages for grantseekers. One common use of the Keyword Search field occurs when a searcher is not familiar with the exact terminology that has been applied by the Center's staff in the Subjects index in the Grants database. If you do not find the terms you're looking for, use the Keyword Search field. For example, if you are seeking funding for a holistic health program that features yoga training, you will not find "yoga" as a Subject. To determine what indexing terms are used, input "yoga" in the Keyword field. You will then ascertain that the authorized term used for yoga—listed in the Subjects index—is "Human services, mind/body enrichment." With that information in hand, you can also do this search again in the Grants database using the Subjects index. Both of these searches, one using Keyword and the other using the authorized indexed terms, will provide results that you'll want to review.

TIP: To broaden a geographic search, use the Keyword feature, inputting the country name(s) in that field. This will return more grant records because it will locate grants with the term anywhere in the record.

As another example, let's say you are seeking funding to develop a distance learning program for your organization, and would like to see what grants have already been made in this area. You'll note that this is a relatively new concept, and there is no entry in the Subjects index that is an exact match. Perhaps the closest match is "Telecommunications," but that is a much broader term than you need. A Keyword search for the term "distance learning," however, will return a list showing grants for programs like the one you are hoping to establish. As further examples, phrases such as "service learning," "civic engagement," and others that are used in common parlance may not be indexed terms. The Keyword field is designed to be of use in these instances.

Figure 6-10. Results of A Grants Search Using Range Fields—
Foundation Directory Online Professional

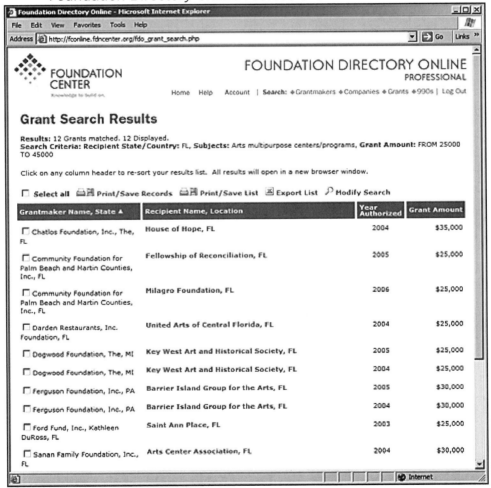

Wildcard Searching

The two wildcards, the asterisk (*) and the question mark (?) help the searcher retrieve records containing variations of words. The asterisk will return records where any form of the root word appears; the question mark, however, replaces only one letter. As already noted, inputting the term "wom?n*" in the Keyword field will locate grant records with woman, women, woman's or women's in any field.

Search 990s

Search 990s is a unique tool available to users of the *Professional* level of *Foundation Directory Online*, allowing them to search across *the entire text* of the contents of the Center's database of more than 400,000 Forms 990 and 990-PF filed with the Internal Revenue Service by private foundations, community foundations, and grantmaking public charities. The most useful elements of Forms 990 and 990-PF are explained in Chapter 5 (pages 61–64 and Figure 5-8). New Forms 990 are added each month as the Center receives them from the IRS. For online information about this document and its uses, refer to the tutorial "Demystifying the 990-PF" at the Center's web site: foundationcenter.org/getstarted/tutorials/demystify.

THE FORM 990—HOW IT CAN HELP YOU LEARN ABOUT A FUNDER, ESPECIALLY SMALLER FOUNDATIONS

Grantseekers use 990 forms primarily to review grants lists. (In this chapter, we'll use the term "990s" to refer to both Form 990 and 990-PF.) It can also be useful to find out if substantial new monies are being contributed *to*

> **TIP:** The Search 990s option is a supplemental search feature and should be utilized in conjunction with—not as a replacement for—more traditional searches that mine the grantmakers and grants databases as already described. Because the 990s for larger grantmakers with substantial investment activities and extensive grants lists may be very long and unwieldy to examine, it's wise to refer to the 990s for foundations for which other resources (web sites, annual reports, published grants lists, and so forth) are *not* available. For example, a recent 990-PF of the Ford Foundation is more than 1,800 pages in length. But the Ford Foundation also has a comprehensive web site, an annual report, and press releases, among other means of communicating its funding priorities to the public. All of these may be better sources of information for the grantseeker than the 990-PF.

foundations, as this may indicate that more money will become available for grants. Other data, such as investments and executives' salaries, might be of interest as well, but are peripheral to the concerns of most nonprofit fundraisers. Keep in mind that for smaller grantmakers, or those that do not publish annual reports or maintain web sites, the 990 may be the *only* complete record of their operations and grantmaking activities. The Search 990s feature in *Foundation Directory Online Professional* offers an efficient way to look through all available 990s at once.

Who files which form with the IRS?

Independent foundations	Form 990-PF
Company-sponsored foundations	Form 990-PF
Operating foundations	Form 990-PF
Grantmaking public charities (including most community foundations)	Form 990
Other nonprofit organizations	Form 990
Corporate direct giving programs	No form required

From one foundation's 990-PF document to the next, there is little uniformity in the appearance of the list of grants. Some foundations give only a few grants each year, and they can fit their list in the space provided on page 11 of the form. For most foundations, however, the list does not fit into the few lines on page 11 and so it is appended at the end of the document. It may be presented in alphabetical order (by name of recipient), in chronological order, grouped into categories, or in some other sequence that cannot readily be determined. You may encounter some lists that are handwritten. The information required by the IRS includes the name of the recipient and the amount of the grant. Some funders also include more detailed information about the grants they award, their mission, and primary grantmaking activity on their IRS form.

The information on Form 990 differs somewhat from that of Form 990-PF. For most grantseekers' purposes, the important fact to remember is that the grants list on both forms (unless a very short list) is most often found toward the end of the entire document. On Form 990, however, information about program activities and associated grants or allocations will also be found on page 3.

990 SEARCH OPTIONS

The Search 990s database in *Foundation Directory Online Professional* offers various search fields: Keyword, Fiscal Year, Grantmaker Name, Grantmaker City, Grantmaker State, Grantmaker Zip Code, and EIN (Employer Identification Number). The Search 990s database does not include indexed or range fields.

Keyword Searching

Searching on one or more words or phrases in the Keyword Search field will retrieve a list of all of the 990s that include those terms. The search terms will be highlighted whenever and wherever they appear within the text of the 990 documents (highlighting *only* occurs for keyword search terms). Figure 6-11 shows a keyword search on the phrase "adult day care" along with a partial list of results.

Figure 6-11. Search 990s Using Keyword, with Partial Results List— *Foundation Directory Online Professional*

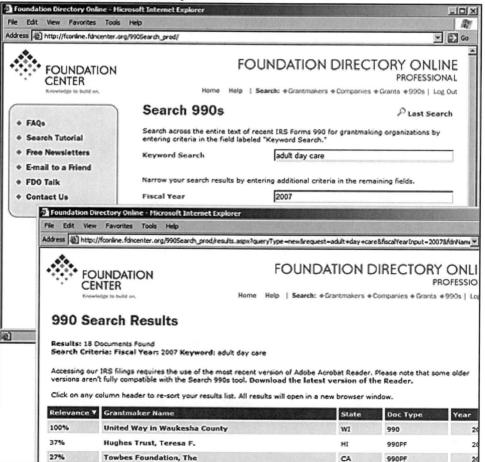

The Keyword option will always retrieve the most inclusive list of results, since it will search the entire 990 document for any words or phrases you enter wherever they occur. This feature can make it possible for you to locate terms or phrases that are used by the grantmakers themselves to describe their own mission(s) or the purpose of grants that are listed on their 990s, or even the names of grant recipients. For example, the keyword phrase "urban sprawl" will locate the Horizons Foundation's description of one aspect of its grantmaking interests, although the same keyword search in the Grantmakers or Grants databases will not locate the Horizons Foundation (because this funder's environmental priorities are described in broader terms.) This capability of drilling down by using very precise terms may well yield more useful results than broad topics such as "environment."

In some cases using the Keyword Search field may return a very large number of records. For example, if you are a grantseeker interested in funding activities in San Francisco, you might wish to review 990s that include the name of your city. In that case, you might input "San Francisco" in the Keyword field. This will return more than 8,500 hits. A more efficient use of the search options in this example might be to input San Francisco in the Grantmaker City field combined with relevant subject terms in the Keyword field. The best approach is to experiment in order to find the most useful searches in your area of interest.

You can use Boolean operators to expand or narrow your searches. Inputting the NEAR operator in the Keyword field can be especially helpful to target your search results if you are using terms that are likely to yield hundreds of documents.

The NEAR function is also helpful in locating people, especially when a document might use a middle initial or full middle name. (Note the different way that the Boolean NEAR is formulated in the 990s Search than in either the Grantmakers or Grants Search.) For example, inputting "hillary w/2 clinton" in the Keyword field will return Forms 990-PF where her name appears as Hillary Clinton, Hillary R. Clinton, or Hillary Rodham Clinton. Names of individuals could appear as executives, board members, donors, or even grantees on Form 990 or 990-PF.

990 Search offers several fields for geographic searches: Grantmaker City, State and Zip Code. Use Zip Code search to locate funders within your area.

Wildcard Searching

The question mark (?) wildcard in 990 Search is a powerful tool and operates in a similar manner here as in the Grantmaker and Grants databases, replacing one letter. It can be used in any field, including the Keyword field. You can very easily expand a zip code search by using the question mark wildcard. A search on a partial zip code (070??) shows grantmakers located in many cities and towns, and in several counties, in northern New Jersey.

COMBINING SEARCH FIELDS

Combining search fields will help to create a more targeted results list. Figure 6-12 shows a search for 990s that include the terms "environment" and "water quality" for grantmakers in New York, California or Illinois for fiscal years 2004 to 2006.

Figure 6-12. Combining Fields in Search 990s—
Foundation Directory Online Professional

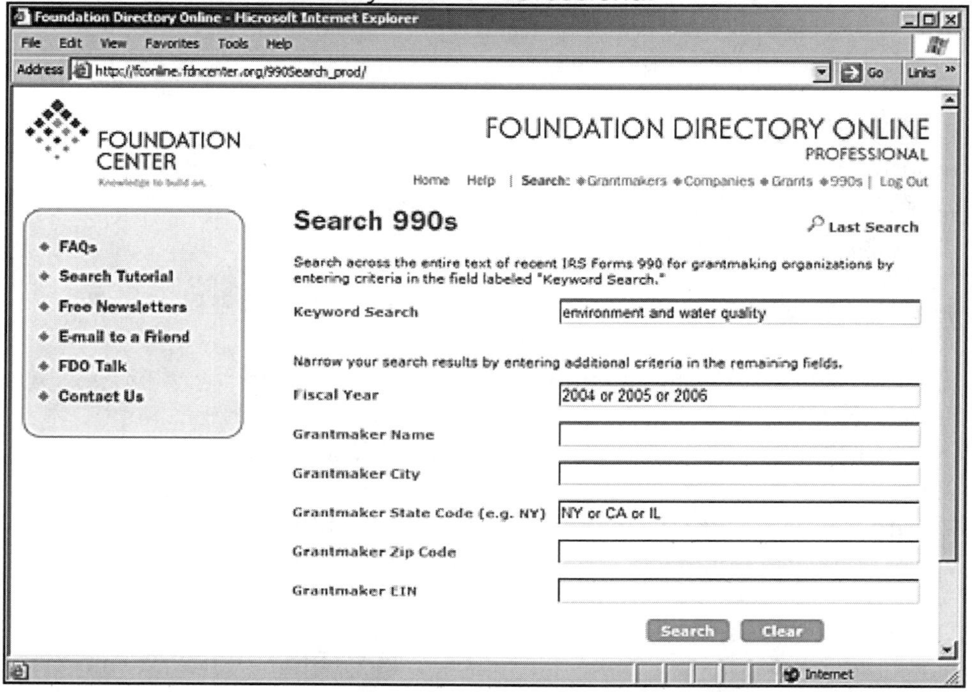

Summary

The savvy searcher will want to learn as much as possible about prospective funders, identify the best possible matches for his or her nonprofit's program, and to do this in the most efficient way possible. Using the Grantmakers, Grants, and 990s databases of *Foundation Directory Online Professional* provides a means for optimizing your search efforts as well as scanning hundreds of thousands of primary documents issued by grantmakers themselves. This capability makes it possible to zero in on the activities and funding interests of the full complement of the nation's grantmakers. In the next chapter, we'll look into options for locating information related to companies and their giving.

Resources for Corporate Funding Research

The fundraising strategies of many nonprofit organizations include seeking support from corporations. In this chapter we'll address what factors make corporate grantmakers unique and the strategies that grantseekers should adopt to find out more about them. According to *Giving USA*, published by the Giving USA Foundation, U.S. business contributions to nonprofits (including both company-sponsored foundation giving and direct giving by corporations) reached $12.72 billion in 2006, which represents approximately 4.3 percent of total charitable giving in that year (see Figure 2-5). It should be noted that nonmonetary support for nonprofits, often called noncash or "in-kind" gifts, is frequently considered an operating expenditure rather than a charitable contribution by the company that incurred the expense, and, hence, is often omitted from corporate contribution statistics such as these. The Conference Board estimates that noncash giving surpassed corporate direct cash and foundation giving for the third consecutive year in 2005, accounting for 52.9 percent of overall giving.[1] Although corporate contributions on average are smaller than grants from independent foundations, nonprofits would be wise to at least consider corporations as part of their overall funding strategies, among other sources of funding. As discussed in Chapter 1, the Foundation Center tracks corporate direct giving (when possible), in addition to giving by company-sponsored foundations, since both can be significant potential sources of support for nonprofits.

---

1. Muirhead, Sophia A. *The 2006 Corporate Contributions Report.* Research Report Number R-1399-06-RR (New York: The Conference Board, 2006).

Why Do Companies Give?

Unlike foundations and other charitable agencies, of course, corporations do *not* exist to give money away. Their allegiance, instead, is to their customers, shareholders, employees, and—most of all—to the bottom line. There is no simple answer as to why corporations support nonprofit organizations and their causes. Many, if not most, contribute out of a combination of altruism and self-interest, and it is nearly impossible to determine where one leaves off and the other begins. It is fair to assume, however, that corporate givers will seek *some* benefit from their charitable activities. These benefits may include consumer goodwill, improved community relations, enhanced employee morale, and other positive results. Recent studies confirm that consumers have a positive response to companies that are seen to support worthwhile causes. Regardless of the motivation behind corporate giving, more than any other factor the attitudes of top management impact the giving philosophies of corporations. Chief executive officers often play a primary role in company giving, with contributions officers usually reporting directly to the CEO or to the chief financial officer. And increasingly, the interests of employees (particularly regarding their volunteer commitments) help determine where philanthropic dollars are expended by businesses.

In this chapter, we'll explore the main vehicles used by corporations to engage in philanthropic activities, describe Foundation Center resources that will prove useful in conducting corporate giving research, recommend specific strategies with examples, provide suggestions for other sources of information, explain how to refine your prospect list, and offer tips on how to approach a corporation.

Company-Sponsored Foundations and Corporate Direct Giving—Their Structure and Unique Features

Corporations may provide support to nonprofit organizations in a variety of ways. Some companies give only through direct giving programs; others choose to channel the majority of their charitable activities through a private foundation; still others use both vehicles to support nonprofit organizations in their communities. Regardless of which method(s) of charitable support the company chooses, it is important for the grantseeker to understand the differences between a company-sponsored foundation and a corporate direct giving program administered within a company. Often a company-sponsored foundation's grantmaking program and the corporation's direct giving program are coordinated under the same general policy and may even be managed by the same staff.

COMPANY-SPONSORED FOUNDATIONS

Company-sponsored foundations (also called corporate foundations) obtain their funds from profit-making companies or corporations, but are legally independent entities whose purpose is to award grants, usually on a broad basis, although not without regard for the business interests of the corporation. In practice, company-sponsored foundations typically maintain close ties to the parent company, and their giving usually is in fields related to corporate activities and/or in communities where the parent company operates. The governing board of a corporate foundation often is composed of officers of the parent company.

Some company-sponsored foundations have substantial endowments from which they make grants. Others maintain small endowments and rely on regular annual contributions (gifts received) from the parent company to support their giving programs. These annual contributions are most often in the form of "pass-through" gifts. They do not increase the corporate foundation's endowment. Rather, they pass through the foundation to the intended beneficiaries in the nonprofit sector. Company-sponsored foundations may not be as subject to the ups and downs of the profit cycle or the vagaries of the stock market as corporate direct giving programs. In years of substantial profits, corporations may use their foundations to set aside funds that can be called upon to sustain their charitable giving in years when corporate earnings are lower.

Since company-sponsored foundations must adhere to the same rules, regulations, and reporting requirements as other private foundations, including meeting the annual payout rate (currently 5 percent of total assets) and filing a yearly Form 990-PF with the IRS, it is much easier for the grantseeker to obtain information about a company-sponsored foundation than it is about a corporate direct giving program.

CORPORATE DIRECT GIVING PROGRAMS

Corporate direct giving—all non-foundation company giving—is based solely on corporate resources and tends to rise and fall with corporate profits. For federal tax purposes companies can deduct up to 10 percent of their pretax income for charitable contributions, but approximately 1 percent is closer to reality. Corporate direct giving is less regulated and usually less public than that of company-sponsored foundations. Corporations are not required to publicize direct giving programs or to sustain prescribed levels of funding. They can also make various other types of contributions, sometimes treated as business expenses, which are not necessarily included in giving statistics or tracked in any systematic way. In fact, when approaching corporations, the lack of information about corporate direct giving may be one of the biggest obstacles the grantseeker faces. A recent uptick in company mergers has had the effect of making research more difficult, complicating the process of tracking a corporate giver over time.

Managers of corporate direct giving programs today increasingly seem to favor nonmonetary, or in-kind, support along with, or in lieu of, cash grants. Such support includes products, supplies, and equipment; facilities and support services (e.g., meeting space or computer services); and public relations (e.g., printing and duplicating, mailings, graphic arts, advertising). As part of noncash support, corporations may also contribute employee expertise in areas such as legal assistance and financial advice, market research, and strategic planning. In addition, many companies encourage and reward employee voluntarism, and some even permit their employees to take time off with pay to perform volunteer work. Corporations tend to support organizations where their employees are involved as volunteers, and some companies donate funds to these organizations exclusively.

Other forms of corporate activity, including event sponsorship and cause-related marketing don't meet the definition of pure "giving." With event sponsorship, a company provides the money and/or volunteers necessary to promote a nonprofit's program or event to a wide audience. In exchange the company receives favorable publicity for "doing good" in the community. Both the business and the nonprofit increase their incomes and communicate with large numbers of customers and donors. Cause-related marketing is a joint venture between a business and a nonprofit group to market products or services through a public affiliation. For example, such an arrangement may take the form of a credit card company donating a percentage of credit card sales to a specified nonprofit organization during a certain timeframe. Although some critics feel that a charitable contribution should not provide the donor with a profit, cause-related marketing has proven effective for a variety of causes, including some non-traditional charities, such as those supporting people with AIDS or battered women. Companies find—and recent surveys are bearing out—that such marketing-related donations increase sales or help target new customer bases.

When looking for corporate funders, grantseekers should employ the same strategies as with other prospective donors. Ask yourself the following questions: (1) Does the funder give in the geographic area served by my organization or project? (2) Is the corporate funder interested in the same subject field and/or population group as my organization or project? (3) Does the company provide the types of support and/or amounts needed by my organization? The geographic and the subject approach are significant in the corporate giving arena, since, whether by means of a company-sponsored foundation or by direct giving, corporate contributions tend to be concentrated in communities where the company operates and/or in fields related to corporate interests. The types of support approach, which is very important when conducting a corporate funding search, permits the grantseeker to expand the search for in-kind and other noncash gifts.

It helps to learn to think like a corporate grants decision maker. Consider how a grant or in-kind gift to your nonprofit would actually benefit the company making the contribution. For instance, ask yourself: Could a partnership between your organization and a specific company help that company sell more products, reach new customers, and/or improve its image in the community? Does your nonprofit organization offer programs or services that could be used by or otherwise benefit the company or its employees?

Resources

As noted, it is far easier for the grantseeker to locate information about company-sponsored foundations than about corporate direct giving programs. Because company-sponsored foundations are private foundations, as defined in the Tax Reform Act of 1969 and its subsequent amendments, the public has access to their Forms 990-PF. On the other hand, since there are no public disclosure laws about a company's direct charitable giving program, we know only about those activities that the company chooses to publicize. With patience and creativity, however, the grantseeker can locate pertinent information about corporate direct giving programs as well. Because public records on direct giving don't exist, the Center mails questionnaires to corporate givers, contacts companies via telephone, reviews corporate web sites, and employs other means to collect information on direct corporate giving.

Information about corporate funders, be they foundations or direct givers, is made available in these major vehicles by the Foundation Center:

Foundation Directory Online includes company-sponsored foundations in the Basic and Plus subscription plans when their giving places them among the 10,000 largest foundations, and in Premium when they are among the 20,000 largest foundations. Platinum and Professional subscription plans include corporate direct giving programs in addition to company-sponsored foundations. The latter two plans feature a sponsoring company section with contact information, business activities, financials, corporate officers and directors, plant, office, and subsidiary locations, and more. The Professional level provides a separate Search Companies database, allowing users to access corporate grantmaker records by searching across the corporate information of sponsoring companies.

Corporate Giving Online is a web-based product that provides access to the corporate grantmakers included in the Platinum and Professional plans of *Foundation Directory Online* as well as the Search Companies database featured in the Professional plan. The same data elements and features, such as direct links to a company's 10-K form, subsidiary names and locations, names of officers and directors, as well as Standard Industrial Classification (SIC) business activities are available in both online products.

The *National Directory of Corporate Giving* is an annual print publication providing comprehensive profiles of corporate donors. Both company-sponsored foundations and corporate direct giving programs are described in depth. All records contain key contact names, application procedures, fields of interest, giving limitations; many records also include selected grants. The book provides multiple indexes: officers, donors, trustees, and administrators; geographic focus; international giving; types of support; subject; type of business; and corporate and corporate grantmaker name.

FC Search: The Foundation Center's Database on CD-ROM provides the same level of detailed information about corporate grantmakers as the Center's online databases; it is published in April and updated in November.

In this chapter, we will look first at the Search Companies option of *Foundation Directory Online Professional,* and then concentrate on the Search Grantmakers database, explaining when to use each.

Search Companies

THE COMPANY PROFILE—WHAT YOU CAN LEARN ABOUT CORPORATE ACTIVITIES

Data elements in a company record vary, depending on the amount of information that is available or appropriate. Most records include: the full legal name of the company, and the "Doing Business As," "Also Known As," and/or former name of the company, if applicable; company address; telephone; URL; establishment information, including the year in which the company, or its predecessor company, was established and other background information; company type (classifications include public company, private company, subsidiary of a public company, subsidiary of a private company, subsidiary of a foreign company, etc.); name of immediate parent company and the name of the company's top-level parent company; company ticker symbol and exchange (for public companies); a general description indicating the principal products and services provided or the types of business conducted by the company; business type (SIC code); financial profile, including the number of worldwide company employees, total assets, sales volume, pre-tax net income, expenses and liabilities; *Fortune* and/or *Forbes* rankings; the names of directors; the names and titles of corporate officers; names and locations of subsidiaries and/or divisions; locations of plants and/or offices; names and locations of joint ventures; countries where the company operates internationally; the names of companies that have merged into the company and the date on which the merger was completed; names of the corporate grantmaker(s) through which the company gives; and the company Employee Identification Number (EIN). See Figure 7-1 for a partial profile of Wal-Mart Stores, Inc.

SUPPLEMENTAL FEATURES

The Company Profile window in *Foundation Directory Online Professional* has several tabs that present supplemental information when it is available. The **People** tab provides information on the officers and board members of the corporation, providing titles and affiliations. An asterisk following a person's name indicates an officer who is also a director. The **10-K** tab launches the U.S. Securities and Exchange Commission's (SEC) web site in a new browser window providing links to the latest available SEC Form 10-K filings by a particular company. The **Grantmakers** tab links to the company's grantmaker profile(s).

COMPANY SEARCH OPTIONS—INDEXED FIELDS

The associated indexes for each of the eight indexed search fields can be opened by clicking on the field name that you wish to search. The indexed fields include: Company Name; Company State and City; Business Type (SIC codes); Officers/Directors; Subsidiary Name; Subsidiary State/Country; and Subsidiary City. Figure 7-2 shows the search screen of the Search Companies database in *Foundation Directory Online Professional.*

> **TIP:** In addition to selecting terms from the indexes, you can type them (full or partial) directly into any search field on the Search screen. The terms used in the search fields will appear in red; terms used in the keyword field will appear in red any place they appear in your results list.

Figure 7-1. Partial Company Profile—*Foundation Directory Online Professional*

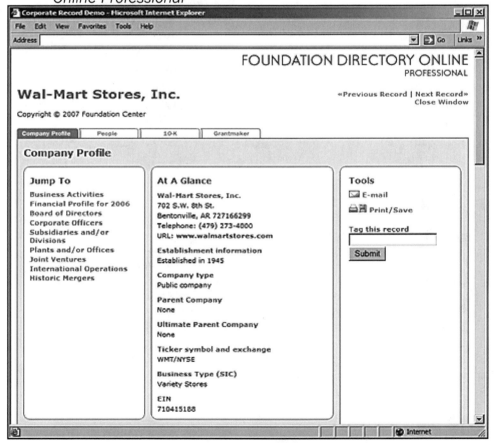

Grantseekers should pay particular attention to the geographic location of potential corporate donors, and not just to the company's headquarters. Find out where plants, field offices, and subsidiary operations are located, since companies tend to spend charitable dollars in these locations as well. Some corporations allow local managers to make decisions regarding charitable donations, while other businesses concentrate this effort solely at headquarters and may even have designated staff to oversee philanthropic activities. Others may divide the responsibility among staff at the foundation or headquarters office, while still permitting some local decisions by regional managers. Keep in mind that company executives may be convinced to support a program because it provides direct service to employees and other community residents, because it brings public recognition and/or prestige to a company and its management, and/or because it will improve customer relations and help build a future customer base in an important market. For

Figure 7-2. Search Companies Search Screen—
Foundation Directory Online Professional

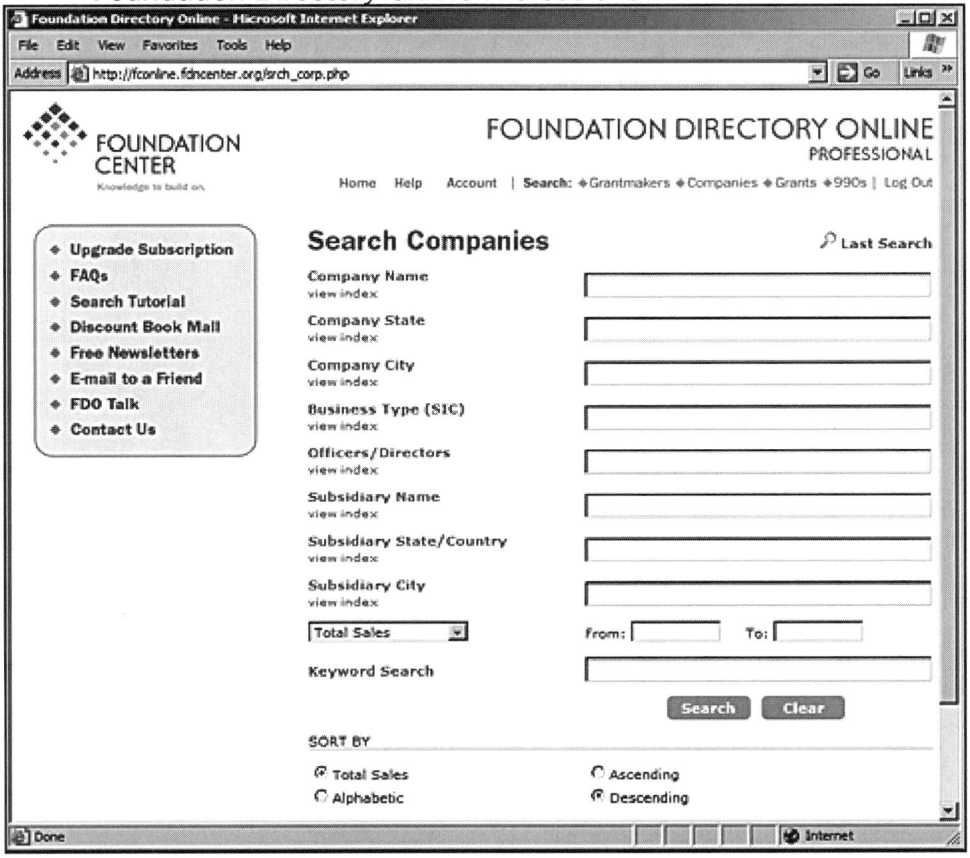

this reason, identifying companies or their subsidiaries in your geographic area is a logical first step, because an interest in enhancing the communities where their employees live and work is very often an important rationale for company giving.

The Search Companies database offers four indexed fields related to geographic locations: Company State, Company City, Subsidiary State/Country, and Subsidiary City.

The field called Business Type—(SIC) is used to search for companies by the principle products and services provided or the types of business conducted. This search option can be particularly helpful to the grantseeker in discovering a common bond between a nonprofit organization and corporate interests and activities. Some shared nonprofit/corporate interests will be rather obvious. A sporting goods manufacturer might subsidize an athletic program for disadvantaged youth; a manufacturer of musical instruments may support a school's music appreciation program; a pharmaceutical company or alcoholic beverage distributor could be a likely candidate to fund a drug-education program. Other common fields of interest may be less obvious. For instance, textile manufacturers predominantly employ women, and child care is frequently an issue for working women. Therefore, an after-school day care center may be able to secure a gift from a local clothing manufacturer whose employees utilize the day care center's services for their children. See Figure 7-3 for an example of a search using the SIC terms.

STANDARD INDUSTRIAL CLASSIFICATION

The SIC list of terms is based on the Standard Industrial Classification (SIC) system, originally developed by the U.S. government in the 1930s and updated on a periodic basis. The SIC system is a four-level hierarchical structure organized into 10 major industry divisions that are further divided by major group, industry group, and industry. For the purpose of classifying sponsoring companies, the Foundation Center uses the terms associated with the first three levels of the SIC structure.

TIP: A Grantmaker State or Grantmaker City search in the Grantmaker directory of *Foundation Directory Online* will yield hits for only those states or cities where the company-sponsored foundation or corporate direct giving program is headquartered. A Corporate Location search will include not only the headquarters city of the company but also any cities where the company has plants, offices, or subsidiaries.

COMPANY SEARCH OPTIONS—RANGE FIELDS

Let's say the grantseeker is looking for corporate givers of a particular size. The range fields, selected by using the drop-down menu, enable the user to specify a particular range in order to narrow a search. The numerical

---

TIP: If the business activity you are seeking is not readily apparent in the Business Type index, try using those terms that seem most logical to you in the Keyword Search field; this will return a preliminary list from which you can determine how the SIC describes this business activity. For example, "women's apparel stores" may not be an obvious term to refer to companies such as Daffy's and Dress Barn. Using the keyword phrase "clothing stores" brings up those records by searching all fields.

Figure 7-3. Business Type (SIC Codes) Search—*Foundation Directory Online Professional*

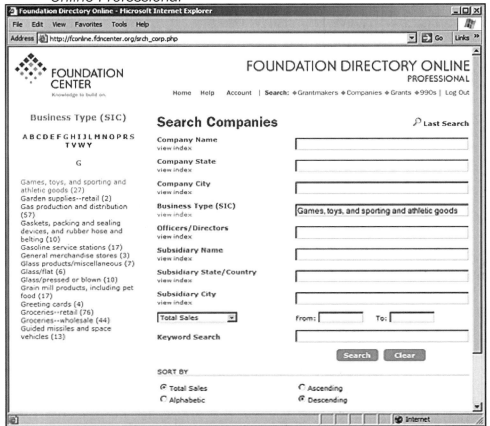

criteria entry boxes for Total Sales and Establishment Year provide two fields into which upper and lower range parameters can be entered. To search on these criteria as "greater than" or "less than," use only upper or lower range limits by typing into only one of the range boxes. To set a lower parameter (greater than) only, type a numerical value into the first box. To set an upper parameter (less than) only, type the numerical value into the second box. The search results will always include the amount typed in as a range parameter. Figure 7-4 shows the results of a search using both indexed and range fields to find Chicago-based sports companies with total sales of $150,000 or more.

> **TIP:** You do not need to use either a dollar sign or commas in the Total Sales search. Note, however, that numeric fields used as search criteria will not be highlighted in red in the actual records as the text index and keyword terms are.

Figure 7-4. Index and Range Field Search Results—
Foundation Directory Online Professional

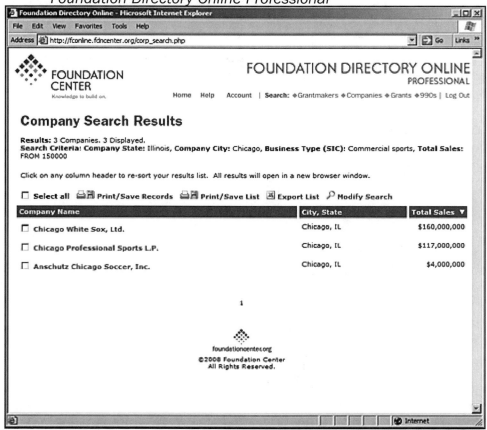

COMPANY SEARCH OPTIONS—KEYWORD SEARCHING

As in most databases, the Keyword Search field is a helpful and practical tool because it scans the entire company profile for the term or phrase that you have entered. As noted previously, one of the most helpful uses of the Keyword field is to search the business activity field information, where the business activity may be expressed in more familiar language than SIC terms. Other keyword phrases that can help to target your list might include "public company" (returns only those businesses that are publicly traded on a stock exchange) and *Fortune* and/or *Forbes* rankings (to focus a search on the largest companies). Figure 7-5 shows the results list of a search for commercial banks with operations in China that are also included in the *Forbes 2000* annual listing.

A Keyword search can also be used to determine the merger activity of companies. Inputting the phrase "historic mergers" will bring up a list of companies that have absorbed other companies, while the phrase "at press time" in the keyword field will return a list of companies engaged in mergers that are not yet finalized.

Figure 7-5. Index and Keyword Search Results—*Foundation Directory Online Professional*

BOOLEAN OPERATORS

As described in the previous chapter, the use of Boolean operators—OR, AND, NOT, and NEAR—lets you combine multiple search criteria in various ways, broadening or narrowing search results based on indexed entries and/or the keywords that you select. Boolean searching is a powerful tool, providing great flexibility in designing complex search strategies.

Search Grantmakers

The Search Companies database zeroes in on corporate information, such as locations, Form 10-K, sales data, and related particulars. But you'll want to use the Grantmakers Database of *Foundation Directory Online Professional* to locate companies by their funding interests, geographic focus, or by the types and amounts of support they provide. To concentrate solely on corporate donors in this database, use the Type of Grantmaker field, selecting either "Company-sponsored foundation" or "Corporate giving program," or both, from the list of six types of grantmakers. The search strategies you'll employ are outlined in Chapter 6. To recap:

There are three primary search fields that can be supplemented by any of the additional indexed and/or range fields that are available. Most searches use the Fields of Interest index to locate terms that relate to your nonprofit's work. This will return profiles of corporate grantmakers with a giving history, or stated commitment, to those areas of endeavor. Figure 7-6 shows a search of the Grantmakers database for companies located in New York that give for theater or performing arts. You may supplement the Field of Interests term(s) with Types of Support, noting that there are several types of support that relate specifically to corporate giving.

TYPES OF SUPPORT

Just as many foundations tend to limit their giving to one or, at most, a few types of support, corporations may specify the types of support that they will consider. To facilitate this aspect of corporate research, *Foundation Directory Online* and related Center publications contain ten types of support categories that relate particularly well to company giving: cause-related marketing, donated equipment, donated products, employee matching gifts, employee volunteer services, employee-related scholarships, in-kind gifts, loaned talent, public relations services, and sponsorships. As mentioned at the beginning of this chapter, recent estimates indicate that noncash giving currently represents more than half of corporate philanthropic dollars. Traditional cash donations from company-sponsored foundations are no more prevalent than various types of in-kind support provided by corporate giving programs or through the marketing, community relations, or public relations offices of major businesses.

Figure 7-6. Subject Search of Corporations in the Grantmakers Database—*Foundation Directory Online Professional*

Figure 7-7 shows the result of a search for donated products that might benefit an educational program related to reading and literacy. For a comprehensive explanation of the types of support used in Foundation Center databases and directories, see Appendix D.

Using the *National Directory of Corporate Giving*

The *National Directory of Corporate Giving*, an annual publication of the Foundation Center, provides comprehensive profiles of both company-sponsored foundations and corporate direct giving programs, along with basic information about the companies themselves. Entries in this directory include plant and subsidiary locations, *Forbes* and/or *Fortune* rankings, descriptions of business activities, financial data, contact persons, giving interests, application

Figure 7-7. Results of a Search for Donated Products— *Foundation Directory Online Professional*

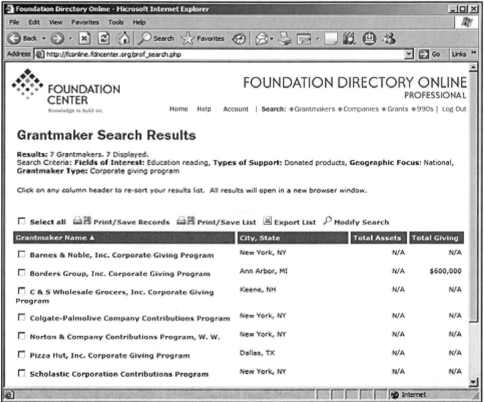

guidelines, and types of support awarded. Figure 7-8 shows portions of the multi-part entry for the Sara Lee Corporation and its philanthropic programs.

Figure 7-8. Sample Entry—*National Directory of Corporate Giving*

SAP—2937

Deadline(s): None
Final notification: Following review
Number of staff: 1 full-time professional.

2938
Sara Lee Corporation
3 First National Plz.
70 W. Madison St.
Chicago, IL 60602-4260 (312) 726-2600

Company URL: http://www.saralee.com
Establishment information: Established in 1939.
Company type: Public company
Company ticker symbol and exchange: SLE/NYSE
Business activities: Manufactures and markets consumer products.
Business type (SIC): Food and kindred products
Financial profile for 2006: Number of employees, 109,000; assets, $14,522,000,000; sales volume, $18,539,000,000
Fortune 500 ranking: 2006—125th in revenues, 277th in profits, and 235th in assets
Forbes 2000 ranking: 2006—460th in sales, 1270th in profits, and 1058th in assets
Corporate officers: Brenda C. Barnes, Chair., Pres., and C.E.O.; L.M. "Theo" de Kool, Exec. V.P. and C.F.O.; Roderick A. Palmore, Exec. V.P., Genl. Counsel, and Secy.; Wayne R. Szypulski, Sr. V.P., Cont., and C.A.O.; George Chappelle, Sr. V.P. and C.I.O.; Lois M. Huggins, Sr. V.P., Human Resources; J. Randall White, V.P., Public Affairs
Board of directors: Brenda C. Barnes, Chair.; J.T. Battenberg; Charles W. Coker; James S. Crown; Willie D. Davis; L.M. "Theo" de Kool; Laurette T. Koellner; Joan D. Manley; Frank Van Oers; Ian Prosser; Rozanne L. Ridgway; Richard L. Thomas; Cornelis J.A. Van Lede
Subsidiaries: Bryan Foods, Inc., West Point, MS; Southern Family Foods, L.L.C., Tupelo, MS
Plants: Champaign, IL; Jackson, Olive Branch, MS; Tarboro, NM; New York, NY; Jefferson, Lumberton, Maxton, Mocksville, Morganton, Raleigh, Sanford, Sparta, Winston-Salem, NC; Mountain City, TN; Galax, Gretna, Hillsville, Martinsville, Rocky Mount, Salem, VA
International operations: Australia; Canada; Denmark; France; Germany; Hungary; Italy; Mexico; Netherlands; South Africa; Spain; United Kingdom
Giving statement: Giving through the Sara Lee Corporation Contributions Program, the Sara Lee Foundation, and the Sara Lee/Kahn's Foundation, Inc.
Company EIN: 362089049

Sara Lee Corporation Contributions Program
3 First National Plz.
Chicago, IL 60602-4260
URL: http://www.saralee.com/ourcompany/communitiesHome.aspx

Financial data (yr. ended 6/28/03): Total giving, $22,924,000, including $6,389,000 for grants and $16,535,000 for in-kind gifts.
Purpose and activities: As a complement to its foundation, Sara Lee also conducts philanthropic activities via various company locations that determine local charitable guidelines. At its headquarters in Chicago, Illinois, Sara Lee makes charitable contributions to nonprofit organizations involved with arts and culture and economically disadvantaged people.
Fields of interest: Arts Economically disadvantaged.

Type of support: Annual campaigns; Continuing support; Donated products; General/operating support; Program development; Sponsorships.
Geographic limitations: Giving primarily in Chicago, IL.
Support limitations: No support for religious organizations, political organizations, or government agencies. No grants for capital campaigns.
Application information: Applications not accepted. Contributes only to pre-selected organizations. The Human Resources Department handles giving.
Number of staff: 5 full-time professional; 2 full-time support.

Sara Lee Foundation
c/o Direct Grants Prog.
3500 Lacey Rd.
Downers grove, IL 60515-5422
FAX: (630) 598-8459; URL: http://www.saraleefoundation.org

Establishment information: Incorporated in 1981 in IL.
Donor: Sara Lee Corp.
Financial data (yr. ended 7/2/05): Assets, $1,846,556 (M); gifts received, $630,443; expenditures, $8,629,546; qualifying distributions, $8,623,867; giving activities include $6,224,152 for 210 grants (high: $350,000; low: $350) and $1,218,071 for 1,252 employee matching gifts.
Purpose and activities: The foundation supports organizations involved with arts and culture, food issues, nutrition and healthy lifestyles, self-sufficiency for women, with diversity and accessibility throughout.
Fields of interest: Arts, equal rights; Visual arts; Museums; Performing arts; Performing arts, dance; Performing arts, theater; Performing arts, music; Arts; Employment, training; Employment; Food services; Nutrition; Civil rights, equal rights Minorities; Women.
Programs:
Community Programs: The foundation supports programs designed to assist individuals in realizing their full potential, specifically through job training; provide services that address issues pertaining to communities of color; help create jobs in low-income communities and/or train people for employment; help tackle the immediate material needs of hunger and nutrition; and reduce barriers to equal opportunity.
Cultural Program: The foundation supports programs designed to broaden accessibility of cultural programs to the public; facilitate artistic growth and innovation; focus on newly created artistic work; and promote artistic expression by people of color and women.
Employee Matching Gifts: The foundation matches contributions made by employees of Sara Lee to hospitals and nonprofit organizations involved with arts and culture, higher education, the environment, health, youth development, and human services on a two-for-one basis from $25 to $1,000 and on a one-for-one basis from $1,000 to $10,000 per employee, per calendar year.
Type of support: Annual campaigns; Donated products; Employee matching gifts; Employee volunteer services; General/operating support; Program development; Sponsorships.
Geographic limitations: Giving primarily in areas of company operations, with emphasis on the greater metropolitan Chicago, IL, area.
Support limitations: No support for organizations with an accumulated deficit, organizations with a limited constituency, religious organizations not of direct benefit to the entire community, political or lobbying organizations, government units, disease-specific hospitals or health organizations,

community development corporations, or discriminatory organizations. No grants for sports-related events or sponsorships.
Publications: Annual report; Application guidelines; Biennial report; Grants list; Program policy statement (including application guidelines).
Application information: General operating support generally does not exceed $15,000. Support is limited to 1 contribution per organization during any given year. Applicants should submit the following:
1) timetable for implementation and evaluation of project
2) results expected from proposed grant
3) population served
4) copy of IRS Determination Letter
5) brief history of organization and description of its mission
6) geographic area to be served
7) copy of most recent annual report/audited financial statement/990
8) how project's results will be evaluated or measured
9) listing of board of directors, trustees, officers and other key people and their affiliations
10) detailed description of project and amount of funding requested
11) copy of current year's organizational budget and/or project budget
12) listing of additional sources and amount of support
Visit Web site for detailed application guidelines.
Initial approach: Complete online letter of inquiry form for organizations located in the Chicago, IL, area; proposal to nearest company facility for organizations located outside the Chicago, IL, area; complete online application form for table sponsorships
Copies of proposal: 1
Deadline(s): None
Final notification: 3 weeks
Officers and Directors:* Randy White, Pres.; Roderick A. Palmore, V.P. and Secy.; L.M. "Theo" de Kool*, V.P. and Treas.; C.J. Fraleigh*, V.P.; Jim Nolan*, V.P.; Brenda C. Barnes; Adriaan Nuhn.
Number of staff: 6 full-time professional.
EIN: 363150460
Selected grants: The following grants were reported in 2005.
$350,000 to United Way of Metropolitan Chicago, Chicago, IL. For general operating support.
$312,500 to Forsyth Medical Center Foundation, Winston-Salem, NC. For Sara Lee Center for Women's Health.
$250,000 to Chicago Symphony Orchestra, Chicago, IL. For Symphony Center Presents Sara Lee Series.
$200,000 to Music and Dance Theater Chicago, Chicago, IL. For general operating support.
$200,000 to New Schools for Chicago, Chicago, IL. For Commercial Club Foundation.
$50,000 to Southwest Women Working Together, Chicago, IL. For Spirit of a Woman event.
$25,000 to Arts and Business Council of Chicago, Chicago, IL. For Anniversary Outreach.
$25,000 to Charities Aid Foundation America, Alexandria, VA. For general operating support.
$15,000 to Chicago Legal Clinic, Chicago, IL. For Domestic Violence Program, Pilsen office.
$10,000 to University of Chicago, Chicago, IL. For general operating support.

Sara Lee/Kahn's Foundation, Inc.
(formerly Kahn's and Company Foundation, Inc.)
P.O. Box 1118
CN-OH-W10X
Cincinnati, OH 45201-1118

Donor: Schloss & Kahn, Inc.

The *National Directory of Corporate Giving* has the following indexes: Officers, Directors, Donors, Trustees, and Administrators; Geographic Location; International Giving; Types of Support; Subject; Types of Business; and Corporation and Corporate Grantmaker Name. These indexes correspond to search fields in *Foundation Directory Online* and make it possible to locate companies that may be suitable prospects. For example, the Types of Business index is helpful for finding those corporations that manufacture products or provide services that may have some relation to your agency's work—a key issue when considering a request for in-kind donations. Another good starting point is the Geographic index, which refers to plant and subsidiary locations as well as to corporate headquarters.

Other Sources of Information About Corporations and Their Giving

FORM 990-PF

As with all private foundation information returns, you can access company-sponsored foundation Forms 990-PF at the Foundation Center's web site, the foundation's own office, or through the attorney general and/or charities registration office in the state in which the foundation is incorporated (see Chapter 5). The grants list on the form is a complete accounting of the grants given in the fiscal year covered in the document. For company foundations, these lists may be very long, since many corporations give numerous smaller grants. A company's direct contributions to charitable causes are reported to the IRS on the company's corporate income tax form. Unlike the Form 990-PF, this information is private and not available for public scrutiny.

CORPORATE GIVING PUBLICATIONS

Some company-sponsored foundations and a few corporate direct giving programs issue annual reports, grants lists, brochures, application guidelines, or other publications. Entries in Foundation Center databases and print publications indicate if a company-sponsored foundation or corporate direct giving program issues these publications. If the company in which you have an interest makes available such documents, you will want to examine them. Foundation Center libraries collect these grantmaker publications and make them available to the public, and increasingly, corporate grantmakers are making these available online at their own web sites. Some Cooperating Collections (see Appendix F) obtain such reports on companies in their local areas. Some companies also issue press releases when they make a significant contribution or participate in a community activity. *Philanthropy News Digest* at the Center's web site (foundationcenter.org/pnd) is a good source for such announcements, as is the web site *PR Newswire* (prnewswire.com).

COMPANY WEB SITES

If you are interested in researching the corporate giving policies of a specific company at that company's web site, you may be disappointed. Although a corporate web site may mention the corporation's direct giving program or its foundation, it often provides little detail about the company's charitable endeavors. Frequently, the corporate giving information is contained on a "page within a page." In other words, you have to click through many different web pages to get to the information you want. The best way to save time when you visit a corporate web site is to find the site map (see Figure 7-9). This is a listing of all of the pages contained within a particular web site, and is often more reliable than the tedious process of reading through each

Figure 7-9. Sample Corporate Web Site

area of the site. Look for items on the site map like "About Us," "History," "Community," "Corporate Relations," "Foundation," and even "News Releases." These headings link to areas most likely to contain information about a company's giving. Even if you are unable to locate specific information about a company's charitable activities, studying the company's web site, as with reading the company's annual report, can provide you with important clues to its interests.

SPECIALIZED REFERENCE TOOLS

Standard reference works about companies, such as *Standard and Poor's Register of Corporations, Directors and Executives* (New York, NY: Standard & Poor's Corporation, annual and online), the *D&B Reference Book of Corporate Management* (New York, NY: Dun & Bradstreet, annual and online), *Directory of Corporate Affiliations* (New Providence, NJ: LexisNexis Group, annual and online), and various Chamber of Commerce directories, typically are available in the business reference department of your local public library. Although some of these directories mention company charitable giving, none provides extensive information on this topic. You can, however, obtain valuable information about the locations of subsidiaries and the activities and interests of a company by referring to these more general resources. The business section of local newspapers, *The Wall Street Journal*, and business journals, such as *Crain's* (with editions for Chicago, Cleveland, Detroit, and New York) can all provide useful business intelligence as well.

Because geography is a significant factor in fundraising from corporations, grantseekers are encouraged to seek support from local businesses and not just from well-known multinational corporations. However, ferreting out information about these smaller, often intensely private, companies can be time-consuming and challenging. You may be able to obtain the names of businesses and corporations in your area simply by consulting the local yellow pages or the Chamber of Commerce. *American Cities Business Journals* (with editions for more than 40 cities—see bizjournals.com) are also good sources of information about businesses, disclosing their "personalities" and financial health and other topics of interest to grantseekers.

INTERNET RESOURCES

Helpful web sites for information about businesses include the Internet Prospector's Newsletter page (internet-prospector.org/—look for the link to Current Newsletter), and the Companies and Executives area of David Lamb's Prospect Research Page (lambresearch.com/CorpsExecs.htm). Both sites have links to sources of business information, and either is a good starting point when looking for corporate information. Those wishing to receive or view corporate annual reports may want to visit the Investor Relations Information Network (irin.com). Here, annual reports issued by more than 11,000 companies can be accessed in PDF format.

One of the most comprehensive sites for corporate information on public and private companies, not only in the United States but abroad, is Hoover's Online (hoovers.com). Hoover's boasts access to records of millions of companies. A paid subscription is needed for full access. Another site for researching corporate information is the Yahoo! Finance Company and Fund Index (biz.yahoo.com/i). This site provides a searchable database of information on more than 9,000 public companies in the United States, and access is free.

When searching for corporate giving information on the web, the specific keywords or subject descriptors you choose can greatly impact the search results you receive. Try searching initially using phrases such as "corporate giving," "community relations," or "corporate contributions." "Corporate responsibility" and "corporate social responsibility" are other terms you might try. Once you have a sense of what kind of information is available on the web, you may be able to narrow your searches further by adding words more specific to your own needs (e.g., "arts corporate giving"). You may also want to try the same search using different search engines to see how your results vary. Other keywords to try are "in-kind gifts" if you are looking for product donations, or "community reinvestment act" for those seeking loans.

If the company you are researching is a public company, that is, one whose stock is publicly traded, the Securities and Exchange Commission's (SEC) database (sec.gov/edgar.shtml) is a good place to locate information. Called EDGAR, this database contains an archive of all the financial documents filed with the SEC since 1993. There are many different types of material about the company and its operation. The 10-K report is the company's annual report to the SEC and will probably be one of the most useful documents for you, as it provides a comprehensive overview of the state of a company's business. As noted, easy access to 10-Ks is available using the Professional level of *Foundation Directory Online*.

During the course of your research you will already have consulted primary sources, such as the IRS Form 990-PF, annual reports, or application guidelines. In the absence of these primary documents related specifically to philanthropic actitivites, you can look at an annual business report of the company. While corporate annual reports usually do not contain actual information on charitable activities, they can aid you in shaping an appeal. Business reports often present a company's philosophy and its plans for the future, which in turn may prove helpful when it comes to linking your funding request to the corporation's interests.

Secondary sources such as articles in newspapers and journals may also prove informative. *Philanthropy News Digest* (PND), the Foundation Center's online summary of the news of the world of philanthropy, delivers current information about companies and their philanthropic efforts. PND summaries will also inform you of recent major grants, funding initiatives, and other such information. You may wish to use PND's search engine to enter the name of a foundation or company and see what, if anything, has been reported about this funder's recent gifts. PND also has requests for proposals issued by corporate givers in its RFP Bulletin.

Refine Your List

Once you have developed a list of possible corporate prospects, you should review it to eliminate those that are not interested in your subject field, that do not give in your geographic area, and/or that do not award the type(s) or amount of support your organization needs. As a grantseeker, it is up to you to determine which attributes of your organization will be attractive to each corporation on your prospect list. For example, a local orchestra or a community center may receive funding because it serves the interests of corporate employees and the larger community, while a clinic providing health services to Latinos may be funded in part because the corporation wants to enhance its image among members of that population who are potential customers.

If you used *Foundation Directory Online* or *FC Search* to construct your list, you probably used multiple search criteria, thereby targeting your prospect list already. The Prospect Worksheet provided in Chapter 4 (see Figure 4-1) is a useful tool that can help you to quickly rule out less appropriate candidates.

You are now ready to scrutinize your list further to determine those corporate funders that are most likely to be interested in your organization or project. As with all prospective funders, you will want to learn all you can about a corporate giver *before* submitting a request. Posing the questions raised in Chapter 4 is a good place to start, whether you are researching a company-sponsored foundation or a direct giving program. Additional questions you might ask that are especially relevant to corporate funders include:

- Do you or does anyone on your board know someone connected with the company?

- What economic conditions might affect the corporate funder's ability to give?

- Can you determine if grants decisions are made at a central headquarters or are they managed by executives at each corporate site or subsidiary location?

Approaching a Corporation

Some corporate funders prefer to receive a preliminary letter of inquiry, others have application forms (some available online at their web sites), and still others require multiple copies of formal proposals. If at all possible, find out the preferred means of approach in advance of submitting a proposal. If you are applying to a company-sponsored foundation, the application procedures will most likely appear in the entries in the Center's resources that we've discussed in this chapter. It's often a wise strategy to approach a corporation first for a small in-kind donation, giving its executives a chance to get to know your organization before applying for a substantial cash grant. Corporations are less likely than some other funders to give on the first approach, so patience may be necessary. See specific tips about submitting a proposal to a corporation in Chapter 10.

For direct giving programs of smaller companies, you will probably need to place a telephone call to ask for application information. If you are unable to identify the correct person to call, ask to be connected to the department of "community affairs," "public affairs," "public relations," "communications," or some other term that connotes a relationship to the larger community. In large cities, the correct contact person might be in the department of "urban affairs." If corporate giving is not operated out of that office, the person you reach by phone will probably be able to put you in touch with the correct individual. If the company is large enough to appear in the business directories, such as *Standard & Poor's Register of Corporations, Directors and Executives* or the *Corporate Affiliations* directory, you may want to refer to one of those books at your local public library to identify a vice president or director responsible for corporate giving.

Personal Contacts

In fundraising, personal contacts help—if for no other reason than to get information—but their impact varies. It makes sense that company-sponsored foundations and corporate direct giving programs with separate staff and explicit guidelines or formal procedures are unlikely to require personal contacts, while companies with informal giving programs and no specific guidelines are more likely to be amenable to personal contacts. The grantseeker who "knows someone" will want to utilize that relationship but to do so judiciously. Grantseekers without personal contacts may want to develop them in order to facilitate receipt of corporate gifts. Establishing a rapport with a corporate funder can be difficult. Such cultivation requires long-term effort. Traditionally, the interests of the company's CEO may have been the decisive factor in determining which nonprofits to support. Today, corporate gifts are also likely to reflect strategic business decisions and employee involvement with various causes.

Summary

Companies make charitable donations of money, products, services, and staff time in the communities in which they do business. These gifts make the community a better place to live and to work, and they enhance the companies' standing among customers and employees. Companies may make their gifts through a private foundation or a direct giving program or both. Finding information about a company-sponsored foundation is relatively easy because of the public disclosure laws governing private foundations. Finding information about corporate direct giving programs is more difficult, since the only public information about such programs is that which the company chooses to divulge. Although company donations, whether from a company-sponsored foundation or from a corporate direct giving program, are usually smaller than contributions by independent foundations to similar causes, corporate funding is a significant part of a strategic fundraising plan for many nonprofits.

Remember not to limit your thinking about corporations to asking only for money or in-kind support. Look to local businesses as sources for board members and volunteer assistance. Keep in mind as well that a good relationship with one company may pave the way for good relationships with others.

Searching CD-ROM and Print Directories

In the past few years, grantseekers conducting funding research have been turning away from traditional tools such as print and CD-ROM directories and relying more and more on online resources. The features and search tips for the Center's web-based *Foundation Directory Online* are fully described in Chapters 5, 6, and 7. But some grantseekers may prefer to use print directories or search tools that do not require access to the Internet. To meet that need, the Foundation Center continues to make available reference tools in both print and CD-ROM format that are easy to use and also provide comprehensive information on U.S.-based foundations. These are *FC Search: The Foundation Center's Database on CD-ROM* and *Foundation Directory, Parts 1, 2,* and *3.* The Center's five libraries have all Center-issued publications available for free public use. Some Cooperating Collections may have *FC Search* rather than *Foundation Directory Online*, but all will have the books in *The Foundation Directory* series. In this chapter, we'll provide information on the primary uses of print and CD-ROM tools for grantseekers.

FC Search: The Foundation Center's Database on CD-ROM

FC Search: The Foundation Center's Database on CD-ROM was introduced in 1996 and quickly became a popular way to search the grantmaking universe for potential funders. *FC Search* is published annually in the spring with an update six months later.

FC Search includes profiles of U.S. grantmakers, corporate givers, and public charities; the names and foundation affiliations of trustees, officers, and donors who make the funding decisions at these institutions; and descriptions of recently reported grants. The number of grantmaker records closely parallels those in *Foundation Directory Online,* except that *Foundation Directory Online* is updated weekly while *FC Search* is updated twice a year. Where Internet access is available, *FC Search* allows the user to link directly to grantmaker web sites and Forms 990.

FC Search offers a browse feature as well as three search modes—Basic Grantmaker, Advanced Grantmaker, and Advanced Grants (see Figure 8-1). There are multiple ways to approach searching, and it's good to be comfortable with a number of them. Don't be surprised if each attempt brings up a different list—that's exactly what you're looking for. Your objective here is to cast a wide net, and then, upon further research, to refine the list to a targeted group of the most likely funders.

Figure 8-1. Main Screen—*FC Search: The Foundation Center's Database on CD-ROM*

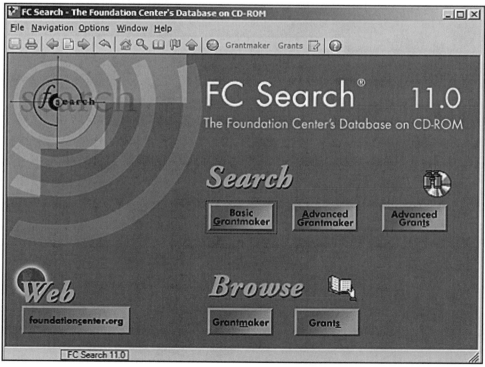

THE GRANTMAKER PROFILE—HOW IT CAN HELP YOU LEARN ABOUT A FUNDER

The goal of your search strategy is to glean information about specific funders. How much can you learn about each one? While the content of a foundation profile depends largely on the size and nature of its grantmaking programs and the availability of information on the foundation, the elements of the grantmaker profile in *FC Search* closely match those found in *Foundation Directory Online*. See Figure 8-2 for a partial profile of the Joyce Foundation.

GRANTMAKER SEARCH OPTIONS—BASIC SEARCH

You can utilize *FC Search's* grantmaker database in either Basic or Advanced Search modes. The Basic Search mode is designed for users new to *FC Search* or for those who wish to employ the most common search criteria. The first four search fields (Grantmaker Name, Grantmaker State, Fields of Interest, and Trustees, Officers, and Donors) have associated indexes from which

Figure 8-2. Partial Grantmaker Profile—*FC Search: The Foundation Center's Database on CD-ROM*

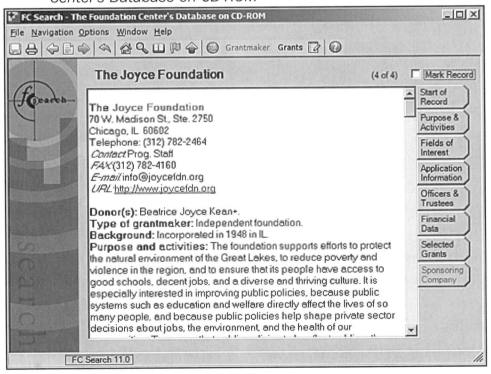

possible search terms can be selected. The fifth field, the Text Search field, finds words or phrases that appear anywhere within the grantmaker record.

When designing a Basic Search, you may choose from any one or all five of the default search criteria. An example of a basic search using two fields is shown in Figure 8-3. In this instance, the grantseeker is conducting a search to identify foundations in South Carolina that are interested in animal welfare. You'll note the use of the index for the Field of Interest.

TIP: Although you can type search terms directly into search fields, it's always better to select terms from the indexes (available for all fields except range and text fields). This prevents errors that occur either due to misspelling or use of a term that is not authorized. The index feature in *FC Search* is very user-friendly, since it provides guided searching through the alphabet.

Figure 8-3. Basic Search Using Two Search Fields—*FC Search*: *The Foundation Center's Database on CD-ROM*

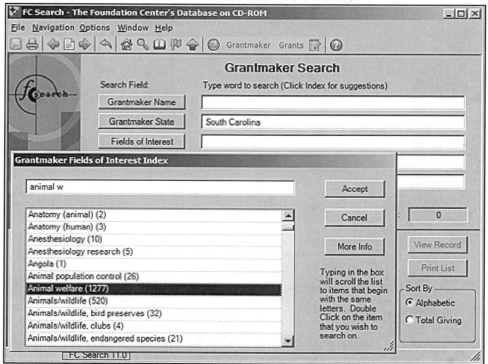

Figure 8-4 shows the results of the search for South Carolina grantmakers interested in animal welfare. Results are displayed in three columns: Grantmaker Name, Grantmaker City and State, and Total Giving for the most recent year available.

GRANTMAKER SEARCH OPTIONS—ADVANCED SEARCH

The Advanced Search mode has capabilities beyond those offered in Basic Search. It is designed for those with some experience using *FC Search* or for those who wish to search on fields that are not available in the Basic Search mode. The additional indexed fields are: Corporate Location, Corporate Name, Geographic Focus, Grantmaker City, Grantmaker Type, and Types of Support, as well as three range fields—Total Assets, Total Giving, and Establishment Date. Drop-down menus offer access to each of these search fields. As described in Chapter 6, most initial searches begin with the fields of interest, geographic parameters, and types of support.

Figure 8-4. Grantmaker Results Screen—*FC Search: The Foundation Center's Database on CD-ROM*

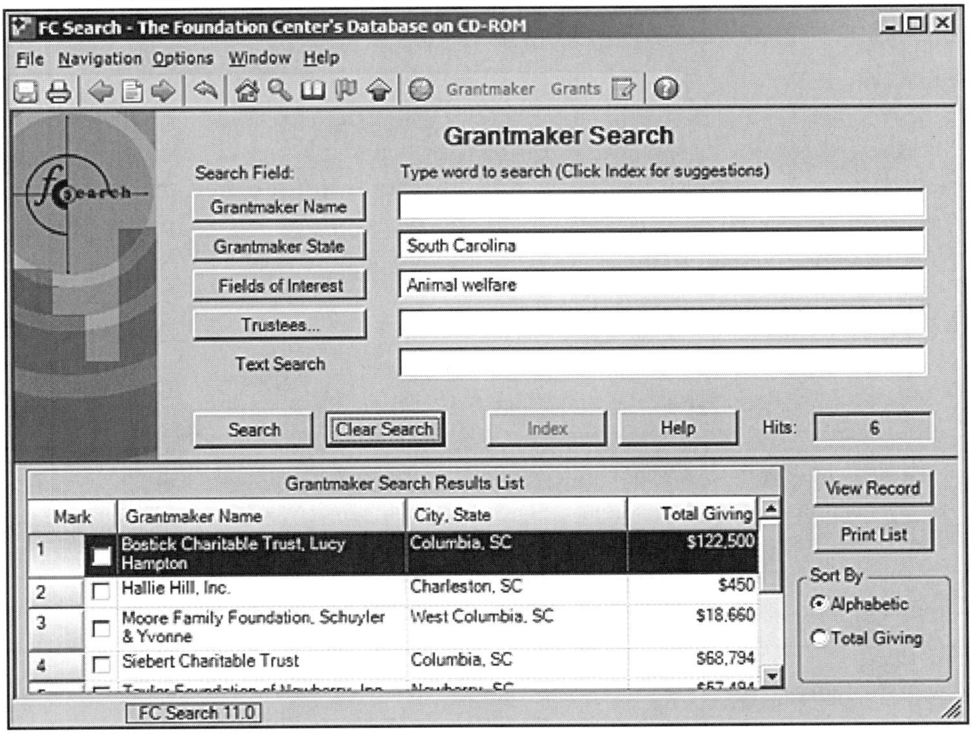

RANGE FIELDS

Searches that utilize the indexed fields will provide results that can be supplemented by use of the range fields: Total Assets, Total Giving, or Establishment Year. The numerical criteria entry boxes provide two fields into which upper and lower range parameters can be entered. Total Assets and Total Giving are helpful for identifying larger (or smaller) grantmakers, while Establishment Year can locate newer (or older) funders.

Once you've completed your search, you'll want to review each foundation profile that appears in your results list, and use *FC Search*'s mark records feature to single out those that are especially relevant so that you can follow up with additional research, such as visiting their web sites and requesting copies of their guidelines.

Boolean Operators

The use of Boolean operators (described in detail in Chapter 6) AND, OR, or NOT is very easy in *FC Search,* since they are accessed by using a drop-down menu located on the left side of the search boxes. The search engine automatically inserts the AND Boolean operator *between* search fields. But OR is automatically inserted between terms *within* indexed fields.

Text Field

Because the terms that are entered into the Text field may appear anyplace in the grantmaker profiles, this search option offers a unique method for finding language embedded within the grantmaker description. Terms in this field can also be truncated, using wildcards (explained on page 136).

TIP: Some grantmaker records, especially for the larger foundations, are quite extensive. The Field Tab feature (see Figure 8-2) makes for easy navigation within a grantmaker profile. Click on a tab on the right-hand side of the screen to advance through a record to a desired field. The tabs provide a useful shortcut when scrolling through long records or when you want to view a specific field, such as Financial Data.

The use of the Text field enhances search capabilities in several ways. One of the most frequent, and helpful, uses of the Text field is to eliminate from your search results those foundations that do not accept applications. Grantseekers find that removing these donors from their target list can be efficient, since then they need to do more research only on those funders that are open to proposals. This is done in *FC Search* by typing this phrase into the text search box: "applications not accepted" and changing the Boolean operator at the left of the field to "NOT." Figure 8-5 shows a screen shot of this often-used function. In this example, we are looking for grantmakers who will consider international projects related to housing or economic development, and that accept applications.

The text search field also provides the ability to use the NEAR operator. It's up to you to determine the number of words that can separate two terms by using the "Preferences" dialog box available under the Options menu. Some experimentation will inform the process.

Figure 8-5. Using the "Applications Not Accepted" Phrase in the Text Field—*FC Search: The Foundation Center's Database on CD-ROM*

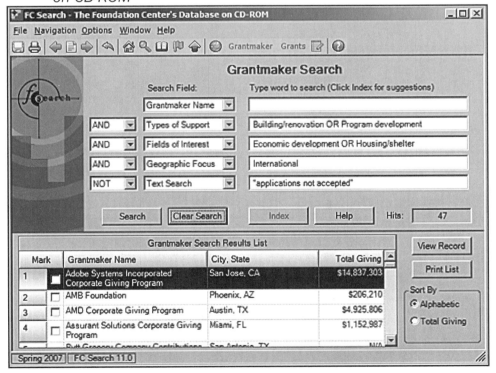

Wildcard Searching

The two wildcard characters you can use in a search are the asterisk (*) and the question mark (?). Wildcards can be used in all non-numeric search fields except the state indexes, but they are most often used in the text search field. The asterisk (*) wildcard finds words with variations on several letters at the beginning or end of a word. On the other hand, using the question mark (?) finds words with variations on a single letter anywhere in a word. One frequent use of the asterisk is to locate funders in a particular geographic area. Figure 8-6 shows a search for funders located in several counties in northern New Jersey with an interest in youth programs.

SORT OPTIONS

FC Search allows you to sort your grantmaker search results lists both before and after conducting the search. The default sort option is in alphabetic order by the name of the grantmakers. The other option, Total Giving, sorts results by the total dollar value of all awards paid by the foundations during the year of record (in the form of grants to organizations or individuals, employee-matching gifts, or in-kind gifts) from the highest amount to the lowest.

Figure 8-6. Use of the Wildcard Option—*FC Search: The Foundation Center's Database on CD-ROM*

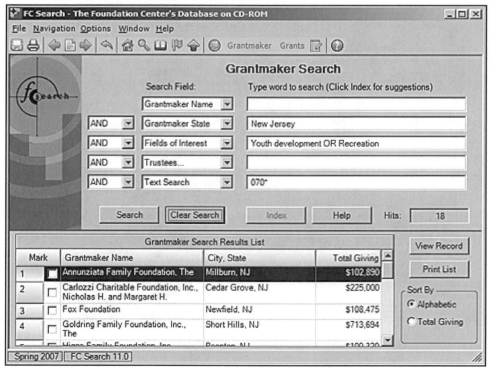

In this overview we introduced the basic search terminology and uses of the Grantmaker file of *FC Search: The Foundation Center's Database on CD-ROM*. Remember, the most targeted results will most likely be the outcome of searches that contain a combination of indexed fields, range fields, and text search. In the next section, we're going to use a similar approach to *FC Search*'s Advanced Grants Search.

ADVANCED GRANTS SEARCH

The structure and functionality of the Advanced Grants file is quite similar to the Advanced Grantmaker file, but the field choices are somewhat different. Grantmaker interests generally are indicated in two ways: by the foundation's own description of its purpose and activities and by the giving priorities reflected in the grants it actually awards. Since some funders' stated program interests are very broad or may change over time, in general the best indication of what a foundation will support is often what it has supported in the recent past. That is one reason why the Advanced Grants option is an essential tool for fundraising research.

THE GRANT RECORD—HOW IT CAN HELP YOU LEARN ABOUT FUNDERS

The grant record in *FC Search* matches that found in *Foundation Directory Online* and provides information about both the funder and the recipient. Details about the purpose of the grant are given when that information is available. See Figure 8-7 for an example of a typical grant record.

Grants in the search results list are displayed in four columns: Grantmaker Name/State, Recipient Name/State, Year Authorized, and Grant Amount.

INDEXED FIELDS

Just as in the Advanced Grantmaker database, the Grants database has both indexed and range fields. The indexed fields include: Grantmaker Name, Grantmaker State, Grantmaker Geographic Focus, Types of Support, Recipient Name, Recipient State/Country, Recipient Type, Recipient City, and Subjects.

RANGE FIELDS

These fields utilize a range entered by the user and offer another strategy for identifying funders whose recent giving patterns most closely match your need. The numerical criteria entry boxes for Grant Amount or Year Authorized will provide two fields into which upper and lower range parameters can be entered. Use the Grant Amount search criteria to narrow your search to grants of a specific size or range. Use Year Authorized to target your search to the newest grants.

Boolean Operators

Boolean operators AND, OR, or NOT can be useful in searching grants to broaden or narrow results. They are accessed by using the drop down menus to the left of the search fields. The NEAR operator limits a search to records that include one or more terms in proximity to one another. The proximity—how near one term is in relation to the other—is one that you determine.

Figure 8-7. Sample Grant Record—*FC Search: The Foundation Center's Database on CD-ROM*

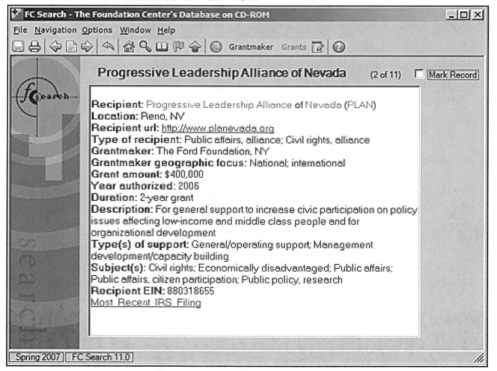

Text Field

Use the Text field to input terms not found in the indexes or partial words that are truncated by a wildcard.

SORT OPTIONS

FC Search allows you to sort your grants search results lists in two ways: alphabetically by the name of the grantmaker (the default option) or by the grant amount, in descending order. You can specify your sort preferences either before or after conducting a search.

In this brief overview we described the primary features of *FC Search: The Foundation Center's Database on CD-ROM*. In the next section, we'll take a close look at print directories that can be employed in grantseeking research.

The Foundation Directory Series

The Foundation Directory series is the most authoritative and widely used print reference tool on private foundations. The three-part set includes descriptions of all active grantmaking foundations in the United States, and is comprised of the following components:

The Foundation Directory profiles the largest 10,000 foundations, which account for approximately 86.3 percent of the total assets owned by foundations and 89.7 percent of the total grant dollars awarded annually by private foundations. More than 67,700 selected grants are included in the most recent edition.

The Foundation Directory Part 2 provides similar information on the second tier of U.S. foundations—the next-largest 10,000 foundations by total giving. These foundations represent hundreds of millions of grant dollars awarded annually to nonprofit organizations. More than 52,500 sample grants are included in the most recent edition.

New in 2008, *The Foundation Directory Part 3* contains profiles on the remaining known active grantmaking foundations in the U.S. with approximately 46,700 entries.

Each *Directory* entry may include the following data elements: foundation name, address, and telephone number; separate application address(es) and contact person(s); fax number and e-mail and/or web addresses; establishment data; donors; foundation type; current financial data, including assets, gifts received, expenditures, qualifying distributions, grants to organizations, grants to individuals, matching gifts, loans or program-related investments, foundation-administered program amounts, and the value of in-kind gifts, if applicable; purpose and activities; fields of interest; international giving interests; types of support awarded; limitations on its giving program(s), including geographic limitations; publications; application procedures; officers, trustees, and staff; the foundation's IRS Employer Identification Number (EIN); and a list of selected grants, when available. Figure 8-8 provides sample grantmaker profiles from *The Foundation Directory*.

Each volume is arranged by state, then alphabetically within state by foundation name. *The Foundation Directory* includes the following seven indexes to help you identify foundations of interest:

- an index of trustees, officers, and donors;

- a geographic index to foundation locations by state and city, including cross-references to foundations with identified giving patterns beyond the states in which they are located;

- an international giving index of countries, continents, or regions where foundations have indicated giving interests, broken down by the states in which the foundations are located;

- an index of types of support offered, broken down by the states in which the foundations are located;

- an index to giving interests in hundreds of subject categories, broken down by the states in which the foundations are located;

- an index listing foundations new to the current edition; and

- an index by foundation name.

In the geographic, subject, and types of support indexes, foundations with national, regional, or international giving patterns are indicated in bold type, while foundations with local giving interests are listed in regular type. As you define the parameters of your funding search, these indexes can help you to focus on locally oriented foundations in your community as well as on national foundations that have an interest in your field of activity.

The Foundation Directory and *The Foundation Directory Part 2* are updated with a *Supplement* volume that is published six months after those volumes are issued. The *Supplement* provides complete revised entries for foundations reporting substantial changes in personnel, name, address, program interests, limitations, application procedures, or other areas by the midpoint of the yearly *Directory* publishing cycle.

Figure 8-8. Sample Grantmaker Profiles—*The Foundation Directory*

8179—Eberly—PENNSYLVANIA

Application information: Application form not required.
 Initial approach: Letter
 Copies of proposal: 1
 Deadline(s): Aug. 1
 Board meeting date(s): Oct.
Officers: Carolyn E. Blaney, Pres. and Treas.; Ruth Ann Carter, V.P. and Secy.
Trustees: Dana Blaney; Carolyn Jill Drost; Paul O. Eberly; Robert E. Eberly, Jr.; Robert E. Eberly III; Patricia H. Miller; Tana M. Shirk.
Number of staff: 2 full-time professional; 1 part-time professional; 2 full-time support.
EIN: 237070246
Selected grants: The following grants were reported in 2005.
$1,400,000 to Pennsylvania State University, University Park, PA.
$500,000 to Fay-Penn Economic Development Council, Uniontown, PA. 2 grants: $250,000 each
$271,647 to Greater Uniontown Heritage Consortium, Uniontown, PA. 4 grants: $76,725, $79,689, $45,456, $69,777
$5,500 to Laurel Highlands School District, Uniontown, PA. 2 grants: $3,000, $2,500
$2,500 to United Negro College Fund, Pittsburgh, PA.

8180
ECOG Research and Education Foundation, Inc. ◇
1818 Market St., Ste. 1100
Philadelphia, PA 19103-3602
Contact: Deborah Deal

Established in 1992 in WI.
Foundation type: Independent foundation.
Financial data (yr. ended 6/30/05): Assets, $11,452,930 (M); gifts received, $7,557,537; expenditures, $2,978,137; qualifying distributions, $2,907,430; giving activities include $2,361,600 for 5 grants (high: $2,044,326; low: $5,000), and $2,983,997 for 4 foundation-administered programs.
Purpose and activities: Giving only for cancer research at academic institutions.
Fields of interest: Health organizations, association; Cancer; Cancer research.
Limitations: Giving primarily in PA and WI. No grants to individuals.
Application information:
 Initial approach: Letter
 Deadline(s): Varies
Officers: Robert L. Comis, Pres.; Donna Marinucci, Secy.-Treas.; Robert Gray, V.P.
Directors: Janice Dutcher; Thomas Habermann; John Kirkwood.
EIN: 391723095

8181
Eden Charitable Foundation ◇
Strafford Bldg. 2
200 Eagle Rd., Ste. 204
Wayne, PA 19087

Established in 1993 in PA.
Donor: Franklin C. Eden Revocable Trust.
Foundation type: Independent foundation.
Financial data (yr. ended 12/31/05): Assets, $9,927,602 (M); expenditures, $634,456;

qualifying distributions, $470,901; giving activities include $374,325 for 86 grants (high: $25,000; low: $500).
Fields of interest: Arts; Education; Health organizations, association; Human services; Christian agencies & churches.
Type of support: General/operating support.
Limitations: Applications not accepted. Giving limited to PA. No grants to individuals.
Application information: Contributes only to pre-selected organizations.
Officer: John M. Kapp, Pres. and Treas.
Trustees: Earl M. Eden; Donald E. Parlee.
EIN: 232706163
Selected grants: The following grants were reported in 2005.
$10,500 to Drexel University, Philadelphia, PA.
$10,500 to Ursinus College, Collegeville, PA.
$10,000 to American Red Cross.
$10,000 to Ebenezer Maxwell Mansion, Philadelphia, PA.
$10,000 to Wynnefield Presbyterian Church, Philadelphia, PA.
$7,000 to Audubon Society, National, New York, NY.
$7,000 to Doylestown Hospital, Doylestown, PA.
$7,000 to Eastern University, Saint Davids, PA.
$5,000 to Community Enrichment Center, Fort Worth, TX.
$700 to Philadelphia Society for the Preservation of Landmarks, Philadelphia, PA.

8182
Eden Hall Foundation ▼ ◇
600 Grant St., Ste. 3232
Pittsburgh, PA 15219 (412) 642-6697
Contact: Sylvia V. Fields, Prog. Dir.
FAX: (412) 642-6698; URL: http://www.edenhallfdn.org

Established in 1984 in PA.
Donor: Eden Hall Farm.
Foundation type: Independent foundation.
Financial data (yr. ended 12/31/05): Assets, $160,987,847 (M); expenditures, $20,068,997; qualifying distributions, $19,480,183; giving activities include $10,028,183 for 100 grants (high: $1,000,000; low: $650; average: $10,000–$300,000).
Purpose and activities: The foundation seeks to improve the quality of life in Pittsburgh and western Pennsylvania through support of organizations whose missions address the needs and concerns of the area. The foundation awards grants over four basic program areas: arts and culture; education; health; and social welfare.
Fields of interest: Arts education; Arts; Higher education; Education; Environment, beautification programs; Health care; Substance abuse, services; Multiple sclerosis; Lupus; Agriculture/food; Recreation, parks/playgrounds; Human services; American Red Cross; YM/YWCAs & YM/YWHAs; Women; Economically disadvantaged.
Type of support: Research; General/operating support; Management development/capacity building; Capital campaigns; Building/renovation; Equipment; Endowments; Program development; Scholarship funds; Program evaluation.
Limitations: Giving limited to southwestern PA. No support for private foundations, sectarian or denominational religious organizations (except those providing direct educational or health care services to the public), or political or fraternal organizations. No grants to individuals, or generally

for operating budgets, endowments, or deficit financing.
Publications: Application guidelines.
Application information: Interviews or visitation may be necessary for additional information. Application form not required.
 Initial approach: Letter
 Copies of proposal: 5
 Deadline(s): None
 Board meeting date(s): Quarterly
Officers and Trustees:* George C. Greer,* Chair. and Pres.; Eve H. Shifler,* V.P.; Debora S. Foster,* Secy.; John M. Mazur,* Treas.
Number of staff: 1 full-time professional; 1 full-time support; 1 part-time support.
EIN: 251384468
Selected grants: The following grants were reported in 2005.
$1,000,000 to Carnegie Museum of Natural History, Pittsburgh, PA. For Dinosaurs in Their World.
$1,000,000 to Pittsburgh Parks Conservancy, Pittsburgh, PA. For capital drive.
$500,000 to Pittsburgh Cultural Trust, Pittsburgh, PA. For cabaret theater and restaurant.
$500,000 to Pittsburgh Project, Pittsburgh, PA. For Leaving Footprints expansion and capital campaign.
$500,000 to Sarah Heinz House Association, Pittsburgh, PA. For Building Character capital campaign.
$334,000 to Carnegie Library of Pittsburgh, Pittsburgh, PA. For Library Capital Improvements Program.
$300,000 to Family Resources, Pittsburgh, PA. For Family Retreat Center Capital Campaign.
$100,000 to Mattress Factory, Pittsburgh, PA. For artistic and educational programming and capital building improvements.
$93,000 to Heartwood Institute, Pittsburgh, PA. For development of middle school curriculum.
$50,000 to Veterans Place of Washington Boulevard, Monroeville, PA. For construction of Service Center.

8183
Jerry and Joan Edwards Family Foundation ◇ ☆
1140 Edwards Dr.
St. Thomas, PA 17252-9758

Established in 2003 in PA.
Donors: D. Gerald Edwards; Joan F. Edwards.
Foundation type: Independent foundation.
Financial data (yr. ended 12/31/05): Assets, $3,832 (M); expenditures, $349,147; qualifying distributions, $347,645; giving activities include $347,645 for 8 grants (high: $100,000; low: $1,000).
Fields of interest: Hospitals (general); Human services; Protestant agencies & churches.
Limitations: Applications not accepted. Giving primarily in Chambersburg, PA. No grants to individuals.
Application information: Contributes only to pre-selected organizations.
Officers and Directors:* D. Gerald Edwards,* Pres.; Joan F. Edwards,* Secy.-Treas.
EIN: 200166041

Each edition of the *Supplement* contains thousands of updated entries. The portions of an entry that have changed are highlighted in bold type to aid you in identifying new information quickly. The *Supplement* entries may also include a section called "Other Changes" that provides additional information about a foundation, including significant growth in its asset base or grants awarded, or to highlight specific changes within the entry, as when a foundation relocates to another state.

State and Local Funding Directories

State and local funding directories, issued by a wide range of publishers throughout the nation, can be very good sources of information, particularly for smaller foundations not covered in depth in major reference works. Those state and regional directories that have a subject index may provide some of the only such access to the giving patterns of smaller foundations. In addition, many of these directories list sample grants, which give you some indication of a local funder's interests. Some directories also include information on corporations that support charitable programs in their geographic area, a very useful complement to foundation information.

The Foundation Center currently publishes six local/regional funding directories, and these are often produced in collaboration with a partnering organization: the *Guide to Greater Washington, DC Grantmakers on CD-ROM* is co-published with Washington Grantmakers; the *Guide to Ohio Grantmakers on CD-ROM* is co-published with the Ohio Grantmakers Forum and the Ohio Association of Nonprofit Organizations; *The Michigan Foundation Directory* is co-published with the Council of Michigan Foundations in both print and CD-ROM formats; the *Directory of Missouri Grantmakers on CD-ROM* is published in collaboration with Gateway Center for Giving; *The Vermont Directory of Foundations* is co-published with the Vermont Community Foundation in print format and as an online database. The *Guide to Georgia Grantmakers on CD-ROM* is published by the Center. All of these regional directories include corporate direct giving programs and grantmaking public charities as well as foundations, and they list grantmakers outside the specified region if they have identified giving interests in the defined geographic area. All CD-ROM regional databases contain 12 searchable fields in both the grantmaker and grants files.

The Center's regional funding publications and many other state and local funding directories are available for public reference in the Center's five libraries. Cooperating Collections often have directories for their own state or region along with bibliographies for their geographic areas. A state-by-state annotated listing of funding directories has been compiled by Center staff and is updated annually on our web site: foundationcenter.org/getstarted/topical/sl_dir.html.

Additional Funding Information Resources

Beyond the resources already described, Foundation Center libraries also maintain collections of a variety of other print resources including annual reports, informational brochures, and newsletters issued by foundations and corporate grantmakers, in addition to files of news clippings, press releases, and historical materials related to philanthropy. These supplementary materials are either primary, meaning that they were issued or posted by the foundation itself, or secondary, meaning that they were produced by outside sources. Along with visits to grantmaker web sites, when available, such resources can be particularly helpful in the final stages of your research as you gather detailed information about the grantmakers you have identified as the most likely funding sources for your organization or project.

Summary

Although it may seem that all information today is available only on the Internet, in grantseeking it is still possible to perform high quality research utilizing traditional publications. In this chapter we have described the typical search capabilities and strategies for *FC Search: The Foundation Center's Database on CD-ROM*, *The Foundation Directory* series, and other print and CD-ROM resources. Be sure to refer back to previous chapters for further information on foundation data and for tips on searching.

9

Resources for Individual Grantseekers

Most grants awarded by foundations are given to nonprofit organizations that have 501(c)(3) designation from the Internal Revenue Service. As explained in Chapter 3, in order to make grants directly to individuals, foundations must adhere to a very specific set of rules covering "expenditure responsibility." Because this involves submitting a number of financial reports, not all foundations are equipped to take on this additional level of responsibility. Corporations are also reluctant to make grants to individuals unless they are related to the company in some way and/or a direct line can be drawn to their business interests. (And even then, most often these are treated as business expenses, not charitable contributions, since corporations receive no tax deduction for grants to individuals.)

Currently about 5,000 independent foundations have giving programs that support individuals directly. Of those, the greatest number—about 70 percent—are for educational support. So simply going by the numbers, the individual grantseeker—especially one who is looking for support beyond pursuit of a formal educational program—should expect to encounter even stiffer competition for grant dollars than the nonprofit organization. Despite advertisements you may see on the Internet and elsewhere that suggest that foundation money is freely available for housing purchases, world travel, and other personal expenses, most private monies awarded to individuals are for traditional college or graduate scholarships, or for specific research and other projects. Similarly, corporate giving programs for individuals typically are for scholarships for employees or the children of employees, and occasionally to support scientific research that is closely tied to corporate interests.

That having been said, individual grantseekers can and do receive foundation support. The Foundation Center's database, *Foundation Grants to Individuals Online* and its corollary book, *Foundation Grants to Individuals*, contain profiles of the 5,000 foundations referenced above and an additional 1,500 grantmaking public charities with funding programs for individuals. Since many of these programs have strict limitations, your search may require perseverance and creativity. Below are some general recommendations for those seeking assistance for educational expenses, and for those who are looking for project support. A very handy chart, with links to both general and specific resources for individual grantseekers can be found at the Center's web site at this address: foundationcenter.org/getstarted/individuals/fundingfor.

Support for Educational Purposes

If you are seeking help with funding for your higher education, you should first contact the financial aid office at the college or university you plan to attend. Foundations often provide financial aid through colleges or universities rather than directly to individual students. Direct financial assistance from the college, federal and state subsidized loans and grants, work-study programs, and support from local clubs, alumni, or religious groups are all possibilities. Be sure to find out if corporations that employ you or your family members offer scholarships or tuition-aid programs. In addition, there are a number of guides and directories that describe grant programs operated by local and state governments, corporations, labor unions, educational institutions, and a variety of trade associations and nonprofit agencies. Many high school and public libraries maintain, and make available free of charge, funding information resources for students.

Several web sites may prove helpful in the individual's quest for funding:

- Michigan State University Grants and Related Resources (www.lib.msu. edu/harris23/grants/3subject.htm) has an extensive collection of links on educational funding for individuals.

- FinAid's FastWeb (fastweb.com) has a free scholarship search engine for students (registration required).

- College Board's Scholarship Search (apps.collegeboard.com/cbsearch_ss/welcome.jsp) allows users to create a personal profile of educational level, talents, and background to search among 2,300 undergraduate scholarships, loans, internships, and other financial aid programs from noncollege sources.

In addition to these resources, you should certainly consider approaching foundations. *Foundation Grants to Individuals Online*, or the annual print directory, *Foundation Grants to Individuals*, are appropriate tools for you to use in your search for funding.

Support for Non-Educational Purposes

As noted, most foundations place highly specific limitations on their giving to individuals, and provisions for grants to individuals require advance approval of the program by the IRS. For this reason, grantmakers are unlikely to make exceptions to their program guidelines, even if you present a compelling case to do so. Many foundations that award grants to individuals are small, have limited assets, and make a modest number of grants each year. In general, foundations that give grants to individuals prefer support for particular projects with start and end dates rather than grants for ongoing personal needs.

Affiliation Options

Depending on the nature of your project, your access to funding opportunities may be improved substantially by engaging in some type of affiliation with a nonprofit organization. Affiliation can take several forms, and careful consideration of the degree of affiliation necessary to your success is an essential preliminary step in the development of your grant proposal. Affiliation may be viewed as a continuum ranging from working almost entirely independently to becoming an employee of a nonprofit institution in order to seek funding for your idea. See the Affiliation Continuum chart in Figure 9-1.

WORK ON YOUR OWN

At one end of the affiliation continuum is the individual whose idea can be developed without either institutional backing or recourse to the skills and expertise of others. Those in the fine arts—poets and fiction writers, in particular—may fall under this rubric. Also in this category are inventors with simple ideas that can be accomplished within a short time period at

Figure 9-1. Affiliation Continuum Chart

The Affiliation Continuum

Work on your own

Level of Affiliation: Work on your own
Examples: Inventors, Sculptors, Poets, Photographers

Level of Affiliation: Form a consortium with other individuals; develop affinity groups; form your own tax-exempt organization
Examples: Self-help groups, Local ecology groups, Sports clubs, Chamber orchestras

Form a consortium

Find a temporary fiscal agent

Level of Affiliation: Find a temporary "in name only" sponsor or umbrella group to serve as a fiscal agent or conduit
Examples: Arts councils, Historical societies, Church groups, Film societies, United funds

Level of Affiliation: Make use of a current affiliation to serve as your formal sponsor, or find a new sponsor
Examples: Professional societies, Trade associations, Clubs, Unions, Alumni groups

Find a formal fiscal sponsor

Level of Affiliation: Become an employee of a nonprofit institution

Become an employee

Examples: Universities, Libraries, Hospitals, Museums

foundationcenter.org

one location. Another group is comprised of applicants for various awards and/or prizes, e.g., architects competing for cash prizes for the best design of a local building; scholars applying for travel funds to present a paper at an international conference; and medical researchers, as well as those in other fields, applying for awards in recognition of past achievement or demonstrated excellence in given disciplines.

FORM YOUR OWN ORGANIZATION

Closely related to applying for grants on your own—and one option available to the grantseeker—is forming your own (typically nonprofit) organization. Such organizations may be loosely or formally structured depending upon the degree of affiliation required by potential funders. They range from affinity groups of individual grantseekers who band together to provide one another moral support to formal tax-exempt 501(c)(3) organizations incorporated for the purpose of seeking grants for specific projects.

Forming your own organization will take time (from three months to one year), money (from several hundred to several thousand dollars in legal, accounting, and/or registration fees), and may be unappealing to the individual grantseeker who shuns formalities and red tape. The primary steps in forming an organization are outlined in Chapter 3, Figure 3-1: "How to Form and Operate a 501(c)(3) Nonprofit Corporation." Obviously, not all ideas lend themselves to the establishment of an organization. For those that do, nonetheless, this is another possibility to consider. It serves as an alternative to seeking institutional affiliation and sponsorship, and is particularly appropriate for longer-term projects as opposed to short-term efforts.

UMBRELLA GROUPS

Forming your own organization need not entail the establishment of a large, formal institution. It may mean simple coalitions, consortia, or affinity groups that have no separate legal status. Such group formations and alignments may be quasi-independent from existing community organizations or technical assistance agencies or may function as arms or chapters of such agencies. Any nonprofit organization is eligible to serve as an "umbrella group" for the purpose of applying for grants. An umbrella group refers to an intermediate agency, usually nonprofit, that receives and disburses funds to individuals. Churches, schools, community organizations, self-help groups, arts councils, and even local clubs, if they are nonprofit, may serve as umbrella groups for grant applicants.

SPONSORSHIP

Fiscal sponsors are third-party groups that collaborate with you to meet funders' requirements. You provide the idea and the labor; the sponsor provides the track record, credibility, and tax-exempt status. Together you form a kind of symbiotic relationship. Schools, colleges, universities, research institutes, educational associations, professional societies, state and local art associations, historical societies, museums, hospitals, health agencies, nonprofit performing groups, sports clubs, scientific societies, social and recreational clubs, fraternal organizations, community foundations, unions, labor, agricultural, and horticultural organizations, veterans' groups, civic leagues, chambers of commerce, and churches and religious groups are all examples of potential sponsors. You are most likely *already* affiliated with several groups that might serve as sponsors for your grant project. In searching for a fiscal sponsor, you should seek out organizations that have demonstrated an interest in programs or projects similar to yours and whose mission is in line with the project that you seek to bring to fruition. It will be easier to find a fiscal sponsor if your project enhances or furthers that organization's charitable purposes and/or if that organization benefits in some way from being associated with your project.

In order to find a sponsor, start with your current affiliations. Make a list of clubs, professional associations, educational institutions, and work-related groups with which you are presently or were formerly affiliated. The Types of Support index in *Foundation Grants to Individuals Online* database includes "Fiscal agent/sponsor" as one choice. Using the "Affiliations Profile" worksheet (Figure 9-2) we have provided will help you get started.

Most affiliations with fiscal sponsors are formal, based on a written contract that spells out who will do what. Some sponsors will expect a fee for this service, which is typically about 5–10 percent of the grant award. If the grant is approved, the funder's check is made out to the sponsoring organization, which in turn administers the project, doling out funds to the individual as needed and often deducting its own administrative fee. Since grants would then be made directly to the sponsoring organization, you and the sponsor should have in advance a clear agreement about the management of funds received and what fees may be subtracted from the grant.

A comprehensive tutorial on the topic of fiscal sponsorship is available on the Foundation Center's web site (foundationcenter.org/getstarted/tutorials/fiscal). It includes links to worksheets as well as examples of policies and

Figure 9-2. Affiliations Profile Worksheet

For Individual Grantseekers and Scholarship Seekers

Affiliations Profile

Answer the following questions before you begin your research.
Your answers will help focus your scholarship or grant search by giving you "key words" or index terms to use.

Your School (Where are you studying? Where do you plan to study? From what school did you graduate?)	
Your Employer(s) or Union(s) (or that of a parent or a spouse or a close relative that may have a scholarship program for employees)	
Your Religious Affiliation(s) (Do you, your spouse or your parents have any religious affiliations?)	
Your Professional or Trade Associations (Do you, your spouse, or your parents belong to any professional or trade associations? Do they offer scholarships or other awards?)	
Community and Civic Organizations or Clubs (Do you or your family members belong to such groups as Boy Scouts, Elks, fraternities, etc., or agencies where you volunteer your time? Do they offer scholarships or awards?)	
Military Status (Are you a veteran dependent of a member of the military, or are you interested in a career in the military?)	
Other Affiliations	

guidelines for sponsorship agreements. It is important that you begin looking for a fiscal sponsor at the same time that you start researching potential funders. Also refer to Appendix A for additional readings and Internet resources on the subject of fiscal sponsorship.

BECOME AN EMPLOYEE

At the opposite end of the affiliation continuum from working on your own is one final possibility—becoming an employee. This is an alternative rarely considered by the individual grantseeker. Yet it is a perfectly viable option. In certain specific instances, it is really the only choice, because some types of grants are awarded solely to institutions, e.g., grants for building or renovation, salaries, general operating expenses, or the purchase of equipment. In these cases and others, the more informal sponsorship arrangement simply is not sufficient to qualify the individual for funding. If the potential funders you've identified make grants only to organizations, or if the idea you have in mind is one for which only an institution may apply for a grant, you may decide to join an institution as an employee.

Which Resource to Use?

If you determine that your best alternatives entail affiliation with a nonprofit that will receive funds on behalf of your project, or if you are successful in partnering with a fiscal sponsor, your primary research tool will be *Foundation Directory Online*, and you can follow the search instructions outlined in Chapter 6. Keep in mind the audience that will be served by your project as you devise your search strategies. If sponsorship or other forms of affiliation with a nonprofit are not an option, *Foundation Grants to Individuals Online* or the print directory, *Foundation Grants to Individuals,* are the appropriate research tools for you to use.

FOUNDATION GRANTS TO INDIVIDUALS ONLINE

This unique online foundation database of more than 6,500 programs that award grants to individuals is convenient to use, and can be accessed from the web. It is updated on a quarterly basis. It is searchable by eight indexed fields and a separate text search field. It is available on a monthly or annual subscription basis and for free use at all Foundation Center library/learning centers and at Cooperating Collections. Figure 9-3 shows the search screen of *Foundation Grants to Individuals Online*.

The Grantmaker Profile—How It Can Help You Learn About Funders

While the content of a foundation profile depends largely on the size and nature of its funding programs and the availability of information on the foundation, most grantmaker profiles include any combination of the following: the grantmaker's name, address, and telephone number; separate application address(es) and contact person(s); fax number and e-mail and/or web addresses; limitations; geographic focus; financial information, including fiscal year-end date, total assets, gifts received, expenditures, amount and

Figure 9-3. Search Screen—*Foundation Grants to Individuals Online*

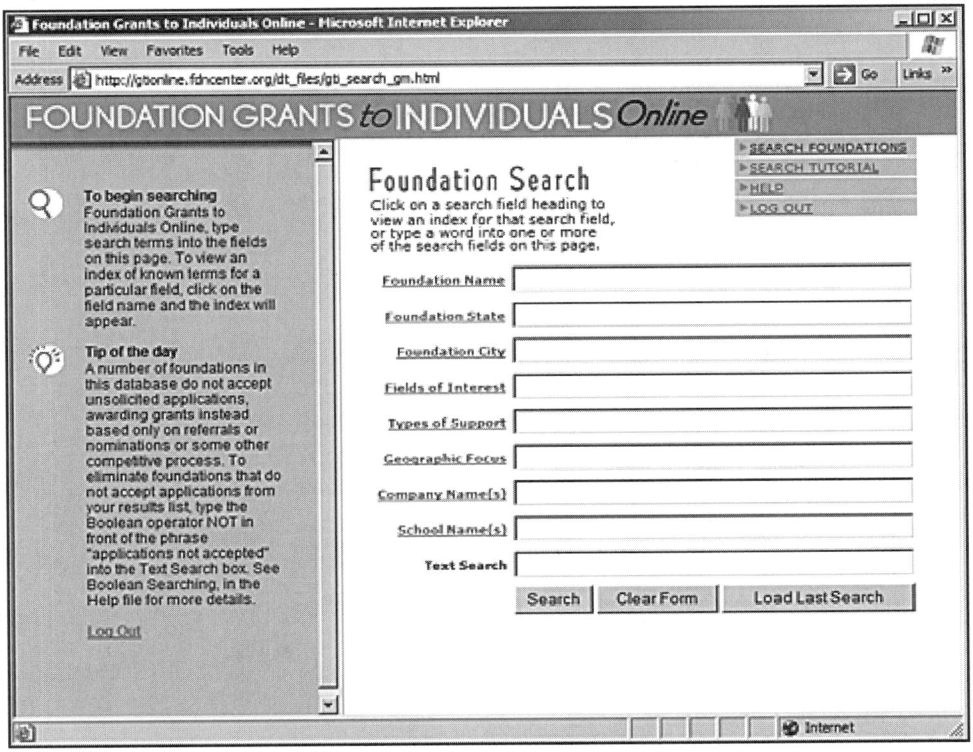

number of grants to individuals, or loans; type of grantmaker; fields of interest reflected in the grantmaker's giving program(s); type(s) of support; application information; publications, if any; program description(s); Employer Identification Number (EIN); and a link to the funder's Form 990-PF or 990.

Figure 9-4 shows a partial grantmaker profile. These profiles are usually quite comprehensive (and in the case of this example, very specific about the funder's geographic preferences). It is the responsibility of the grantseeker to determine, to the greatest extent possible, the potential match between your needs and the funder's interests. If it appears that you don't qualify, don't apply.

Figure 9-4. Grantmaker Profile—*Foundation Grants to Individuals Online*

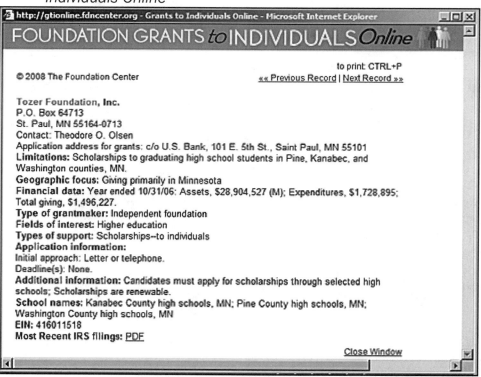

SEARCHING *FOUNDATION GRANTS TO INDIVIDUALS ONLINE*

The indexed fields in *Foundation Grants to Individuals Online* are: Foundation Name, Foundation State, Foundation City, Fields of Interest, Types of Support, Geographic Focus, Company Name(s), School Name(s); a Text Search field is also available. Using Boolean operators—AND, OR, NOT, or NEAR—in search fields will either broaden the search (OR) or narrow it (AND).

The examples that follow will illustrate several search techniques and strategies that you can employ with this database. Be sure to try your search in a variety of ways. Try not to utilize too many fields at any one time, since this tends to limit the number of "hits" you will receive. Performing sequential searches, using a variety of terms that apply to your situation as separate searches, and utilizing only two to three search fields at once, will probably yield the best results. Text search, which scans all the words in a record, is a particularly useful feature with this database.

Scholarship Seekers

Let's consider the example of an African-American high school senior from New York who will need a scholarship to be able to attend a New York State school. The Fields of Interest options might include both "Minorities" and "African Americans/Blacks." By using the Boolean operator OR between the terms (the default option) the search returns all records with at least one (or both) of those terms. In addition, since many foundations give only to residents of their home states (as shown in Figure 9-4), in order to target this search, you can include "New York" as a search term in the Geographic Focus field (and add "National" in this field as well, to include those foundations with no geographic restrictions). In the Types of Support index, select "Scholarships—to individuals" and "Undergraduate support" from the choices available. Figure 9-5 shows a partial results list from this search.

> **TIP:** When using this database keep in mind that the *Foundation Grants to Individuals Online* search engine automatically inserts the AND Boolean operator *between* search fields. But OR is automatically inserted between terms *within* indexed fields.

If you know the academic field that you plan to pursue, locate the term in the Field of Interest index—and broaden it as necessary. For example, if you hope to major in engineering, you may want to select all of these Fields of Interest terms: Engineering, Engineering school/education, Engineering/technology, Physical/earth sciences, and Science. Since some foundations designate scholarships for students who attend specific institutions, be sure to check the School Name(s) field for the high school you attend and/or the college or university that you intend to enroll in. And look at the listings in the Company Name(s) field for businesses that employee your family members and offer scholarships or tuition-aid programs.

Graduate Students

Let's consider the example of a female graduate student who is about to complete a Ph.D. in women's studies. She is planning to write a book related to women's issues upon graduation, and is seeking financial support during the course of the project. Three different options from the Types of Support index are appropriate: "Fellowships," "Publication," and "Program

Figure 9-5. Scholarship Search—*Foundation Grants to Individuals Online*

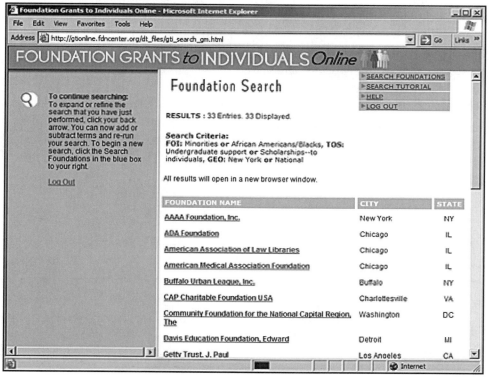

development" (all separated by the OR Boolean operator). Using all three will broaden the search. In the Field(s) of Interest category, select both "Women" and "Women's studies." This search (Figure 9-6) yields more than 20 potential funders.

Filmmakers

Independent filmmakers often use *Foundation Grants to Individuals Online*, and, if they have secured a fiscal sponsor, search *Foundation Directory Online* as well. Let's look at an example of a filmmaker who is creating a documentary about the plight of undernourished children in famine-impacted areas of Africa. The term "Media, film/video" is one of the Field(s) of Interest. In order to add additional relevance and lend focus to the search, you can include the root of the word documentary, which would be "documentar*." This term, with the addition of the asterisk (*) wildcard will retrieve records containing all variations on the word, anywhere in the profile—see Figure 9-7 for a partial results list. This search can be completed with the addition of terms that relate to the subject matter of

Figure 9-6. Graduate Fellowship Search—*Foundation Grants to Individuals Online*

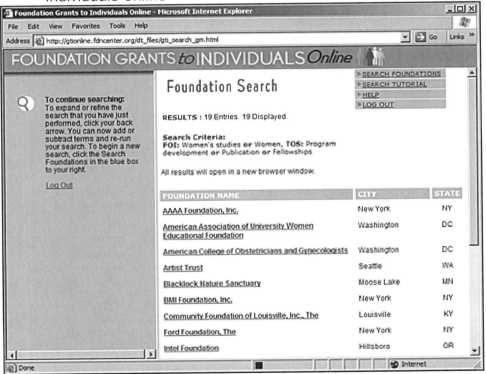

the documentary. Keep in mind that each of the examples provided here demonstrates only one among many potential scenarios you could create to retrieve useful results.

Artists

Many artists look to multiple sources of support for their creative work, and foundations may account for one source of substantial funding for them. Painters, photographers, sculptors, ceramicists, and others will find these specialties itemized as subheadings under the broader term "Visual arts," in *Foundation Grants to Individuals Online* but may also benefit by including both "Visual arts" and even "Arts" to their search. As an alternate approach to seeking a grant, with ingenuity, some artists may be able to convince corporations to treat their creative output as a business expense.

Figure 9-7. Search Using a Wildcard—*Foundation Grants to Individuals Online*

Medical Researchers

In some fields of research, foundations may require applicants to be nominated by their sponsoring institutions in order to be eligible for funding. Using the Boolean operator NOT, a grantseeker can filter out foundations that make this a requirement. For example, a doctor at a hospital looking for support to do advanced independent cancer research could construct a search using "Medical research" OR "Cancer research" as the Field of Interest. In order to construct this search, select "Awards/grants by nomination only" from the Types of Support index, but then type in the word "NOT" in front of that term (leave one space between "NOT" and the term).

Foundation Grants to Individuals

This annual print directory features 6,500 profiles of grantmakers that award educational, general welfare, and arts and cultural support, as well as awards, prizes, grants by nomination, and funding for international applicants, company employees, students and graduates of specific schools, and research and professional support. The content closely mirrors that of the online database. Seven indexes are provided to help target prospective grants (geographic focus, international giving, company name, specific school, type of support, subject, and grantmaker name). When referring to the print

Figure 9-8. Example of a Request for Proposal—*Philanthropy News Digest*

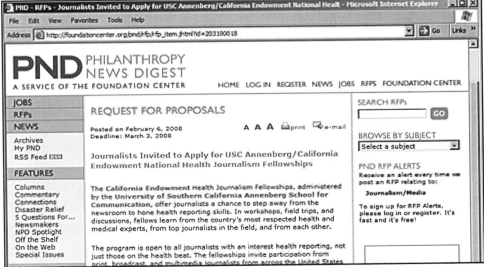

version of *Foundation Grants to Individuals*, it's a good idea to review the table of contents and the appropriate indexes to locate those entries that describe the type of funding you seek.

Requests for Proposals

Requests for Proposals (RFPs) are documents that funders disseminate to invite applications on a specific topic. RFPs are becoming increasingly popular vehicles for grantmakers to publicize new program initiatives. A number of these are for programs of relevance to individual grantseekers. For recent RFPs arranged by subject area, refer to the RFP listings in *Philanthropy News Digest* (foundationcenter.org/pnd/rfp). The most recently posted RFPs will be found in the middle of the page (organized by category). To access other currently active RFPs, use the subject listings on the right-hand side of the screen. As shown in Figure 9-8, RFP records provide the date posted, the deadline for applications, links to relevant organizations, and a link to the full RFP (usually residing on the funder's web site). You can search the entire active RFP file by keyword, and you can also subscribe to a free e-mail RFP newsletter, which will be sent to your inbox once a week.

Summary

The individual grantseeker has a variety of resources to call upon, and knowing how to use each one is key to your ultimate success. Exploring options for affiliation will enhance the likelihood that a project will be considered by a wider group of funders. Many institutions are interested in helping individuals fulfill their educational and creative goals, and with patience and perseverance, you can succeed in bringing your projects to fruition. Tips for compiling your grant request as an individual are included in the next chapter.

10

Presenting Your Idea to a Funder

By now you should have a short list of grantmakers that seem likely to fund your project on the basis of a match you've established between the funders' interests and your nonprofit organization's mission and the project you have in mind. And you have thoroughly researched each funder on your list to uncover as much current information as possible about these grantmakers, being sure that they fund in your geographic area and provide the type and amount of support you require. It is time to present your idea to those funders on your list and convince them to provide support for it.

While some foundations are quite flexible about the format and timing of grant applications, many have developed specific guidelines and procedures to facilitate the decision-making process. In an effort to save time for both grantmaker and grantseeker, some regional associations of grantmakers have adopted a common grant application format so that grant applicants can produce a standard proposal including all the elements required by participating grantmakers. Common grant application forms can be downloaded from the Find Funders directory of the Foundation Center's web site (foundationcenter.org/findfunders/cga.html). Before applying to a funder that accepts a common grant application form, you must, of course, ascertain whether your project matches the funder's stated interests and determine if the funder would prefer a letter of inquiry in advance of a full proposal. You'll also need to determine the funder's deadline(s) for proposals, and how many copies of the proposal are required.

Whether the grantmaker uses a common grant application form or has its own individual format, follow the stated procedures to the letter. You'll want to review the notes you made during the course of your research about a potential funder, including items from web sites, funder-issued annual reports, application guidelines, or informational brochures. Knowing whom to contact and how to submit your application can be critical in ensuring that your request receives serious consideration.

If no guidelines are provided by the grantmaker, use the format set forth in this chapter. The Proposal Writing Short Course in the Get Started directory at the Foundation Center's web site (foundationcenter.org/getstarted/tutorials/shortcourse/index.html) provides a useful framework to assist you in crafting a compelling grant proposal. *The Foundation Center's Guide to Proposal Writing*, and *The Foundation Center's Guide to Winning Proposals*, and other books, listed in Appendix A, are available at Center libraries and many Cooperating Collections.

Timing and Deadlines

Timing is an essential element of the grant application process. Grant decisions are often tied to funders' board meetings, which can be held as infrequently as once or twice a year. Many foundations need to receive grant applications at least two to three months in advance of board meetings to allow time for review and investigation, and some require an even longer lead time. If a prospect on your list has no specified application deadline, try to determine when its board meets and submit your request as far in advance of its next board meeting as possible. Then be prepared to wait three to six months, or even longer, for the proposal review process to run its course.

Initial Inquiries

Based on the information you uncover about a foundation, you may find that a funder does not require a full proposal as the initial approach. Many are now asking grantseekers to call them first for the purpose of determining, on a preliminary basis, how well your organization and the anticipated project matches the funder's current guidelines. The funding representative may encourage you to submit more information, or they may be able to save you time by letting you know during this brief contact that your project isn't right for their funding interests. In order to make effective use of this telephone call, you should have at hand all the basics about your project, such as what you hope to accomplish and why it's necessary, who will do the work, and how much the project will cost over what period of time. Some novice grantseekers find it helpful to rehearse this phone call in advance. And be aware that you will probably not find yourself speaking with the president of the foundation, but, hopefully, with a knowledgeable staff person or other representative who can provide guidance about next steps. Keep in mind that most of the smaller foundations do not have staff at all; so there may well be no one with whom to have this conversation.

Many foundations, both large and small, prefer to have grant applicants send a letter of inquiry before, or even in place of, a formal proposal. Based on their reading of this letter, some grantmakers may be willing to offer advice and/or assistance in preparing the final proposal for applicants whose ideas seem particularly relevant to their funding initiatives. If the foundation cannot provide funding because of prior commitments or a change in its program focus, starting with a letter of inquiry can also save you the time and effort of preparing a full proposal application. Some grantmakers make their funding decisions based solely on a letter of inquiry.

Unless the funder specifies otherwise, your letter of inquiry should be brief, no more than two to three pages. It should describe in clear, concise prose both the purpose of your organization and the parameters of the project for which you are seeking funds. You should be specific about the scope of your project, how it fits with the grantmaker's own program, the type and amount of support you are seeking, and other funders being approached. Your opening paragraph should summarize the essential ingredients of your request, including the amount of money and type of support you are seeking. Most grantmakers will also want to see a copy of the IRS letter determining your organization's tax-exempt status. Depending on what you have learned about the funder, offer to send a full proposal for their consideration or ask about the possibility of a meeting with foundation staff or officials to discuss your project.

Sample letters of inquiry can be found in *The Foundation Center's Guide to Winning Proposals* as well as the FAQ "Where can I find examples of letters of inquiry?" (foundationcenter.org/getstarted/faqs/html/loi.html) at the Center's web site.

You may need to be somewhat persistent in your approach to foundations. Give the funder adequate time to respond to your written inquiry, but don't be afraid to follow up with a phone call or e-mail about two weeks after you've sent your letter to confirm that it was received, and if not, to offer to send another copy. The call also provides the opportunity to ask whether you can supply additional information and to inquire about the timing of the review process.

The Proposal

The full grant proposal may be your *only* opportunity to convince a grantmaker that your program is worthy of its support. Depending on what you've uncovered about a funder's application procedures, it will either be your first direct contact with the funder or will follow an initial exchange of letters, e-mails, or conversations with staff and/or trustees. The proposal should make a clear and concise case for your organization and its programs. Grant decision makers receive and review hundreds, sometimes thousands, of proposals every year. In reviewing your proposal, they need to be able to identify quickly and efficiently how you intend to put the requested grant funds to work to benefit the community or to further the cause(s) in which you and the grantmaker have an interest.

At this stage your executive director and/or board may feel that it's time to turn to outside help and hire a consultant to develop your proposal. Although bringing in a professional proposal writer can bolster your confidence, it is rarely necessary and may even prove inadvisable, since no one knows your project better than a representative of your own organization. Grantmakers are not impressed by slick prose and fancy packaging. They want the facts, presented clearly and concisely, and they want to get a feeling for the organization and the people who run it.

As already noted, there are a number of excellent books on the proposal-writing process, and you may find it useful to review several of them before you get started. Many of these titles, listed in Appendix A, can be found at Foundation Center libraries or Cooperating Collections. Some may be found in your local public library. *The Foundation Center's Guide to Proposal Writing* takes you step-by-step through the proposal-writing process, supplementing advice from the author, an experienced fundraiser, with excerpts from actual proposals, and offering helpful hints from grantmakers interviewed in the preparation of the *Guide*.

There is also help available in the form of a wide assortment of educational courses. The *Guide* serves as the basis for the Center's full-day Proposal Writing Seminars, held throughout the year in many locations across the country. Announcements of upcoming seminars appear on the Center's web site and in newsletters issued by Center libraries. Interactive online training offered through the Center's web site provides a comprehensive e-course that covers the entire proposal document. This e-learning vehicle is a convenient way to participate in formal training at your own pace.

While application criteria and proposal formats vary, most funders expect to see the following components in a special project grant proposal:

TABLE OF CONTENTS

If your proposal is lengthy, you may wish to include a table of contents at the beginning. The table of contents makes it easier for the prospective funder to find specific components of the proposal. While your proposal should be brief (most funders recommend limiting it to ten pages or less), a table of contents helps you organize your presentation and outline the information it contains.

EXECUTIVE SUMMARY

The summary briefly describes the problem or need your project hopes to address; your plan of action, including how and where the program will operate, its duration, and how it will be staffed; a reference to the budget for the project, including the specific amount requested from the funder and your plans for long-term funding; the anticipated results; and a brief statement of the name, history, purpose, and activities of your agency and its capacity to carry out this project. The summary should be presented as the first section of your proposal and can be as short as one or two paragraphs; it should never be longer than a page. Be sure to clearly identify your organization in the executive summary because this one page is likely be separated from the rest of the proposal and photocopied for distribution to several people at the foundation, who may not ever see the full document.

Even though the executive summary is the first item in the proposal, it should be the last thing you actually write. By that point you will have thought through and thoroughly documented the need you plan to address, your plan of action, and the projected outcomes for your project, making it easier to pull out the salient facts for the summary.

STATEMENT OF NEED

This part of the proposal is where you state as simply and clearly as possible the problem, need, or opportunity your project will address. Be sure to narrow the issue to a definable problem that is solvable within the scope of your project. A broad picture of the many problems that exist within your community will only detract from your presentation. You want to paint a compelling picture of a pressing need that might inspire a funder to support you. You should avoid describing a problem that is overwhelming in its size and/or complexity, making the situation seem hopeless to the prospective funder.

Be sure to document the problem you've identified with citations from recent studies and current statistics pertaining to your geographic area, statements by public officials and/or professionals, and previous studies by your agency and/or other agencies. Your object is to convince the funder that the problem or need is compelling and real, and that your approach builds upon the lessons others have learned. Show the funder that you have researched the problem carefully and that you have a new or unique contribution to offer toward its resolution. It may also be appropriate to humanize the issue by portraying the people who will be served, perhaps by including short quotations, condensed case studies, or descriptions of their situations.

PROJECT DESCRIPTION

Now that you've presented the problem, you need to clarify exactly what it is you hope to accomplish. Here's where you state the goals and objectives of the project, the methods you plan to use to accomplish these objectives, a time frame in which the project will take place, and how you will determine the success or effectiveness of your project or program. The complexity of your project will help determine the length of this section of your proposal.

GOALS AND OBJECTIVES

Goals are abstract and subject to conditions. As such, they may not always be fully attainable. Objectives, on the other hand, are based on realistic expectations and therefore are more specific. Since clearly stated objectives also provide the basis for evaluating your program, be sure to make them measurable and time-limited. The realization of each stated objective will be another step toward achieving your goal. For example, if the problem you've identified is high unemployment among teenagers in your area, your objective might be to provide 100 new jobs for teenagers over the next two years. The goal of the project would be a significant reduction in or even the elimination of teenage unemployment in your community.

Don't confuse the objective of a program with the means to be used in achieving that end. You might achieve your objective of providing 100 new jobs for teenagers through a variety of methods, including working with local businesses to create jobs, running a job placement or employment information center, or providing jobs by means of a program operated by your agency. But your measurable objective remains the same: to provide 100 new jobs for teenagers over the next two years.

IMPLEMENTATION METHODS AND SCHEDULE

The methods section of your proposal should describe the plan of action for achieving your goals and objectives, as well as how long it will take. Why have you chosen this particular approach? Who will actually implement the plan? If you're involving staff or volunteers already active in your program or consultants from outside your organization, note their qualifications and include abbreviated versions of their resumes in the appendix to your proposal. If you'll need to hire new staff, include job descriptions and describe your plans for recruitment and training. You should also provide a timetable for the project, making sure to indicate the projected starting and completion dates for each phase of the program. Be sure to allow ample time for each stage, bearing in mind the possibility of delays while you await funding.

EVALUATION CRITERIA AND PROCEDURES

Evaluation provides a means for determining how effective your project has been in achieving its stated objectives. If your objectives are specific and measurable, it will be easier to evaluate your success. Although evaluating the outcome and end results of a project is a primary concern, don't overlook the need to evaluate the process or procedures as well. A good evaluation plan will enable you and others to learn from your efforts.

Most grantmakers today require an evaluation component as part of your proposal. Crafting the evaluation component of a proposal often presents a major stumbling block to the inexperienced grantseeker. Try to remember that evaluation is nothing more than an objective means by which both you and the funder determine whether or not you have accomplished what you set out to do. It is an important part of your proposal because, among other things, it demonstrates that you are aware of the responsibility implicit in receiving a grant. Evaluation should *not* be an afterthought. It should be built into the design of your procedures as a continuous monitoring system. An effective evaluation procedure will attempt to answer the following questions:

- Did you operate as intended, following the methods outlined in your procedures section?

- What beneficial changes have been brought about that are directly attributable to your project?

- Is your project the only variable responsible for these changes?

- What conclusions may be drawn from this evaluation?

- What future directions may be projected for your organization as a result of your accomplishments under this grant project?

BUDGET

Developing a proposal budget requires both candor and common sense. For example, if your proposal involves hiring staff, don't forget that Social Security payments, worker's compensation, and benefits have to be included. Try to anticipate your full expenses in advance. It's unrealistic to expect grantmakers to provide additional funding at a later date to cover needs overlooked in your initial request.

Remember, too, that foundation and corporate donors are experienced in evaluating costs. Don't pad your budget, but don't underestimate the amount you need, either. If other funders have contributed to your project, be sure to say so. The fact that others have confidence in your organization is a plus. If you expect to receive in-kind donations of equipment, office space, or volunteer time, be sure to mention these as well. Many funders want your budget (or your accompanying narrative) to reflect any staff time, resources, or overhead costs your organization will contribute to the cost of the project.

When seeking funds for a specific project, be sure to supply both the budget for your project and, in the appendix, the overall operating budget of your organization. Typically, the budget for a nonprofit organization includes two sections: personnel and nonpersonnel costs (see Figure 10-1). When in doubt, seek professional assistance from an accountant or someone with financial expertise in compiling a budget.

In addition to lists of current institutional donors to your organization, most funders will want to know your future funding plans, and how you plan to sustain your project after their grant money has run out. Even with requests for one-time support (e.g., the purchase of equipment), you should describe how you'll handle related expenditures, such as ongoing maintenance.

Figure 10-1. Sample Budget Format for a Nonprofit Organization's Grant Project

Pleasant Valley Community Center
Knowledge Exchange Project Expense Budget Fiscal 2008

Costs:

Personnel Costs (1):	Annual Salary	Project %		
Salaries:				
Sally Smith, Executive Director	$75,000	10%	$	7,500
Ben Jones, Project Director/				
Instructor	40,000	50%		20,000
Ruth Givens, Instructor	40,000	25%		10,000
Two teaching assistants				18,000 (2)
			$	55,500
Payroll taxes and fringe benefits		25%		13,875
Total Personnel costs			**$**	**69,375**

Other than Personnel costs:		
Consultant—evaluation	$	5,000 (3)
Books and other reading materials		2,400 (4)
Rent		5,200 (5)
In-kind rent (donated)		5,200
Van		1,800 (6)
Nutritious snacks		4,000 (7)
Supplies		300
Total Direct Costs	**$**	**93,275**
Administrative Costs/Overhead		**18,655 (8)**
Total Costs	**$**	**111,930**

Budget Narrative:

(1) Personnel costs include a portion of the salaries plus fringe benefits of an additional 25% of salaries for the 5 employees directly involved in the project as itemized above.

(2) Two teaching assistants at $15/hr. for 3 hours per day.

(3) A consultant will be hired to conduct pre-program and post-program testing of each participating student and an overall evaluation of the entire program at the end of the year.

(4) This represents the cost of books and other reading materials that will be given to each of the estimated 160 students participating in the program at an estimated cost of $15 per student.

(5) This represents the cost of renting space on the south side of town.

(6) This represents the program's share of a contract with a local transportation service.

(7) This represents the cost of nutritious snacks at 50¢ per student, per day.

(8) This represents a proportionate share of PVCC's organizational overhead, which is 20% of direct costs.

Vague references to alternative funding sources are not enough. Grant decision makers want *specifics*. Do you plan to solicit additional support from the public or other grantmakers? Do you expect the program ultimately to become self-supporting through client fees or sales of products or services? Is there a local institution or government agency that will support your program once it has demonstrated its value? Show the funder that you have thought through the question of sustainability by listing other potential funding sources (for example, government grants or individual donations) and income-producing activities (fees for services or sale of products, etc.)

BACKGROUND ON YOUR ORGANIZATION

Even if your organization is large and relatively well known, you should not assume that the grant decision makers reading your proposal will be familiar with your programs or accomplishments. In fact, they may not be aware of your existence. Therefore, you need to provide them with enough background information to build confidence in your group and its ability to carry out the program you are proposing. You can begin to do the groundwork for this section by keeping a "credibility file" that documents your progress and activities. State the mission of your organization succinctly and provide a brief history of your activities, stressing relevant accomplishments and recognition as well as your present sources of support. You may want to call attention to well-known individuals on your board or staff who have played a major role in your organization. Remember, your purpose is to convince the prospective funder that you are capable of producing the proposed program results and are deserving of support. Keep it short and to the point. The background statement should be no longer than a page.

CONCLUSION

Close your proposal with a paragraph or two that summarizes the proposal's main points. Reiterate what your organization seeks to accomplish and why it is important. Since this is your final appeal, at this juncture, you are justified in employing language intended to be persuasive. But remember, a little emotion goes a long way; you do not want to overdo it.

APPENDIX

The appendix to your proposal should include all appropriate supporting documents for your request, including a copy of your agency's tax-exempt determination letter from the IRS, a list of your board of directors (with affiliations), your current operating budget and an audited financial statement, a list of recent and current funding sources (both cash and in-kind), and brief résumés of key staff members and consultants. Include letters of endorsement and news clippings only if essential to the review of the request. By carefully saving letters of encouragement and praise, newspaper articles, and studies that support your work you'll have much of this material already at hand. Soliciting letters of endorsement from individuals and organizations that have benefited from your organization's activities is perfectly acceptable, and you may want to include some in the appendix. But keep in mind, appendices may not be read that carefully by grant decision makers. If something is essential, include it in the body of the text.

If the Proposal Is for General Operating Support

A general-purpose proposal requests operating support for your agency. Therefore, it focuses more broadly on the overall activities of your organization, rather than on a specific project. All of the information in the proposal should be present, but there will not be a separate component describing the organization. That information will be the main thrust of the entire proposal. Also, your proposal budget will be the budget for the entire organization, so it need not be duplicated in the appendix.

Two components of the general purpose proposal deserve special attention. They are the need statement and program information, which replaces the "project description" component. The need section is especially important. You must make the case for your organization itself, and you must do it succinctly. What are the circumstances that led to the creation of your agency? Are those circumstances still urgent today? Use language that involves the reader, but be logical in the presentation of supporting data. For example, a local organization should cite local statistics, not national ones. Program information will refer to your agency's mission, the activities engaged in to accomplish that mission, and especially the audiences served.

If the Proposal Is for a Project or Initiative of an Individual Grantseeker

In general, proposals submitted by individuals do not exceed five single-spaced pages, in addition to the cover letter and the budget. The text should be divided into short paragraphs, with headings and subheadings used for clarification. If you are applying to more than one funder (which is common), you should mention this fact in your cover letter. Stating this up front helps to reinforce your personal integrity and should not hurt your chances. The typical components of a proposal for an individual grantseeker are not dissimilar from other funding proposals. Begin with a cover letter addressed specifically to the appropriate contact person at the foundation, followed by an abstract that describes very concisely (250 words or fewer) the information that will follow. The introduction helps to establish your credibility as a grant applicant (one sentence to two paragraphs). Devote about one page to each of the next four components: a statement of need that describes a problem and explains why you require a grant to address the issue; objectives that refine your idea and tell exactly what you expect to accomplish in response to the need; procedures that describe the methods you will use to accomplish your objectives within a stated time frame; and an evaluation method for determining how you and the funder will measure your results. This should closely correspond to the objectives you set forth. If the project is ongoing, include a paragraph about its future funding, with specific plans for feasible, continuing support. A separate one-page budget depicts in dollars precisely how much money will be required and how and when it will be spent in order to accomplish your objectives. Typical components of the budget include: wages for personnel (usually your own salary is "donated"), space and equipment costs, travel expenses, telephone, printing, postage, and other direct costs.

Presenting Your Ideas to a Corporate Giver

While for the most part your proposal to a corporate funder will follow the format already provided, there are a few tips that are particularly applicable to corporations. First, make an effort to understand the corporate infrastructure. At some companies, nonmonetary support and sponsorships may be handled by the marketing department, while employee voluntarism may be coordinated in the human resources department. Second, draw up a realistic budget and be prepared to divulge your sources of income. Corporate grant decision makers are likely to scrutinize the bottom line, and many will ask for evidence of your nonprofit's fiscal responsibility and of efficient management. Third, and possibly most importantly, focus on company self-interest more than presumed benevolence by considering what a business stands to gain by giving your organization a gift, now or in the future, directly or indirectly. For example, a corporate giver may want to develop a trained pool of potential employees, support research for future products, expand its markets, respond to related social issues, ward off criticism of company policies, and, of course, increase sales. Speak to these concerns clearly in the proposal. If your program is innovative, if it tackles an emerging issue of importance to the company or its customer base or employees, or if it concentrates on a need that few other agencies are addressing, emphasize that fact, without undue self-promotion and in as noncontroversial a fashion as possible.

Cover Letter

A cover letter should accompany every proposal. The cover letter is typically on your organization's letterhead and signed by your board chairman, president, or chief executive officer, and it highlights the features of your proposal most likely to be of interest to the grantmaker. It should point out how you selected the funder and why you believe that particular grantmaker will be interested in your proposal, thus establishing an immediate link between the two organizations. It also includes the amount of money and type of support you are seeking and refers to any prior contacts with the funder about the proposal/request. The letter usually ends with an offer to answer any questions, and provides telephone and e-mail contact information.

Writing Style and Format

Make your proposal readable by using active language and by being specific about what it is you hope to accomplish. Keep the document succinct and to the point.

Within your organization, it is a good idea to use the group approach to generate ideas, but let one writer draft the proposal. Writing by committee doesn't work when you need a concise and well-organized final product (see Figure 10-2). Ask colleagues outside your organization who have been successful in securing foundation grants to review the proposal. You may also want to have someone unfamiliar with your project read the proposal to be sure its meaning is clear and that it avoids specialized jargon.

Prior to submission, review the application procedures issued by the grantmaker, if any. Have you fulfilled the requirements and addressed any concerns that might crop up? Do your proposal and cover letter establish strong connections between your project and their interests? Grantseekers often ask whether they should tailor proposals to individual funders. Unfortunately, the answer to this question is "yes and no." While it is generally not a good idea to develop a proposal or make major adjustments in your operations to conform to the interests of a particular funding source, it is perfectly acceptable and, in fact, recommended practice to customize your basic proposal to each funder's requirements. And you should be sure that your cover letter reflects any connections that exist between you and the grantmaker you have targeted. Establishing links is what fundraising is all about.

Figure 10-2. Stylistic Hints for Proposal Writers

SUGGESTIONS FOR GOOD WRITING

1. Use the active rather than the passive voice.

2. Avoid jargon; use acronyms only when absolutely necessary.

3. Stick to simple declarative sentences.

4. Keep your paragraphs short; employ headings and subheadings.

5. Address yourself to a human being: picture the grant decision maker across the desk from you as you write. Always address your cover letter to an individual. Never begin with "Dear Sir" or "To Whom It May Concern."

6. Write with the needs of the people you hope to help in mind, making sure to demonstrate how your program will be of benefit to them.

7. Unless you have evidence to the contrary, assume that the reader is unfamiliar with your organization.

8. Do not resort to emotional appeals; base your arguments on documented facts.

What Happens Next?

Submitting your proposal is nowhere near the end of your involvement in the grantseeking process. About two weeks after you have submitted your proposal, follow up with a phone call or e-mail to make sure your materials were received, if this has not already been acknowledged. If the grantmaker seems open to the idea, you may want to request a meeting with foundation representatives to discuss your program or project.

Grant review procedures at foundations vary widely, and the decision-making process can take anywhere from a few weeks to six months or longer. During the review process, the funder may ask for professional references or for additional information. This is a difficult time for the grantseeker. You need to be patient but persistent. Some foundations outline their review procedures on their web site, in annual reports, or in application guidelines. If you are unclear about the process or timetable, don't hesitate to ask.

Rejection Is Not the End

Most grantmakers receive many more worthwhile proposals than they can possibly fund in a given year. Just because a grantmaker is unable to fund a particular proposal in a given grantmaking cycle does not mean the door is closed forever. An increasing number of funders are willing to discuss with you why your proposal was declined. You can ask whether the funder needed additional information. Would they be interested in considering the proposal at a future date? Could they suggest other sources of support you should pursue? Such follow-up conversations may be particularly helpful if the grantmaker has demonstrated a commitment to funding projects in your geographic area and subject field.

Rejection is not necessarily the end of the relationship. In fact, it may be worthwhile to cultivate the funder's interest for the future. Put grant decision makers on your mailing list so that they can become further acquainted with your organization. Remember, there's always next year.

When You Get the Grant

Congratulations! You have received formal notification of your grant award and are ready to implement your program. Before you begin to hire staff or purchase supplies, however, take a few moments to acknowledge the funder's support with a letter of thanks. You also need to pay careful attention to the wording of the grant award letter to determine if the funder has specific forms, procedures, and deadlines for reporting the progress of your project under the grant. Clarifying your responsibilities as a grantee at the outset, particularly with respect to financial reporting, will prevent misunderstandings and serious problems at a later date. Be sure you understand all the qualifications attached to your grant before you start to spend the money.

While you must respect the wishes of grantmakers that request anonymity, you will find that many appreciate acknowledgment of their support in press releases, publications, and other products resulting from or concerning grant-related activities. A few of the larger, staffed foundations offer assistance to grantees in developing press releases and other publicity materials. Again, if you are unsure about the grantmaker's expectations, be sure to ask.

Keep detailed records of all grant-related activities, including contacts with and payments from the funder. Prepare a schedule of deadlines for reports and follow-up phone calls. Communicate with funders selectively. Don't inundate them with mail or invitations, but don't forget to keep them advised of important events or developments relating to your project. This is the beginning of what you hope will be a long and fruitful relationship. Treat it with the care and attention it deserves.

Summary

Many foundations have very specific guidelines and procedures for handling grant requests. It is up to the grantseeker to find out what these are and to adhere to them. If no guidelines are provided, use the format and suggestions set forth in this chapter. Since the full written proposal may be your only opportunity to convince a grants decision maker to support your project, you will want to spend significant time and effort compiling this document. There are many resources available in print, online, and in the form of free and fee-based training offered by the Foundation Center and others to help you learn more about proposal writing. Your proposal format and submission strategies may vary a bit if you are seeking general operating support as opposed to project support, if you are an individual grantseeker, or if you are approaching a corporate funder. Whether or not you receive a grant the first time you apply to a particular funder, this may be just the beginning of a relationship, either as a responsible grant recipient or as a potential grantee who needs to conduct additional cultivation in order to succeed.

Good luck with all your foundation fundraising endeavors!

Appendix A
Additional Readings
and Resources

Chapter 1: What Is a Foundation?

Beggs, Sarah, Erica C. Johnson, and Jack Thomas, eds. *The New Foundation Guidebook: Building a Strong Foundation.* Bethesda, MD: Association of Small Foundations, 2003.

> Experts and representatives from various philanthropies provide advice on starting a foundation. Topics covered include vision and mission statements, board members, tax and legal issues, financial management, grantmaking, and grantmaker associations.

Commonfund Benchmarks Study: Foundations Report. Wilton, CT: Commonfund Institute, 2007.

> Covers investments, spending, management, staffing, and operational practices of 279 private, community, and public foundations.

Edie, John A. *First Steps in Starting a Foundation.* 5th ed. Washington, DC: Council on Foundations, 2001.

> Discusses in non-technical language the various types of organizations that are all generally labeled as foundations by the public, and the requirements for establishing, and regulations governing, each type.

Esposito, Virginia, ed. *Splendid Legacy: The Guide to Creating Your Family Foundation.* Washington, DC: National Center for Family Philanthropy, 2002.
> The book is composed of contributions by various specialists on topics ranging from start-up to grantmaking, and is illustrated throughout with examples and lessons from those involved with family philanthropies.

Fleishman, Joel L. *The Foundation: A Great American Secret—How Private Wealth Is Changing the World.* New York, NY: PublicAffairs, 2007.
> Fleishman's study is based on interviews with senior officers or trustees at approximately 100 of the (mostly) largest foundations. He explains how foundations operate in practice, some of the motivations for donors, and the unique—often paradoxical—place that foundations have in American society.

Foundations Today series. New York, NY: The Foundation Center, annual.
> Provides comprehensive statistical analysis of foundation growth, funding priorities, and giving trends.

Freeman, David F., John A. Edie, and Jane C. Nober. *The Handbook on Private Foundations.* 3rd ed. Washington, DC: Council on Foundations, 2005.
> Designed primarily for new foundation staff and trustees, a substantial portion of the book explains legal and regulatory requirements.

Hopkins, Bruce R. and Jody Blazek. *Private Foundations: Tax Law and Compliance.* Hoboken, NJ: John Wiley & Sons, 2003.
> Covers federal tax laws related to the establishment of private foundations, and the distinction between private foundations, public charities, and donor-advised funds. Updated by annual supplements.

Kiger, Joseph C. *Philanthropic Foundations in the Twentieth Century.* Westport, CN: Greenwood Press, 2000.
> A comprehensive treatment of the growth of foundations in modern times, with a narrative of the worldwide historical antecedents to their growth. Details the numerous investigations of the field, including the Walsh Commission, the Cox Committee, the Patman Investigation, and the Filer Commission.

Muirhead, Sophia A. *Corporate Contributions: The View from 50 Years.* New York, NY: Conference Board, 1999.
> Provides a history of corporate philanthropy in the U.S. from the time when it was considered illegal to the present, dividing the growth into four developmental periods.

Simone, Kelly Shipp. *How to Calculate the Public Support Test.* 3rd ed. Washington, DC: Council on Foundations, 2006.
> This guide is designed to be of use to the board and staff of community foundations and other public charities, as well as to private foundations concerned that their grants may adversely affect the status of their grantees by causing them to fail the public support test.

Internet Resources:

Association of Small Foundations (smallfoundations.org)
> The web site offers program information, a calendar of events, links to philanthropy organizations, a listing of members by state, links to members' sites, an online version of the association's newsletter, and more.

Council on Foundations (cof.org)
> The national membership organization for grantmakers offers a "Learn" section on its web site to answer basic questions on philanthropy and foundations.

Forum of Regional Associations of Grantmakers (givingforum.org)
> The Forum of Regional Associations of Grantmakers (RAGs) is a membership association of the nation's largest RAGs across the country. The forum's web site includes the Regional Association Locator, which lists contact information for each individual RAG in the United States.

Foundation History: A Resource List (foundationcenter.org/getstarted/topical/fdnhist.html)
> Contains citations for resources documenting the history of philanthropy, voluntarism, and foundations, including company-sponsored and community foundations.

Strengthening Transparency, Governance, and Accountability of Charitable Organizations: A Final Report to Congress and the Nonprofit Sector (nonprofitpanel.org/Report/index.html)

> The 2005 report from the Panel on the Nonprofit Sector states: "The recommendations provide approaches that maintain the crucial balance between legitimate oversight and protecting the independence that charitable organizations need to remain innovative and effective." This report builds upon the ideas in the Panel's earlier interim report, issued in March 2005. A supplement to the report was issued in April 2006.

Chapter 2: Where Foundations Fit in the Total Funding Picture

Indiana University Center on Philanthropy and Melissa S. Brown, ed. *Giving USA*. Glenview, IL: Giving USA Foundation, annual.

> Statistical analysis of charitable contributions by corporations, foundations, individuals, and through bequests. Also provides giving data organized by type of recipient organization.

Wing, Kennard T., Thomas H. Pollak, Amy Blackwood, and Linda M. Lampkin. *The Nonprofit Almanac 2008.* Washington, DC: Urban Institute Press, 2008.

> A statistical profile of the nonprofit sector that examines its size and scope. Also includes data related to charitable giving and voluntarism.

Internet Resource:

Key Facts on Family Foundations. New York, NY: The Foundation Center, 2007.

> Statistical report available at foundationcenter.org/gainknowledge/ research/pdf/key_facts_fam_2007.pdf.

EARNED INCOME AND MEMBERSHIP:

Larson, Rolfe. *Venture Forth! The Essential Guide to Starting a Moneymaking Business in Your Nonprofit Organization.* Saint Paul, MN: Amherst H. Wilder Foundation, 2002.

> A guide for developing nonprofit business ventures that align with an organization's mission and financial goals.

Oster, Sharon M., Cynthia W. Massarsky, and Samantha L. Beinhacker, eds. *Generating and Sustaining Nonprofit Earned Income: A Guide to Successful Enterprise Strategies.* San Francisco, CA: Jossey-Bass Publishers, 2004.
> Various experts contribute chapters on multiple aspects of nonprofit entrepreneurship, including planning, legal and tax issues, securing capital, marketing, and evaluation.

Robinson, Andy. *Selling Social Change (Without Selling Out): Earned Income Strategies for Nonprofits.* San Francisco, CA: Jossey-Bass Publishers, 2002.
> Robinson discusses the growing importance of social entrepreneurship in the nonprofit sector and identifies specific steps to help an organization generate more money from its programs.

Robinson, Ellis M. M. *The Nonprofit Membership Toolkit.* San Francisco, CA: Jossey-Bass Publishers, 2003.
> This publication is directed primarily to the smaller nonprofit and is a comprehensive workbook and guide to establishing or enhancing the membership base. Includes numerous worksheets, sample documents, calendars, and other practical items for the development office.

INDIVIDUAL DONORS AND PLANNED GIVING:

Burnett, Ken. *Relationship Fundraising: A Donor-Based Approach to the Business of Raising Money.* San Francisco, CA: Jossey-Bass Publishers, 2002.
> The guidebook discusses prospect research, donor attitudes, marketing, donor relations, bequests, common mistakes, and new challenges.

Dove, Kent E., Alan M. Spears, and Thomas W. Herbert. *Conducting a Successful Major Gifts and Planned Giving Program: A Comprehensive Guide and Resource.* San Francisco, CA: Jossey-Bass Publishers, 2002.
> Explains how to identify prospects for major gifts, and how this level of philanthropy relates to planned giving.

Greenfield, James M. *Fundraising Fundamentals: A Guide to Annual Giving for Professionals and Volunteers.* Hoboken, NJ: John Wiley & Sons, 2002.
> The guidebook explains various fundraising methods and describes how to manage a comprehensive annual giving program.

Jordan, Ronald R., Katelyn L. Quynn, and Carolyn M. Osteen. *Planned Giving: Management, Marketing, and Law*. 3rd ed. Hoboken, NJ: John Wiley & Sons, 2004.

> Divided into eight parts: managing a planned giving program; marketing planned giving; the planned giving donor; planned giving assets; planned giving options; related disciplines; policies and procedures, and planned giving in context.

Internet Resource:

National Committee on Planned Giving (ncpg.org)

> Professional association for people whose work involves developing, marketing and administering charitable planned gifts.

GOVERNMENT FUNDING:

Dumouchel, J. Robert. *Government Assistance Almanac*. Detroit, MI: Omnigraphics, Inc., annual.

> Outlines more than 1,600 federal domestic programs currently available, providing information about the type or types of assistance offered, with complete contact details.

Federal Grants Management Handbook. Washington, DC: Thompson Publishing Group, updated monthly.

> This guide explains how to comply with federal grants management rules, including developing an accounting system, indirect cost rates, procurement procedures, reports, audits, and other topics.

Internet Resources:

FirstGov for Nonprofits (www.usa.gov/Business/Nonprofit.shtml)

> A starting point for information about services from federal agencies.

Grants.gov (grants.gov)

> The federal government's portal for grant opportunities for state and local governments, nonprofits, and academia can be browsed by subject.

National Assembly of State Arts Agencies (nasaa-arts.org)

> Sponsored by the National Endowment for the Arts, this site is a clearinghouse of Internet information for arts organizations. Browse the "News from NASAA" section for legislative updates.

Chapter 3: Who Gets Foundation Grants?

Kirschten, Barbara L. *Nonprofit Corporation Forms Handbook.* Eagan, MN: West Group, annual.
> Provides model corporate documents to facilitate the incorporation of nonprofit organizations in various jurisdictions, as well as guidance in applying to the IRS for recognition of exemption from federal income tax.

Mancuso, Anthony. *How to Form a Nonprofit Corporation.* 8th ed. Berkeley, CA: Nolo Press, 2007.
> A soup-to-nuts guide to forming and operating a tax-exempt corporation under Section 501(c)(3) of the Internal Revenue Code.

Ober-Kaler and Thomas K. Hyatt, ed. *The Nonprofit Legal Landscape.* Washington, DC: BoardSource, 2005.
> Each chapter deals with significant decisions that need to be made in the life cycle of a nonprofit, from establishing the legal, tax, and governance structures, intellectual property, employment law, antitrust law, litigation and dispute resolution. Appendices provide information on Form 990, a sample whistleblower policy, and bibliographical references.

Olenick, Arnold J. and Philip R. Olenick. *A Nonprofit Organization Operating Manual: Planning for Survival and Growth.* New York, NY: The Foundation Center, 1991.
> This manual addresses the essential financial and legal aspects of managing a nonprofit organization.

Quotah, Eman. "Getting a Head Start." *Chronicle of Philanthropy,* vol. 19 (5 April 2007): p. 35–7.
> Explains the advantages and drawbacks of fiscal sponsorship arrangements that support organizations without 501(c)(3) tax-exempt status.

Internet Resources:

Alliance for Nonprofit Management (allianceonline.org)
> Members of the Alliance include management support organizations, individual professionals, and a range of national/regional, umbrella, research and academic, publishing, and philanthropic organizations that provide training and consulting to nonprofits.

BoardSource (boardsource.org)
> Useful information about recruiting board members and developing
> board job descriptions.

The Foundation Center's Frequently Asked Questions (foundationcenter.
org/getstarted/faqs)
> The Nonprofit Management Section of the FAQs includes information
> on establishing a nonprofit organization.

Free Management Library (managementhelp.org)
> A no-frills library of free management courses in topics such as board
> roles and responsibilities, communications skills, finance and taxes,
> program development, program evaluation, and consultants.

The Nonprofit FAQ (idealist.org/npofaq)
> An online resource of information and advice about nonprofits, taken
> from discussions on e-mail lists and other sources.

Chapter 4: Planning Your Funding Research Strategy

Brown, Larissa Golden and Martin John Brown. *Demystifying Grant Seeking:
What You Really Need to Do to Get Grants.* San Francisco, CA: Jossey-Bass
Publishers, 2001.
> Confronts some common ideas about the fundraising process and offers
> the building blocks of a systematic grants effort.

Ciconte, Barbara L. and Jeanne G. Jacob. *Fundraising Basics: A Complete
Guide.* 2nd ed. Gaithersburg, MD: Aspen Publishers, 2001.
> Drawing from numerous sources, provides a thorough treatment of the
> fundraising effort, from establishing a philanthropic environment to
> working with consultants.

Dove, Kent E. *Conducting a Successful Fundraising Program: A Comprehensive
Guide and Resource.* San Francisco, CA: Jossey-Bass Publishers, 2001.
> Chapters cover different types of fundraising, including annual
> campaigns, major gifts, planned giving, foundation and corporate
> grants, with additional chapters on how to choose among the
> fundraising options, how to motivate volunteers, use of technology,
> and accountability.

Greenfield, James M., ed. *The Nonprofit Handbook: Fund Raising.* 3rd ed. Hoboken, NJ: John Wiley & Sons, 2001.
> This compilation provides contributions by numerous experts who share information on the entire scope of fundraising, including the "how to" of actual solicitation activities.

Robinson, Andy. *Grassroots Grants: An Activist's Guide to Grantseeking.* 2nd ed. San Francisco, CA: Jossey-Bass Publishers, 2004.
> Provides step-by-step guidance on obtaining funds for grassroots organizations; contains several sample proposals.

Rosso, Henry A. and Eugene R. Tempel, ed. *Hank Rosso's Achieving Excellence in Fund Raising.* 2nd ed. San Francisco, CA: Jossey-Bass Publishers, 2003.
> Comprehensive coverage of successful and ethical fundraising principles, concepts, and techniques.

Seltzer, Michael. *Securing Your Organization's Future: A Complete Guide to Fundraising Strategies.* Rev. ed. New York, NY: The Foundation Center, 2001.
> A step-by-step approach to creating and sustaining a network of funding sources.

Weinstein, Stanley. *The Complete Guide to Fundraising Management.* 2nd ed. Hoboken, NJ: John Wiley & Sons, 2002.
> A comprehensive treatment of fundraising principles and practices, including information about creating case statements, record keeping, prospect research, cultivating donors, major gifts, grants, direct mail, telemarketing, special events, planned giving, and capital campaigns.

Internet Resources:

Association of Fundraising Professionals (afpnet.org)
> The membership organization offers educational programs and support for career development.

Foundation Center's Guide to Funding Research (foundationcenter.org/getstarted/tutorials/gfr)
> Primer on the funding research process for both individuals and nonprofits seeking grants.

The Grantsmanship Center (tgci.com)
> The Center provides training in grantsmanship and proposal writing for nonprofit organizations and government agencies.

Chapter 5: Online Resources for Funding Research

Hogan, Cecilia. *Prospect Research: A Primer for Growing Nonprofits.* Sudbury, MA: Jones and Bartlett Publishers, 2004.
> Explains the terminology, tools, and procedures for prospect research of individuals, corporations, foundations, and government agencies.

Internet Resources:

Association of Professional Researchers for Advancement (aprahome.org)
> Professional association for prospect researchers whose web site contains links to private and government resources.

David Lamb's Prospect Research Page (lambresearch.com)
> Provides recommendations for research tools available on the Internet.

Research 101 (jankowskiresearch.com/Research101.htm)
> Online tutorial covering the major components of foundation research strategy.

Stanford University Development Research (stanford.edu/dept/ OOD/RESEARCH)
> Provides links to resources for researching foundations, corporations, and individuals.

Selected Periodicals:

Alliance (alliancemagazine.org)

Chronicle of Philanthropy (philanthropy.com)

Nonprofit Quarterly (nonprofitquarterly.org)

NonProfit Times (nptimes.com)

Stanford Social Innovation Review (ssireview.org)

Chapter 6: The Savvy Searcher

Internet Resource:

Foundation Directory Online Professional (fconline.foundationcenter.org)
   Provides comprehensive and accurate information on U.S. grantmakers
   and their funding activities. The guided tour demonstrates basic search
   options.

Chapter 7: Resources for Corporate Funding Research

Corporate Contributions. New York, NY: Conference Board, annual.
   The survey of major U.S. corporations provides a detailed overview,
   complete with charts and tables on their contributions.

Corporate Giving Directory. Medford, NJ: Information Today, annual.
   Provides detailed descriptive profiles of 1,000 of the largest corporate
   charitable giving programs in the United States. Each company profiled
   makes annual contributions of at least $200,000, including nonmonetary
   donations.

National Directory of Corporate Giving. New York, NY: The Foundation
Center, annual.
   A directory of more than 3,700 corporations that make contributions
   to nonprofit organizations through corporate foundations or direct
   giving programs.

National Directory of Corporate Public Affairs. Washington, DC: Columbia
Books, annual.
   Provides profiles of nearly 1,500 companies identified as having public
   affairs programs and lists approximately 13,000 corporate officers
   engaged in the informational, political, and philanthropic aspects of
   public affairs.

Zukowski, Linda M. *Fistfuls of Dollars: Fact and Fantasy About Corporate
Charitable Giving.* Redondo Beach, CA: EarthWrites Publishing, 1998.
   Covers the basics of corporate giving solicitation, as well as the
   elements of proposals and budgets. Also discusses how to respond to
   a funding decision.

Internet Resources:

The Committee Encouraging Corporate Philanthropy
(corporatephilanthropy.org)
> CECP's mission is to lead the business community in raising the level
> and quality of corporate philanthropy.

Corporate Giving Online (cgonline.foundationcenter.org)
> An online database of corporate donors that support nonprofit
> organizations and programs through grants as well as in-kind donations
> of equipment, products, professional services, and volunteers.

PR Newswire (prnewswire.com)
> News from corporations worldwide; frequently contains information on
> major corporate gifts.

Chapter 8: Searching CD-ROM and Print Directories

FC Search: The Foundation Center's Database on CD-ROM. New York, NY:
The Foundation Center, annual.
> The comprehensive search tool includes profiles of foundations, corporate
> donors, and public charities.

The Foundation Directory series. New York, NY: The Foundation Center,
annual.
> The three-volume set contains key facts on the nation's foundations.
> Updated information is provided in *The Foundation Directory Supplement.*

FUNDING DIRECTORIES:

The Catholic Funding Guide: A Directory of Resources for Catholic Activities.
5th ed. Washington, DC: Foundations and Donors Interested in Catholic
Activities, Inc., 2007.

Eckstein, Richard M., ed. *Directory of Matching and Endowment Grants.*
Loxahatchee, FL: Research Grant Guides, 2005.

Eckstein, Richard M., ed. *Directory of Operating Grants.* 8th ed. Loxahatchee,
FL: Research Grant Guides, 2006.

Environmental Grantmaking Foundations. 11th ed. Rochester, NY: Resources for Global Sustainability, Inc., 2005.

Guide to Funding for International & Foreign Programs. New York, NY: The Foundation Center, 2008.

Morris, James McGrath and Laura Adler, eds. *Grant Seekers Guide: Foundations That Support Social & Economic Justice.* 6th rev. ed. Kingston, RI: Moyer Bell, 2005.

Internet Resource:

Foundation Center's Topical Resource Lists (foundationcenter.org/getstarted/topical)
> Identify grantmaker directories specific to a geographic area by browsing these resource lists: "State and Local Funding Directories" and "International Directories of Foundations."

Chapter 9: Resources for Individual Grantseekers

Colvin, Gregory L. *Fiscal Sponsorship: 6 Ways to Do It Right.* 2nd ed. San Francisco, CA: Study Center Press, 2005.
> Describes the six forms of fiscal sponsorship recognized by the Internal Revenue Service, with examples, charts, and diagrams.

Dean, Carole Lee. *The Art of Film Funding: Alternative Financing Concepts.* Studio City, CA: Michael Wiese Productions, 2007.
> Topics covered in this guide include proposals, researching funders, fundraising from individuals and businesses, public funding, branding, partnerships, tax laws, and other areas.

Goodwin, Ariane. *Writing the Artist Statement: Revealing the True Spirit of Your Work.* Haverford, PA: Infinity Publishing, 2002.
> The guide describes what artist statements are, discusses why they are important, and explains how to develop them by using creative writing exercises.

Liberatori, Ellen. *Guide to Getting Arts Grants.* New York, NY: Allworth Press, 2006.
> The handbook provides practical advice to help artists obtain grants from foundations and government agencies.

FUNDING DIRECTORIES:

Annual Register of Grant Support: A Directory of Funding Sources. Medford, NJ: Information Today, annual.
> Includes details of the grant support programs of government agencies, public and private foundations, corporations, community trusts, unions, educational and professional associations, and special-interest organizations.

Awards, Honors, and Prizes. Farmington Hills, MI: Thomson Gale, annual.
> Directory containing information on more than 7,500 organizations and 23,000 awards.

Dramatists Sourcebook: Complete Opportunities for Playwrights, Translators, Composers, Lyricists and Librettists. 24th ed. New York, NY: Theatre Communications Group, 2006.
> Contains a "Fellowships and Grants" section listing foundations and organizations that offer funding to playwrights, composers, translators, librettists, and lyricists.

Financial Aid for the Disabled and Their Families. El Dorado Hills, CA: Reference Service Press, biennial.
> Provides current information about more than 1,200 scholarship, fellowship, loan, grant, and award programs established and designed primarily or exclusively for the disabled or members of their families.

Funding for United States Study: A Guide for International Students and Professionals. New York, NY: Institute of International Education, 2007.
> Provides information on more than 500 grants, fellowships, and scholarships for undergraduate and graduate study, as well as doctoral and postdoctoral research in the United States. In addition, the guide provides informative articles on financial assistance and university funding options.

Grants Register: The Complete Guide to Postgraduate Funding Worldwide. New York, NY: Palgrave Publishers, annual.

Lists more than 3,500 scholarships, fellowships, and awards at all levels of graduate study. Fellowships and awards span a variety of subjects, many of which are open to international students.

Musical America Worldwide. East Windsor, NJ: Commonwealth Business Media Inc., annual.

Includes a listing of North American and international contests, foundations, and awards in the fields of music and performing arts.

Internet Resources:

American Music Center (amc.net)

The organization's *Opportunities in New Music Directory* is a subscription-based database that lists ongoing American and foreign competitions, grants, commissioning programs, workshops, calls for scores, and artist's colonies.

Federal Student Aid (studentaid.ed.gov)

The U.S. Department of Education's Federal Student Aid (FSA) programs, described on this web site, are the largest source of student aid in America. The information provided is designed to assist college planning. It provides access to and information about the products and services needed throughout the financial aid process, including a link to the FAFSA (Free Application for Federal Student Aid) form.

The Foundation Center's Web Portal for Individual Grantseekers (foundationcenter.org/getstarted/individuals)

Visit the individual grantseekers area at the Foundation Center's web site to find useful tips and learn about training opportunities.

Foundation Grants to Individuals Online (gtionline.foundationcenter.org)

The Foundation Center's online database of more than 6,500 foundation and public charity programs that provide support to individuals.

GovBenefits.gov (govbenefits.gov)

Includes information on a variety of Federal and state benefit and assistance programs for veterans, seniors, students, teachers, children, people with disabilities, disaster victims, caregivers, and others.

Institute of International Education Online (iie.org)

Includes information about international education and training programs, including Fulbright scholarships.

New York Foundation for the Arts (nyfa.org)
> The "For Artists" area of the web site provides information on fellowships and fiscal sponsorship for artists, including "NYFA Source," a national database of awards, services, and publications for artists of all disciplines.

PEN American Center (pen.org)
> The membership organization offers a subscription service, *Grants and Awards Available to American Writers,* that contains more than 1,000 listings of domestic and foreign grants, literary awards, fellowships, and residencies.

Social Science Research Council (ssrc.org)
> The SSRC offers fellowship and grant programs mostly targeting the social sciences, though many are also open to applicants from the humanities, natural sciences, and relevant professional and practitioner communities.

Chapter 10: Presenting Your Idea to a Funder

Anderson, Cynthia. *Write Grants, Get Money.* Worthington, OH: Linworth Publishing, 2001.
> A proposal writing guidebook for school media specialists and other K-12 librarians to improve library programs and facilities.

Carlson, Mim. *Winning Grants Step by Step: The Complete Workbook for Planning, Developing and Writing Successful Proposals.* 2nd ed. San Francisco, CA: Jossey-Bass Publishers, 2002.
> Contains instructions and exercises designed to help with proposal planning and writing skills and to meet the requirements of both government agencies and private funders.

Collins, Sarah, ed. *The Foundation Center's Guide to Winning Proposals.* New York, NY: The Foundation Center, 2003.
> The guide reprints in their original form 20 proposals and four letters of inquiry that succeeded in securing foundation support. Each proposal is accompanied by commentary by the funder who awarded the grant and proposal writing advice.

Geever, Jane C. *The Foundation Center's Guide to Proposal Writing*. 5th ed. New York, NY: The Foundation Center, 2007.
> Guides the grantwriter from pre-proposal planning to post-grant follow-up. Incorporates excerpts from actual grant proposals and interviews with foundation and corporate grantmakers about what they look for in a proposal.

Geever, Jane C. and Silvia R. Sanusian, trans. *Guía para escribir propuestas*. New York, NY: The Foundation Center, 2008.
> A Spanish translation of *The Foundation Center's Guide to Proposal Writing*, 5th ed. Includes an appendix of technical assistance providers that will assist Hispanic nonprofits.

Hall, Mary Stewart. *Getting Funded: A Complete Guide to Proposal Writing*. 4th ed. Portland, OR: Continuing Education Publications, 2003.
> This guidebook to proposal writing is organized along a logical pattern of planning, beginning with a discussion of ideas for projects and ending with considerations about submissions, negotiation, and project renewal.

Miner, Jeremy T. and Lynn E. Miner. *Models of Proposals Planning & Writing*. Westport, CT: Praeger, 2005.
> Provides a step-by-step strategy for creating proposals and other documents for applying to both private funders and government agencies.

Quick, James Aaron and Cheryl Carter New. *Grant Seeker's Budget Toolkit*. Hoboken, NJ: John Wiley & Sons, 2001.
> In this guidebook on project budgets, the authors explain the calculation of direct costs, with chapters specifically describing personnel and travel costs.

Wells, Michael K. *Understanding Nonprofit Finances*. Portland, OR: Portland State University, 2006.
> Explains how to work with financial and accounting documents in preparing the budget for a proposal or grant application.

Internet Resources:

The Foundation Center's Proposal Writing Short Course (foundationcenter. org/getstarted/tutorials/shortcourse/index.html)
    Basic information about proposal writing, excerpted from *The Foundation Center's Guide to Proposal Writing.*

The Foundation Center's Frequently Asked Questions on Proposal Writing (foundationcenter.org/getstarted/faqs/section_3d.html)
    Includes links to examples of "already-written" proposals and proposal templates.

Grantproposal.com (grantproposal.com)
    Provides free resources for both advanced grantwriting consultants and inexperienced nonprofit staff.

Appendix B
State Charities Registration Offices

ALABAMA
Rhonda Barber
Office of the Attorney General
Alabama State House
11 South Union Street, 3rd Floor
Montgomery, AL 36130
(334) 242-7335
www.ago.state.al.us/consumer_charities.
cfm

ALASKA
Cathy Stone
State of Alaska
Department of Law
Attorney General's Office
1031 West 4th Avenue, Suite 200
Anchorage, AK 99501
(907) 269-5200
E-mail: cathy_stone@law.state.ak.us
www.law.state.ak.us/department/civil/
consumer/cp_charities.html

ARIZONA
Office of the Secretary of State
Charities Division
1700 West Washington Street, 7th Floor
Phoenix, AZ 85007
(602) 542-6187
Fax: (602) 542-7386
www.azsos.gov/business_services/Charities/
Default.htm

ARKANSAS
Office of the Attorney General
Consumer Protection Division
323 Center Street, Suite 200
Little Rock, AR 72201-2610
(501) 682-2341
Fax: 501-682-8118
E-mail: consumer@ag.state.ar.us
www.ag.state.ar.us/consumers_protection_
charitable_registration.html

CALIFORNIA

Registry of Charitable Trusts
P.O. Box 903447
Sacramento, CA 94203-4470
(916) 445-2021
caag.state.ca.us/charities/forms.htm

COLORADO

Russell K. Subiono, Charities Program
  Assistant
Charitable Solicitations Section
Colorado Secretary of State
1700 Broadway
Denver, CO 80290
(303) 894-2200 x6421
Fax: (303) 869-4871
E-mail: charitable@sos.state.co.us
www.sos.state.co.us/pubs/charities/
  charitable.htm

CONNECTICUT

Public Charities Unit
c/o Office of the Attorney General
55 Elm Street
P.O. Box 120
Hartford, CT 06141-0120
(860) 808-5030
www.ct.gov/ag/cwp/browse.
  asp?a=2074&agNav=|

DELAWARE

*No registration required for nonprofits
  in Delaware.*
Office of the Attorney General
Carvel State Building
820 North French Street
Wilmington, DE 19801
(302) 577-8400
E-mail: attorney.general@state.de.us
www.attorneygeneral.delaware.gov

DISTRICT OF COLUMBIA

Government of the District of Columbia
DCRA
Corporations Division
941 North Capitol Street NE
Washington, DC 20002
Send forms to:
PO Box 92300
Washington, D.C. 20090
(202) 442-4432
www.dcra.dc.gov

FLORIDA

Florida Department of Agriculture &
  Consumer Services
2005 Apalachee Parkway
Tallahassee, FL 32399-6500
Send forms to:
Solicitation of Contributions
PO Box 6700
Tallahassee, FL 32314-6700
 (850) 488-2221
E-mail: cswebmaster@doacs.state.fl.us
doacs.state.fl.us/onestop/cs/solicit.html

GEORGIA

Office of the Secretary of State
Division of Securities and Business
  Regulations
2 Martin Luther King, Jr. Drive, SE,
Suite 802, West Tower
Atlanta, GA 30334
(404) 656-3920
Fax: (404) 657-8410
www.sos.state.ga.us/securities

HAWAII

*No registration required for nonprofits
in Hawaii.*
Department of Commerce & Consumer
Affairs
Office of Consumer Protection
Leiopapa A Kamehameha Building
235 South Beretania Street, Suite 801
Honolulu, Hawaii 96813
(808) 586-2630
Fax: (808) 586-2640
E-mail: ocp@dcca.hawaii.gov
www.hawaii.gov/dcca/ocp

IDAHO

*No registration required for nonprofits
in Idaho.*
Office of the Attorney General
Consumer Protection Unit
P.O. Box 83720
Boise, ID 83720-0010
(208) 334-2400
Email: consumer_protection@ag.idaho.gov
www2.state.id.us/ag/consumer/index.htm

ILLINOIS

Illinois Attorney General
Charitable Trust Bureau
100 West Randolph Street, 11th Floor
Chicago, IL 60601
(312) 814-2595
www.ag.state.il.us/charities

INDIANA

*No registration required for nonprofits
in Indiana.*
Office of the Indiana Attorney General
Consumer Protection Division
302 West Washington Street, 5th Floor
Indianapolis, IN 46204
(317) 232-6330
www.indianaconsumer.com/consumer_
guide/charitable_info.asp

IOWA

Iowa Secretary of State
Business Services Division
First Floor, Lucas Building
321 East 12th Street
Des Moines, IA 50319
(515) 281-5204
Fax: (515) 242-5953
E-mail: sos@sos.state.ia.us
www.sos.state.ia.us/business/Nonprofits/
index.html

KANSAS

Kansas Secretary of State
Business Services Division
Memorial Hall, 1st Floor
120 SW 10th Avenue
Topeka, KS 66612-1594
(785) 296-4564
E-mail: corp@kssos.org
www.kssos.org/business/business_
charitable.html

KENTUCKY

Secretary of State
Business Filings Office
P.O. Box 718
700 Capitol Avenue, Suite 154
Frankfort, KY 40602
(502) 564-2848
sos.ky.gov/business/filings/nonprofit.htm

LOUISIANA

Office of the Attorney General
Consumer Protection Section
1885 North 3rd Street
Baton Rouge, LA 70802
Send forms to:
P.O. Box 94005
Baton Rouge, LA 70804-9005
(225) 326-6465
Fax: (225) 326-6499
E-mail: consumerinfo@ag.state.la.us
www.sos.louisiana.gov/tabid/94/Default.
aspx

MAINE

Department of Professional & Financial
    Regulation
Office of Licensing & Registration
35 State House Station
Augusta, ME 04333
(207) 624-8603
Fax: (207) 624-8637
E-mail: charitable.sol@maine.gov
www.maine.gov/pfr/professionallicensing/
    professions/charitable/index.htm

MARYLAND

Kim Smith
Office of the Secretary of State
Charitable Organizations Division
State House
Annapolis, MD 21401
(410) 974-5534
E-mail: KSmith@sos.state.md.us
www.sos.state.md.us/Charity/Charityhome.
    htm

MASSACHUSETTS

Office of the Attorney General
Division of Public Charities
One Ashburton Place
Boston, MA 02108
(617) 727-2200 ext. 1701
www.ago.state.ma.us

MICHIGAN

Department of the Attorney General
Charitable Trust Section
P.O. Box 30214
Lansing, MI 48909
(517) 373-1152
Fax: (517) 373-3042
E-mail: miag@michigan.gov
www.michigan.gov/ag/0,1607,7-164-
    17334_18095—-,00.html

MINNESOTA

Charities Division
Suite 1200, Bremer Tower
445 Minnesota Street
St. Paul, MN 55101-2130
(651) 296-6172
www.ag.state.mn.us/Charities/

MISSISSIPPI

Office of the Secretary of State
Regulation & Enforcement Division
700 North Street
Jackson, MS 39202
Send forms to:
P.O. Box 136
Jackson, MS 39205
(601) 359-2663
www.sos.state.ms.us/regenf/charities/
    charities.asp

MISSOURI

Missouri Attorney General's Office
Attn: Rhonda Johnson
P.O. Box 899
Jefferson City, MO 65102
(573) 751-1197
E-mail: rhonda.johnson@ago.mo.gov
www.ago.mo.gov/checkacharity/
    charityregistration.htm

MONTANA

*No registration required for nonprofits
    in Montana.*
Anthony Johnstone, Assistant Attorney
    General
Office of the Attorney General
P.O. Box 201401
Helena, MT 59620-1401
(406) 444-2026
Fax: (406) 444-3549
E-mail: contactdoj@mt.gov
doj.mt.gov/consumer/nonprofit/default.asp

NEBRASKA

No registration required for nonprofits in Nebraska.
Office of the Attorney General
2115 State Capitol
Lincoln, NE 68509
(402) 471-2682
www.ago.state.ne.us

NEVADA

Nevada Secretary of State
Business Center
206 North Carson Street
Carson City, NV 89701-4299
(775) 684-5708
E-mail: newfilings@sos.nv.gov
www.secretaryofstate.biz/business/forms/
    nonprofit.asp

NEW HAMPSHIRE

Terry M. Knowles
Office of the New Hampshire Attorney
    General
Charitable Trust Unit
33 Capitol Street
Concord, NH 03301
(603) 271-3658
E-mail: terry.knowles@doj.nh.gov
www.doj.nh.gov/charitable

NEW JERSEY

New Jersey Office of the Attorney General
Division of Consumer Affairs
Office of Consumer Protection
Charities Registration
153 Halsey Street
Newark, NJ 07102
(973) 504-6215
E-mail: askconsumeraffairs@lps.state.nj.us
www.njconsumeraffairs.gov/ocp/charities.
    htm

NEW MEXICO

Attorney General of New Mexico
Registry of Charitable Organizations
111 Lomas Boulevard, NW, Suite 300
Albuquerque, NM 87102
(505) 222-9046
E-mail: Charity.Registrar@ago.state.nm.us
www.nmag.gov/office/Divisions/Civ/
    charity/default.aspx

NEW YORK

Office of the Attorney General
Department of Law
Charities Bureau-Registration Section
120 Broadway
New York, NY 10271
(212) 416-8000
E-mail: Charities.Bureau@oag.state.ny.us
www.oag.state.ny.us/charities/charities.html

NORTH CAROLINA

Charitable Solicitation Licensing Section
North Carolina Secretary of State
P.O. Box 29622
Raleigh, NC 27626-0622
(919) 807-2214
E-mail: csl@sosnc.com
www.secretary.state.nc.us/csl

NORTH DAKOTA

Secretary of State
Nonprofit Services
600 East Boulevard Avenue, Department
    108
Bismarck, ND 58505-0500
(701) 328-2900
Fax: (701) 328-2992
E-mail: sos@nd.gov
www.nd.gov/sos/nonprofit

OHIO

Ohio Attorney General
State Office Tower
30 East Broad Street, 17th Floor
Columbus, OH 43215-3428
(614) 466-4320
www.ag.state.oh.us/business/charitable.asp

OKLAHOMA

Secretary of State's Office
Business Filing Division/Charitable
    Organizations
2300 North Lincoln Boulevard, Suite 101
Oklahoma City, OK 73105-4897
(405) 521-3912
www.sos.state.ok.us/business/business_
    filing.htm

OREGON

Charitable Activities Section
Oregon Department of Justice
1515 SW Fifth Avenue, Suite 410
Portland, OR 97201-5451
(971) 673-1880
Fax: (971) 673-1882
E-mail: charitable.activities@doj.state.or.us
www.doj.state.or.us/charigroup/howto.
    shtml

PENNSYLVANIA

Bureau of Charitable Organizations
207 North Office Building
Harrisburg, PA 17120
(717) 783-1720
Fax: (717) 783-6014
E-mail: ST-CHARITY@state.pa.us
www.dos.state.pa.us/char/site/default.asp

RHODE ISLAND

Department of Business Regulation
Securities Division
233 Richmond Street, Suite 232
Providence, RI 02903-4232
(401) 222-3048
Fax: (401) 222-6654
E-mail: securitiesinquiry@dbr.state.ri.us
www.dbr.state.ri.us/divisions/banking_
    securities/charitable.php

SOUTH CAROLINA

Carolyn Hatcher
Secretary of State's Office
Public Charity Division
Edgar Brown Building, Capitol Complex
1205 Pendleton Street
Columbia, SC 29211
Send forms to:
P.O. Box 11350
Columbia, SC 29211
(803) 734-1790
Fax: (803) 734-1604
E-mail: cjhatcher@infoave.net
www.scsos.com/charities.htm

SOUTH DAKOTA

*No registration required for nonprofits in
    South Dakota, unless registered as a
    corporation.*
Office of the Attorney General
Division of Consumer Protection
1302 East Hwy 14
Suite 3
Pierre, SD 57501
(605) 773-4400
Fax: (605) 773-7163
E-mail: consumerhelp@state.sd.us
www.state.sd.us/attorney/office/divisions/
    consumer

To register as a corporation:
Secretary of State
State Capitol
500 East Capitol Road
Pierre, SD 57501

(605) 773-4845
Fax: (605) 773-4550
E-mail: corporations@state.sd.us
www.sdsos.gov/busineservices/corporations.
    shtm

TENNESSEE
Tennessee Department of State
Charitable Solicitations
312 Eighth Avenue North
8th Floor, William R. Snodgrass Tower
Nashville, TN 37243
(615) 741-2555
E-mail: charitable.solicitations@state.tn.us
www.state.tn.us/sos/charity.htm

TEXAS
*Under Texas law, most charities or non-
    profit organizations are not required to
    register with the state. Exceptions exist,
    however, for organizations that solicit for
    law enforcement, public safety, or veterans'
    causes.*
Secretary of State
Corporations Section
P.O. Box 13697
Austin, TX 78711-3697
(512) 463-5555
Fax: (512) 463-5709
E-mail: corpinfo@sos.state.tx.us
www.sos.state.tx.us/corp/nonprofit_org.
    shtml

UTAH
Division of Consumer Protection
Heber M. Wells Building
160 East 300 South, 2nd Floor
SM 146704
Salt Lake City, UT 84114
(801) 530-6601
Fax: (801) 530-6001
E-mail: consumerprotection@utah.gov
www.consumerprotection.utah.gov/
    registration/charitableorganization.html

VERMONT
Secretary of State
Corporations Division
81 River Street
Montpelier, VT 05609-1101
(802) 828-2386
Fax: (802) 828-2853
E-mail: bpoulin@sec.state.vt.us
www.sec.state.vt.us/tutor/dobiz/noprof/
    Nonprofit/nphome.htm

VIRGINIA
Department of Agriculture and Consumer
    Services
Office of Consumer Affairs
Charitable Solicitations
P.O. Box 526
Richmond, VA 23218
(804) 786-1343
Fax: (804) 225-2666
E-mail: webmaster.vdacs@vdacs.virginia.
    gov
www.vdacs.virginia.gov/consumers/
    registrations.shtml

WASHINGTON
Office of the Secretary of State
Charities Program
P.O. Box 40234
Olympia, WA 98504-0234
(360) 753-0863
E-mail: charities@secstate.wa.gov
www.secstate.wa.gov/charities

WEST VIRGINIA
Charitable Organizations Assistant,
    Secretary of State
Building 1, Suite 157-K
1900 Kanawha Boulevard East
Charleston, WV 25305-0770
(304) 558-6000
Fax: (304) 558-5758
E-mail: charities@wvsos.com
www.wvsos.com/charity/main.htm

WISCONSIN

Department of Regulation & Licensing
P.O. Box 8935
Madison, WI 53708-8935
(608) 266-2112
E-mail: web@drl.state.wi.us
drl.wi.gov/boards/rco/index.htm

WYOMING

Corporations Division
Wyoming Secretary of State's Office
The Capitol Building, Room 110
Cheyenne, WY 82002
(307) 777-7311
Fax: (307) 777-5339
E-mail: corporations@state.wy.us
soswy.state.wy.us/corporat/np.htm

Appendix C
The Foundation Center's Grants Classification System and the National Taxonomy of Exempt Entities (NTEE)

The Foundation Center began to record and categorize grants in 1961. It established a computerized grants reports system in 1972. From 1979 to 1988, the Center relied on a "facet" classification system, employing a fixed vocabulary of four-letter codes that permitted categorization of each grant by subject, type of recipient, population group, type of support, and scope of grant activity.

In 1989, following explosive growth in the number of grants indexed annually, the Center introduced a new classification system with links to the National Taxonomy of Exempt Entities (NTEE), a comprehensive coding scheme developed by the National Center for Charitable Statistics. This scheme established a unified national standard for classifying nonprofit organizations while permitting a multidimensional structure for analyzing grants. The new system also provided a more concise and consistent hierarchical method with which to classify and index grants.

The Center's Grants Classification System uses two- or three-character alphanumeric codes to track institutional fields and entities, governance or auspices, population groups, geographic focus, and types of support awarded. The universe of institutional fields is organized into 26 "major field" areas (A to Z), following the ten basic divisions established by the NTEE:

I.	Arts, Culture, Humanities	A
II.	Education	B
III.	Environment/Animals	C, D
IV.	Health	E, F, G, H
V.	Human Services	I, J, K, L, M, N, O, P
VI.	International/Foreign Affairs	Q
VII.	Public Affairs/Society Benefit	R, S, T, U, V, W
VIII.	Religion	X
IX.	Mutual/Membership Benefit	Y
X.	Nonclassifiable Entities	Z

The first letter of each code denotes the field, such as "A" for Arts and "B" for Education. Within each alpha subject area, numbers 20 to 99 identify services, disciplines, or types of institutions unique to that field, organized in a hierarchical structure. These subcategories cover most activities in the nonprofit field. As a result, hundreds of specific terms can be researched with consistent results and grant dollars can be tallied to determine distribution patterns.

While based on NTEE, the Center's system added indexing elements not part of the original taxonomy, including the ability to track awards to government-sponsored organizations such as public schools, state universities, and municipal or federal agencies; a secondary set of codes to classify 56 specific types of grant support; and a third set of codes to track 41 different grant beneficiary populations. More evolutionary than revolutionary, the new system introduced two new fields not previously tracked by the Foundation Center: Auspices (NTEE's governance codes are used) and Country of Activity (not part of NTEE). This last field is used to track the foreign locations of grant activities, for example, an award to the New York office of UNESCO for relief services in Ethiopia.

In 2005 a new set of codes was adopted to track the U.S. domestic geographic focus of individual grant activity. The codes include all the 2-letter state codes as well as codes for regions in the U.S., such as GL for Great Lakes, GP for Great Plains, RU for rural areas, WE for West, etc. These codes allow for the tracking of specific geographic areas of grant funding when the program location is different from the recipient's location.

For more information on "How the Foundation Center Indexes Grants," see foundationcenter.org/gainknowledge/grantsclass/how.html. The complete list of all the NTEE terms and definitions can be found at the Center's web site at foundationcenter.org/ntee. The complete lists of the population beneficiary codes, the type of support codes, and the recipient auspice codes can also be found at the Center's web site at foundationcenter.org/gainknowledge/grantsclass/ntee_gcs.html.

Appendix D
Types of Support Definitions

A grantmaker may limit its giving to certain types of support. The types of support indexes in Foundation Center print and electronic publications are used to locate grants that are in the form of a specific type of funding. The following is a list of terms in these indexes with their definitions.

Please note: *Foundation Directory Online* and *FC Search: The Foundation Center's Database on CD-ROM* have separate lists of types of support terms for their Grantmaker and Grants files. These are similar but not identical to each other. Unless otherwise noted, the following terms are used in both the Grantmaker and Grants files of these electronic databases.

Annual campaigns: Any organized effort by a nonprofit to secure gifts on an annual basis; also called annual appeals.

Awards/prizes/competitions: Grants for artists' awards, prizes, competitions, housing, living space, and workspace. Grants file only.

Building/renovation: Grants for constructing, renovating, remodeling, or rehabilitating property. Includes general or unspecified capital support awards.

Business startups/expansion: An area of activity supported by the investments of foundations or funders, the purpose of which is to stimulate the business sector. Grants file only.

Capital campaigns: Campaigns to raise funds for a variety of long-term purposes such as building construction or acquisition, endowments, land acquisition, etc.

Cause-related marketing: The practice of linking gifts to charity with marketing promotions. This may involve donating products that will then be auctioned or given away in a drawing with the proceeds benefiting a charity. The advertising campaign for the product will be combined with the promotion for the charity. In other cases it will be advertised that when a customer buys the product a certain amount of the proceeds will be donated to charity. Grantmaker file only.

Charitable use real estate: Program-related investments in properties that are used for charitable purposes. In most cases, a property such as a building is held by a foundation, which in turn donates or leases it at below market rates to a nonprofit organization. In other cases, a property consists of either land or buildings that are held for a period of time by a foundation and then either given away as a grant or sold to a nonprofit or to a government agency. Grants file only.

Collections acquisition: Grants to libraries or museums to acquire permanent materials as part of a collection, usually books or art. Grants file only.

Collections management/preservation: Grants for maintenance, preservation, and conservation of materials. Grants file only.

Commissioning new works: Grants to support the creation of new artistic works. Grants file only.

Computer systems/equipment: Grants to purchase or develop automated systems. Grants file only.

Conferences/seminars: Includes workshops.

Consulting services: Professional staff support provided by the foundation to a nonprofit to consult on a project of mutual interest or to evaluate services (not a cash grant). Grantmaker file only.

Continuing support: Grants renewed on a regular basis.

Curriculum development: Awards to schools, colleges, universities, and educational support organizations to develop general or discipline-specific curricula.

Debt reduction: Grant to reduce the recipient organization's indebtedness; also referred to as deficit financing. Frequently refers to mortgage payments.

Donated equipment: Surplus furniture, office machines, paper, appliances, laboratory apparatus, or other items that may be given to charities, schools, or hospitals. Grantmaker file only.

Donated land: Land or developed property. Institutions of higher education often receive gifts of real estate; land has also been given to community groups for housing development or for parks or recreational facilities. Grantmaker file only.

Donated products: Companies giving away what they make or produce. Product donations can include periodic clothing donations to a shelter for the homeless or regular donations of pharmaceuticals to a health clinic resulting in a reliable supply. Grantmaker file only.

Electronic media/online services: Grants for support of projects on the Internet and World Wide Web, including online publications and databases, development of web sites, electronic networking and messaging services, CD-ROM products, and interactive educational programs. Grants file only.

Emergency funds: One-time grants to cover immediate short-term funding needs of a recipient organization on an emergency basis.

Employee matching gifts: Usually made by corporate foundations to match gifts made by corporate employees.

Employee volunteer services: Effort through which a company promotes involvement with nonprofits on the part of employees. Grantmaker file only.

Employee-related scholarships: Scholarship programs funded by a company-sponsored foundation usually for children of employees; programs are frequently administered by the National Merit Scholarship Corporation which is responsible for selection of scholars. Grantmaker file only.

Endowments: Bequests or gifts intended to be kept permanently and invested to provide income for continued support of an organization.

Equipment: Grants to purchase equipment, furnishings, or other materials.

Equity investments: An ownership position in an organization or venture taken through an investment. Returns on the investment are dependent on the profitability of the organization or venture. Grants file only.

Exchange programs: Usually refers to funds for educational exchange programs for foreign students. Grantmaker file only.

Exhibitions: Awards to institutions such as museums, libraries, or historical societies specifically to mount an exhibit or to support the installation of a touring exhibit. Grants file only.

Faculty/staff development: Grants to institutions or organizations to train or further educate staff or faculty members. Grants file only.

Fellowships: Indicates funds awarded to educational institutions or organizations to support fellowship programs. A few foundations award fellowships directly to individuals.

Film/video/radio: Grants to fund a specific film, video, or radio production.

Foundation-administered programs: Funds expended for programs administered by the foundation. Grants file only.

General/operating support: Grants for the day-to-day operating costs of an existing program or organization or to further the general purpose or work of an organization; also called "unrestricted grants."

Grants to individuals: These awards are given directly to individuals, not through other nonprofit organizations. Many grantmakers have a specific limitation stating no grants to individuals. In order to make grants to individuals, a foundation must have a program that has received formal IRS approval. Grantmaker file only.

In-kind gifts: Contributions of equipment, supplies, or other property as distinct from monetary grants.

Income development: Grants for fundraising, marketing, and to expand audience base.

Interim financing (bridge loans, cash flow financing): Short-term loan to provide temporary financing until more permanent financing is available. Grants file only.

Internship funds (institutional support): Funds awarded to an institution or organization to support an internship program, rather than a grant to an individual.

Land acquisition: Grants to purchase real estate property.

Line of credit: Agreement by a bank that a company may borrow at any time up to an established limit. Grants file only.

Linked deposits (usually CDs): A deposit in an account with a financial institution to induce that institution's support for one or more projects. By accruing no interest or low interest on its deposit, a foundation essentially subsidizes the interest rate of the project borrowers. Grants file only.

Loaned talent: Usually involves employee-loaned professionals and executive staff who are helping a nonprofit in an area involving their particular skills. Grantmaker file only.

Loan guarantee: A pledge to cover the payment of debt or to perform some obligation if the person liable fails to perform. Grants file only.

Loans for loan funds: Funding for nonprofit or for-profit institutions that have specialized lending capacities. They obtain capital in the form of equity and low-interest loans (program-related investments) from a variety of sources, including foundations and other funders, to form a "lending pool." Grants file only.

Loans/promissory notes: See "Program-related investments/loans." Grants file only.

Loans—to individuals: Assistance distributed directly to individuals in the form of loans. Grantmaker file only.

Management development/capacity building: Grants for salaries, staff support, staff training, strategic and long-range planning, budgeting, and accounting.

Matching/challenge support: Grants made to match funds provided by another donor and grants paid only if the donee is able to raise additional funds from another source.

Mortgage financing: Funds to lending organizations providing low-interest mortgages to needy individuals. Grants file only.

Performance/productions: Grants to cover costs specifically associated with mounting performing arts productions. Grants file only.

Professorships: Grants to educational institutions to endow a professorship or chair.

Program development: Grants to support specific projects or programs as opposed to general purpose grants.

Program evaluation: Grants to evaluate a specific project or program; includes awards both to agencies to pay for evaluation costs and to research institutes and other program evaluators.

Program-related investments/loans: Loans or other investments (as distinguished from grants) to organizations to finance projects related to the foundation's stated charitable purpose and interests. Student loans are classified under "Student aid funds." Grantmaker file only.

Public relations services: May include printing and duplicating, audio-visual and graphic arts services, helping to plan special events such as festivals, piggyback advertising (advertisements that mention a company while also promoting a nonprofit), and public service advertising. Grantmaker file only.

Publication: Grants to fund reports or other publications issued by a nonprofit resulting from research or projects of interest to the funder.

Research: Funds to cover the costs of investigations and clinical trials, including demonstration and pilot projects. (Research grants for individuals are usually referred to as fellowships.)

Scholarship funds (institutional support): Grants to educational institutions or organizations to support a scholarship program, mainly for students at the undergraduate level; the donee institution then distributes the funds to individuals through their own programs.

Scholarships—to individuals: These are funds awarded to individuals through programs administered by the grantmaker. Grantmaker file only.

Seed money: Grants to start, establish, or initiate new projects or organizations; may cover salaries and other operating expenses of a new project; also called "start-up funds."

Sponsorships: Endorsements of charities by corporations or corporate contributions to charitable events. Grantmaker file only.

Student aid (institutional support): Assistance in the form of educational grants, loans, or scholarships. Grants file only.

Student loans—to individuals: These are loans distributed directly to individuals through programs administered by the grantmaker. Grantmaker file only.

Technical assistance: Operational or management assistance given to nonprofit organizations, including fundraising assistance, budgeting and financial planning, program planning, legal advice, marketing, and other aids to management.

Use of facilities: May include rent-free office space for temporary periods, dining and meeting facilities, telecommunications services, mailing services, transportation services, or computer services. Grantmaker file only.

Appendix E
Resources of the
Foundation Center

From searchable online directories of funding sources to grantseeker training courses to research reports on the philanthropic and nonprofit sectors, the Center provides a full spectrum of fundraising and educational resources.

The Foundation Center's award-winning web site, foundationcenter.org, is the leading online information tool for grantseekers, grantmakers, researchers, the press, and the general public. Registered visitors gain access to a world of valuable information geared to their region and fields of interest. In addition, the Center's web site features *Philanthropy News Digest* (PND), the daily source for the latest philanthropic news, reviews, requests for proposals, and job openings.

Please note: you may order any of the Foundation Center's publications and subscription services at foundationcenter.org/marketplace, or by calling (800) 424-9836. For the most current details on any Foundation Center resource, please visit our web site, foundationcenter.org. These are some of the highlights.

Online Directories

FOUNDATION DIRECTORY ONLINE

Updated weekly, *Foundation Directory Online* is the nation's premier grantseeking database.

For top-tier intelligence, *Foundation Directory Online Professional* provides four searchable databases: Grantmakers, Companies, Grants, and IRS 990s. It includes detailed profiles of U.S. foundations, grantmaking public charities, and corporate donors, as well as over one million recently awarded grants, and key contact names. Each *Professional* database includes up to 19 indexed search fields plus keyword-search capability.
$179.95/MONTH; $1,295/YEAR

To meet the needs of grantseekers at every level, *Foundation Directory Online* offers these additional subscription plans.

Platinum—complete profiles of all U.S. foundations, grantmaking public charities, and corporate giving programs; recent grants; trustee, officer, and donor names.
$149.95/MONTH; $995/YEAR

Premium—complete profiles of the top 20,000 U.S. foundations; recent grants; trustee, officer, and donor names.
$59.95/MONTH; $595/YEAR

Plus—complete profiles of the top 10,000 U.S. foundations plus recent grants; trustee, officer, and donor names.
$29.95/MONTH; $295/YEAR

Basic—complete profiles of the top 10,000 U.S. foundations; trustee, officer, and donor names.
$19.95/MONTH; $195/YEAR

All FDO plans are available with monthly, annual, and two-year subscription options. With every plan, subscribers can save and store their search strategies, and tag, save, and print grantmaker records. Annual and two-year subscribers receive substantial discounts on Foundation Center publications. For complete details and to subscribe, visit fconline.foundationcenter.org

CORPORATE GIVING ONLINE

This directory, updated weekly, provides the fastest, most accurate path to America's corporate funders. It includes detailed company profiles, descriptions of company-sponsored foundations, key facts on corporate direct giving programs, and summaries of recently awarded grants. With three databases, subscribers to *Corporate Giving Online* can search companies, grantmakers, and grants.

$59.95/MONTH; $595/YEAR

TO SUBSCRIBE, VISIT CGONLINE.FOUNDATIONCENTER.ORG.

FOUNDATION GRANTS TO INDIVIDUALS ONLINE

This unique directory, updated quarterly, is focused on foundations that provide support to students, artists, researchers, and other individuals. Updated quarterly, it includes nine search fields. Foundation profiles include name, address, and contact information, fields of interest, types of support, and application information. One-month, three-month, and annual subscriptions are available.

ONE MONTH: $9.95.

TO SUBSCRIBE, VISIT GTIONLINE.FOUNDATIONCENTER.ORG.

Annual CD-ROM Directories

FC SEARCH

FC Search: The Foundation Center's Database on CD-ROM contains in-depth profiles of U.S. foundations, grantmaking public charities, and corporate donors. *FC Search* includes detailed funder profiles, descriptions of recently awarded grants, key contact names and addresses, and links to current IRS 990-PF returns.

SINGLE-USER LICENSE: $1,195, INCLUDING UPDATE DISK.

GUIDE TO OHIO GRANTMAKERS ON CD-ROM

Profiles of thousands of grantmakers that support nonprofits in the state. Includes grants awarded to Ohio nonprofits or from Ohio-based funders.

SINGLE-USER: $125

GUIDE TO GREATER WASHINGTON, DC GRANTMAKERS ON CD-ROM

Details on grantmakers focused on supporting nonprofits within greater Washington, DC. Includes grants awarded to nonprofits in the Washington, DC area or from funders in the region.

SINGLE-USER: $75

DIRECTORY OF GEORGIA GRANTMAKERS ON CD-ROM

Details on grantmakers focused on supporting nonprofits in the state. Includes grants awarded to nonprofits in Georgia or from funders within the state.

SINGLE-USER: $75

DIRECTORY OF MISSOURI GRANTMAKERS ON CD-ROM

Profiles of grantmakers in the state or with an interest in supporting Missouri nonprofits. Includes descriptions of recently awarded grants.

SINGLE-USER: $75

Annual Print Directories

THE FOUNDATION DIRECTORY

This classic directory profiles the 10,000 largest U.S. foundations. Key facts include fields of interest, contact information, financials, names of decision-makers, and thousands of sample grants. Indexes help you quickly locate your best leads. $215

THE FOUNDATION DIRECTORY PART 2

Broaden your funding base with details on the next 10,000 largest foundations. Each year, up to 2,000 new entries are added to this annual directory. Includes thousands of sample grants. $185

THE FOUNDATION DIRECTORY PART 3

The Directory Part 3 completes the universe of U.S. foundation profiles, with more than 46,000 organizations not included in *The Foundation Directory* or *The Foundation Directory Part 2*. Detailed entries for smaller foundations include contact information, current assets, giving amounts, and geographic limitations. $225

THE FOUNDATION DIRECTORY SUPPLEMENT

This volume provides updates for hundreds of foundations included in the *Directory* and *Directory Part 2*. New entries include changes in financial data, contact information, and giving interests. $125

NATIONAL DIRECTORY OF CORPORATE GIVING

The most comprehensive information available in print on America's corporate donors. Complete profiles feature giving priorities and background on each company. $195

FOUNDATION GRANTS TO INDIVIDUALS

The only directory devoted entirely to foundation grant opportunities for qualified individual applicants. Includes contact information, giving limitations, and application guidelines. $65

GRANT GUIDE SERIES

Twelve subject-specific directories of grants awarded to organizations in particular fields of interest. Each *Grant Guide* includes Subject, Geographic, and Recipient indexes. $75 EACH

Fundraising Guides

THE FOUNDATION CENTER'S GUIDE TO PROPOSAL WRITING

Our best-selling *Guide* includes comprehensive instructions on crafting breakthrough grant proposals. Includes interviews with funders, revealing the latest trends among decision-makers in evaluating proposals. $34.95

GIA PARA ESCRIBIR PROPUESTAS

The Spanish-language edition of *The Foundation Center's Guide to Proposal Writing*. $34.95

THE FOUNDATION CENTER'S GUIDE TO WINNING PROPOSALS

Twenty actual proposals that were approved and funded by leading grantmakers. $34.95

THE GRANTSEEKER'S GUIDE TO WINNING PROPOSALS

Forty actual funded proposals with commentary from the grantmakers that said 'yes' to them. $34.95 (SUMMER 2008)

Nonprofit Management Guides

WISE DECISION-MAKING IN UNCERTAIN TIMES
Edited by Dr. Dennis R. Young, this book provides practical guidelines for nonprofits coping with escalating demand for services, economic downturns, and reduced government funding. $34.95

EFFECTIVE ECONOMIC DECISION-MAKING BY NONPROFIT ORGANIZATIONS
Practical guidelines to advance your mission while balancing the interests of funders, trustees, government, and staff. Edited by Dr. Dennis R. Young. $34.95

INVESTING IN CAPACITY BUILDING
Author Barbara Blumenthal shows nonprofit managers how to get more effective support, and helps grantmakers and consultants design better methods to help nonprofits. $34.95

THE BOARD MEMBER'S BOOK
Author Brian O'Connell shows how to find and develop the best board members and executive director, with strategies for fundraising and financial planning. $29.95

PHILANTHROPY'S CHALLENGE
Author Paul Firstenberg explores the roles of grantmaker and grantee within various models of social venture grantmaking. $39.95, HARDCOVER; $29.95, SOFTCOVER

SECURING YOUR ORGANIZATION'S FUTURE
Author Michael Seltzer explains how to strengthen your nonprofit's capacity to raise funds and achieve long-term financial stability. $34.95

AMERICA'S NONPROFIT SECTOR
Author Lester Salamon defines the scope, structure, and operation of the sector, and examines its relation to government and the business community. $14.95

BEST PRACTICES OF EFFECTIVE NONPROFIT ORGANIZATIONS
Author Philip Bernstein focuses on procedures that help practitioners define goals, adhere to mission, and respond to change by adjusting operations and services. $29.95

Research Reports

FOUNDATIONS TODAY SERIES
Published annually. The series includes:

FOUNDATION GIVING TRENDS: UPDATE ON FUNDING PRIORITIES
Examines grantmaking patterns of a sample of more than 1,000 large U.S. foundations and compares current giving priorities with previous trends. FEBRUARY, $45

FOUNDATION GROWTH AND GIVING ESTIMATES: CURRENT OUTLOOK
Includes the new top 100 foundations list and the outlook for the current year. APRIL, $20

FOUNDATION YEARBOOK: FACTS AND FIGURES ON PRIVATE AND COMMUNITY FOUNDATIONS
Documents the growth in number, giving amounts, and assets of all active U.S. foundations since 1975. JUNE, $45
COMPLETE SERIES AVAILABLE FOR $95

THE PRI DIRECTORY: CHARITABLE LOANS AND OTHER PROGRAM-RELATED INVESTMENTS BY FOUNDATIONS
This indexed directory lists leading providers and includes tips on how to seek out and manage PRIs. $75

SOCIAL JUSTICE GRANTMAKING
Providing quantitative benchmarks of grantmaking priorities, geographic distribution of funds, and giving by foundation type, this report includes grants awarded for civil rights, educational reform, and community development. $24.95

CALIFORNIA FOUNDATIONS
A PROFILE OF THE STATE'S GRANTMAKING COMMUNITY

Based on a Foundation Center survey, this report covers the latest foundation trends in California. It illuminates critical issues facing the state's funders, and includes an essay on the overall health of California philanthropy. $24.95

On-call Research Assistance

ASSOCIATES PROGRAM

Our members-only service for fundraisers. To find the best funding prospects and develop the most compelling proposals, let our research staff do the legwork for you. They have access to the full spectrum of Foundation Center databases, biographical information, studies, and reports on the field. For more information, call (800) 634-2953.

EDUCATIONAL SERVICES

Full-day training courses: The Foundation Center takes an interactive approach to sharing its wealth of information in classrooms coast-to-coast, fostering team-building through small group exercises and topical discussions. As a participant, you will learn the latest strategies to address the challenges facing grantseekers, and share your experiences with other nonprofit professionals from your region. Course topics: fundraising fundamentals, proven techniques for crafting winning proposals, and strategies for building organizational capacity.

Online training courses—Designed for any nonprofit professional who wants to become a more effective grantseeker, our online courses provide self-paced lessons, interactive exercises and assignments, case studies, and a final exam. Course topics: grantseeking basics, proposal writing. Our webinars provide the opportunity to interact with colleagues and pose questions of live instructors.

Contract training—Schedule as many full-day classroom training courses as your team needs, and the Foundation Centers experts will present in the location you prefer. This special service includes course materials and publications.

Free basic training—If you want a brief overview of some of the most popular topics for grantseekers, introductory courses from 60 to 90 minutes are presented at no cost in each of our regional centers.

REGIONAL CENTERS

For current information on foundations and corporate donors with expert library assistance, visit one of our five regional centers in New York, Washington, DC, Atlanta, Cleveland, and San Francisco. Our extensive network of Cooperating Collections provides free access to the Center's online and print directories, fundraising guides, nonprofit management books, periodicals, and research findings on U.S. philanthropy.

To view the complete list of Cooperating Collections in all 50 states, Puerto Rico, and Mexico, visit foundationcenter.org/collections.

LOG ON TO FOUNDATIONCENTER.ORG

Continuously updated and expanded, the Foundation Center's web site is visited daily by tens of thousands of grantseekers, grantmakers, researchers, and others who are interested in the world of philanthropy. Find answers to your questions about seeking funds, nonprofit management, and how to start a nonprofit organization. Search recent IRS 990s at no cost. Check statistics on U.S. foundations, their assets, distribution of their grant dollars, and the top recipients of their gifts. Search the Catalog of Nonprofit Literature, our comprehensive bibliographic database, or look up a foundation-sponsored report on a topic of interest in PubHub.

The Foundation Center provides a host of free and affordable services and information resources all focused on strengthening the nonprofit sector's ability to serve its constituents. Take a moment to register at our site, foundationcenter.org. It's free and each time you log on, you'll find information tailored to your interests and geographic region.

You may order any of the Foundation Center's publications and register for training courses at foundationcenter.org/marketplace, or by calling (800) 424-9836. For the most current details on any Foundation Center resource, please visit our web site, foundationcenter.org.

Appendix F
The Foundation Center's
Cooperating Collections

ALABAMA

Anniston: Anniston Public Library, 108 E. 10th St. (256) 237-8501

Birmingham: Birmingham Public Library, Government Documents Dept., 2100 Park Place (205) 226-3620

Huntsville: Huntsville-Madison County Public Library, Information and Periodicals Dept., 915 Monroe St. (256) 532-5940

Mobile: Mobile Public Library, West Regional Library, 5555 Grelot Rd. (251) 340-8555

Montgomery: Auburn University at Montgomery, 74-40 East Dr. (334) 244-3200

ALASKA

Anchorage: Consortium Library, 3211 Providence Dr. (907) 786-1848

Juneau: Juneau Public Library, 292 Marine Way (907) 586-5267

ARIZONA

Flagstaff: Flagstaff City-Coconino County Public Library, 300 W. Aspen Ave. (928) 779-7670

Phoenix: Phoenix Public Library, Information Services Dept., 1221 N. Central Ave. (602) 262-4636

Tucson: Pima County Public Library, 101 N. Stone Ave. (520) 791-4393

Yuma: Yuma County Library District, 350 3rd Ave. (928) 782-1871

ARKANSAS

Fayetteville: Fayetteville Public Library, 401 W. Mountain St. (479) 571-2222

Fort Smith: Boreham Library, University of Arkansas—Fort Smith, 5210 Grand Ave. (479) 788-7204

Little Rock: Central Arkansas Library System, 100 Rock St. (501) 918-3000

CALIFORNIA

Bakersfield: Kern County Library, Beale Memorial Library, 701 Truxtun Ave. (661) 868-0701

Bayside: Rooney Resource Center, Humboldt Area Foundation, 373 Indianola Rd. (707) 442-2993

Camarillo: Ventura County Community Foundation, Resource Center for Nonprofit Organizations, 1317 Del Norte Rd., Ste. 150 (805) 988-0196

Fairfield: Solano Community Foundation, 1261 Travis Blvd., Ste. 320 (707) 399-3846

Fresno: Fresno Nonprofit Advancement Council, 1752 L St.   (559) 264-1513

Lompoc: Lompoc Public Library, 501 E. North Ave.   (805) 875-8789

Long Beach: Long Beach Nonprofit Partnership, 3635 Atlantic Ave.   (562) 290-0018

Los Angeles: Center for Nonprofit Management in Southern CA, Nonprofit Resource Library, 1000 N. Alameda St., Ste. 250   (213) 687-9511

Los Angeles: Southern California Library for Social Studies and Research, 6120 S. Vermont Ave.   (323) 759-6063

Milpitas: Compasspoint Nonprofit Services, Nonprofit Development Library, 600 Valley Way, Ste. A   (408) 719-1400

Modesto: Stanislaus County Library, 1500 I St.   (209) 558-7800

Monterey: Community Foundation for Monterey County, 2354 Garden Rd.   (831) 375-9712

North Hills: Los Angeles Public Library, Mid-Valley Regional Branch Library, 16244 Nordhoff St.   (818) 895-3654

Pasadena: Philanthropy Resource Center, Flintridge Foundation, 1040 Lincoln Ave., Ste. 100   (626) 449-0839

Redding: Center for Nonprofit Resources, Shasta College, 1504 Market St., Ste. 200   (530) 225-4385

Richmond: Richmond Public Library, 352 Civic Center Plaza   (510) 620-6561

Riverside: Resource Center for Nonprofit Management, The Bobby Bonds/Cesar Chavez Community Center, 2060 University Ave., Ste. 201 (951) 686-4402

Riverside: Riverside Public Library, 3581 Mission Inn Ave.   (951) 826-5201

Sacramento: Nonprofit Resource Center, 828 I St., 2nd Fl.   (916) 264-2772

San Diego: Funding Information Center, San Diego Foundation, 2508 Historic Decatur, Ste. 200   (619) 235-2300

San Diego: Nonprofit Management Solutions, 8265 Vickers St., Ste. C   (858) 292-5702

San Pedro: Los Angeles Public Library, San Pedro Regional Branch, 931 S. Gaffey St.   (310) 548-7779

San Rafael: Center for Volunteer and Nonprofit Leadership of Marin, 555 Northgate Dr.   (415) 479-5710

Santa Ana: Volunteer Center Orange County, 1901 E. 4th St., Ste. 100   (714) 953-5757

Santa Barbara: Santa Barbara Public Library, 40 E. Anapamu St. (805) 962-7653

Santa Monica: Santa Monica Public Library, 601 Santa Monica Blvd.   (310) 458-8600

Santa Rosa: Sonoma County Library, 3rd and E Sts.   (707) 545-0831

Seaside: Seaside Branch Library, 550 Harcourt Ave.   (831) 899-2055

Sonora: Sierra NonProfit Support Center, 39 N. Washington St. #F (209) 533-1093

Soquel: Community Foundation of Santa Cruz County, 2425 Porter St., Ste. 17   (831) 477-0800

Truckee: Truckee Tahoe Community Foundation, 11071 Donner Pass Rd.   (530) 587-1776

Ukiah: Catalyst (North Coast Opportunities), 776 S. State St., Ste. 102B   (707) 462-2984

Victorville: High Desert Resource Network, Victorville City Library, 15011 Circle Dr.   (760) 949-2930

COLORADO

Colorado Springs: El Pomar Nonprofit Resource Center, Penrose Library, 20 N. Cascade Ave.   (719) 531-6333

Denver: Denver Public Library, 10 W. 14th Ave. Parkway   (720) 865-1111

Durango: Durango Public Library, 1188 E. 2nd Ave.   (970) 375-3380

Greeley: Weld Library District, Farr Branch
Library, 1939 61st Ave.
(970) 506-8518

Pueblo: Pueblo City-County Library
District, 100 E. Abriendo
Ave.   (719) 562-5600

CONNECTICUT

Greenwich: Greenwich Library, 101 W.
Putnam Ave.   (203) 622-7900

Hartford: Hartford Public Library, 500
Main St.   (860) 695-6295

New Haven: New Haven Free Public
Library, 133 Elm St.   (203) 946-7431

Westport: Westport Public Library,
Arnold Bernhard Plaza, 20 Jesup
Rd.   (203) 291-4840

DELAWARE

Dover: Dover Public Library, 45 S. State
St.   (302) 736-7030

Newark: Hugh Morris Library,
University of Delaware, 181 S. College
Ave.   (302) 831-2432

Wilmington: University of Delaware,
Center for Community Research
and Service, 100 W. 10th St., Ste.
812   (302) 573-4475

FLORIDA

Bartow: Bartow Public Library, 2151 S.
Broadway Ave.   (863) 534-0131

Boca Raton: Junior League of Boca Raton,
261 NW 13th St.   (561) 620-2553

Daytona Beach: Volusia County Library
Center, City Island, 105 E. Magnolia
Ave.   (386) 257-6036

Fort Lauderdale: Nova Southeastern
University, Library, Research, and
Information Technology Center, 3100
Ray Ferrero Jr. Blvd.   (954) 262-4613

Fort Myers: Southwest Florida Community
Foundation, 8260 College Parkway, Ste.
101   (239) 274-5900

Fort Pierce: Learning Resources Center,
Indian River Community College, 3209
Virginia Ave.   (866) 866-4722

Gainesville: Alachua County Library
District, 401 E. University
Ave.   (352) 334-3900

Jacksonville: Jacksonville Public Libraries,
Nonprofit Resource Center, 303 N.
Laura St.   (904) 630-2665

Miami: Miami-Dade Public Library,
Humanities/Social Science Department,
101 W. Flagler St.   (305) 375-5575

Orlando: Orange County Library System,
Social Sciences Dept., 101 E. Central
Blvd.   (407) 835-7323

Pinellas Park: JWB Children's Services
Council of Pinellas County Grants
Resource Center, 6698 68th Ave. N.,
Ste. A   (727) 547-5670

Sarasota: Selby Public Library, 1331 1st
St.   (941) 861-1100

Stuart: Martin County Library System,
Blake Library, 2351 SE Monterey
Rd.   (772) 288-5702

Tampa: Hillsborough County Public
Library Cooperative, John F. Germany
Public Library, 900 N. Ashley
Dr.   (813) 273-3652

West Palm Beach: Community
Foundation for Palm Beach and Martin
Counties, 700 S. Dixie Highway, Ste.
200   (561) 659-6800

Winter Park: Rollins College, Philanthropy
and Nonprofit Leadership Center
Library, 200 E. New England Ave., Ste.
250   (407) 975-6414

GEORGIA

Atlanta: Atlanta-Fulton Public Library
System, One Margaret Mitchell
Square, Ivan Allen Jr. Reference
Dept.   (404) 730-1900

Augusta: Georgia Center for Nonprofits,
East Central Georgia Regional Office,
630 Ellis St.   (706) 823-9718

Brunswick: Coastal Georgia Nonprofit
Center, 1311 Union St.
(912) 265-1850

Gainesville: Hall County Library System,
127 Main St. NW   (770) 532-3311

Greensboro: Reynolds Plantation
Foundation, 1021 Parkside
Commons   (706) 767-2143

Macon: Methodist Home, Rumford
Center, 304 Pierce Ave., 1st
Fl.   (478) 751-2800

Savannah: Georgia Center for Nonprofits,
Coastal Georgia Regional Office, 428
Bull St.   (912) 234-9688

Thomasville: Thomas County
Public Library, 201 N. Madison
St.   (229) 225-5252

Vienna: Southwest Georgia United, 1150
Industrial Dr.   (229) 268-7592

HAWAII

Honolulu: Hamilton Library, University of
Hawaii at Manoa, Business/Humanities/
Soc. Science Reference Dept., 2550 The
Mall   (808) 956-7214

IDAHO

Boise: Funding Information Center,
Boise Public Library, 715 S. Capitol
Blvd.   (208) 384-4024

Pocatello: Marshall Public Library, 113 S.
Garfield   (208) 232-1263

ILLINOIS

Carbondale: Carbondale Public Library,
405 W. Main St.   (618) 457-0354

Chicago: Donors Forum of Chicago
Library, 208 S. LaSalle, Ste.
740   (312) 578-0175

Chicago Heights: Prairie State College,
South Metropolitan Philanthropy
Center, 202 S. Halstead
(708) 709-3500

Evanston: Evanston Public Library, 1703
Orrington Ave.   (847) 866-0300

Glen Ellyn: College of DuPage,
Philanthropy Center, Student Resource
Center, 425 Fawell Blvd.
(630) 942-3364

Grayslake: College of Lake County, Lake
County Philanthropy Center, John C.
Murphy Memorial Library, 19351 W.
Washington St.   (847) 543-2071

Oak Forest: Acorn Public Library District,
15624 S. Central Ave.   (708) 687-3700

Quincy: John Wood Community College,
1301 S. 48th St.   (217) 224-6500

Rock Island: Rock Island Public Library,
401 19th St.   (309) 732-7323

Schaumburg: Schaumburg Township
District Library, Northwest Suburban
Philanthropy Center, 130 S. Roselle
Rd.   (847) 985-4000

Springfield: University of Illinois at
Springfield, Central Illinois Nonprofit
Resources Center, Brookens Library,
One University Plaza, MS BRK
140   (217) 206-6633

INDIANA

Bloomington: Monroe County
Public Library, 303 E. Kirkwood
Ave.   (812) 349-3050

Evansville: Evansville Vanderburgh Public
Library, 200 SE Martin Luther King Jr.
Blvd.   (812) 428-8218

Fort Wayne: Allen County Public Library,
Paul Clarke Nonprofit Resource Center,
900 Library Plaza   (260) 421-1238

Gary: Indiana University Northwest, 3400
Broadway   (219) 980-6580

Indianapolis: First Samuel Missionary
Baptist Church, 1402 N. Belleview
Place   (317) 636-7653

Indianapolis: Indianapolis-Marion County
Public Library, 202 N. Alabama
St.   (317) 269-1700

Muncie: Muncie Public Library, 2005 S.
High St.   (765) 747-8204

Terre Haute: Vigo County Public Library,
One Library Square   (812) 232-1113

Valparaiso: The Christopher Center for
Library and Information Resources,
Valparaiso University, 1410 Chapel
Dr.   (219) 464-5364

IOWA

Ames: Iowa State University, 204 Parks
Library   (515) 294-3642
Cedar Rapids: Cedar Rapids Public Library,
500 1st St. SE   (319) 398-5123
Council Bluffs: Council Bluffs Public
Library, 400 Willow Ave.
(712) 323-7553
Creston: Learning Resource Center,
Southwestern Community College,
1501 W. Townline Rd.
(641) 782-7081
Des Moines: Des Moines Public Library,
1000 Grand Ave.   (515) 283-4152
Dubuque: Community Foundation of
Greater Dubuque, 700 Locust St., Ste.
195   (563) 588-2700
Sioux City: Sioux City Public Library,
Siouxland Funding Research Center,
529 Pierce St.   (712) 255-2933

KANSAS

Colby: Pioneer Memorial Library, 375 W.
4th St.   (785) 460-4470
Ellis: Ellis Public Library, 907 Washington
St.   (785) 726-3464
Liberal: Liberal Memorial Library, 519 N.
Kansas   (620) 626-0180
Salina: Salina Public Library, 301 West
Elm   (785) 825-4624
Topeka: Topeka and Shawnee County
Public Library, Adult Services, 1515 SW
10th Ave.   (785) 580-4400
Wichita: Wichita Public Library, 223 S.
Main St.   (316) 261-8500

KENTUCKY

Bowling Green: Helm-Cravens Library,
Western Kentucky University, 110
Helm Library   (270) 745-6163
Covington: Kenton County Public Library,
502 Scott Blvd.   (859) 962-4060
Lexington: Lexington Public Library, 140
E. Main St.   (859) 231-5520
Louisville: Louisville Free Public Library,
301 York St.   (502) 574-1617

Somerset: Pulaski County Public Library,
107 N. Main St.   (606) 679-8401

LOUISIANA

Alexandria: Community Development
Works, 1101 4th St., Ste.
101B   (318) 443-7880
Baton Rouge: East Baton Rouge Parish
Library, River Center Branch, 120 St.
Louis St.   (225) 389-4967
Baton Rouge: Louisiana Association of
Nonprofit Organizations (LANO), 4560
North Blvd., Ste. 117   (225) 343-5266
DeRidder: Beauregard Parish Library, 205
S. Washington Ave.   (337) 463-6217
Lake Charles: Louisiana Association of
Nonprofit Organizations (LANO), 220
Louie St.   (337) 310-9540
Monroe: Ouachita Parish Public Library,
1800 Stubbs Ave.   (318) 327-1490
New Orleans: Louisiana Association of
Nonprofit Organizations (LANO), 1824
Oretha Castle Haley Blvd.
(504) 309-2081
New Orleans: New Orleans Public Library,
Business and Science Division, 219
Loyola Ave.   (504) 596-2580
Shreveport: Louisiana Association of
Nonprofit Organizations (LANO), 2924
Knight St., Ste. 406   (318) 865-5510
Shreveport: Shreve Memorial Library, 424
Texas St.   (318) 226-5894

MAINE

Portland: University of Southern Maine,
Glickman Family Library, 314 Forest
Ave., Room 321   (207) 780-5039

MARYLAND

Baltimore: Enoch Pratt Free Library,
Social Science and History Dept., 400
Cathedral St.   (410) 396-5320
Hyattsville: Prince George's County
Memorial Library, Hyattsville Branch
Library, 6530 Adelphi Rd.
(301) 985-4690

Rockville: Rockville Library, 21 Maryland
Ave.   (240) 777-0140

Salisbury: Community Foundation of
the Eastern Shore, 1324 Belmont
Ave.   (410) 724-9911

Waldorf: Charles County Public Library,
P.D. Brown Memorial Branch, 50
Village St.   (301) 645-2864

Wye Mills: Chesapeake College Library,
1000 College Dr.   (410) 827-5860

MASSACHUSETTS

Boston: Associated Grant Makers (AGM),
55 Court St., Ste. 520   (617) 426-2606

Boston: Boston Public Library, Social
Sciences Reference Dept., 700 Boylston
St.   (617) 536-5400

Pittsfield: Berkshire Athenaeum, One
Wendell Ave.   (413) 499-9480

Springfield: Springfield City Library, 220
State St.   (413) 263-6828

Worcester: Worcester Public Library,
Grants Resource Center, 3 Salem
Square   (508) 799-1654

MEXICO

San Jeronimo, D.F.: International Resource
Center for Civil Society Organizations in
Mexico, Periferico Sur 3453, Tower B,
Office 101   (011) 52- 55-5025-9216

MICHIGAN

Alpena: Alpena County Library, 211 N. 1st
St.   (989) 356-6188

Ann Arbor: University of Michigan, Harlan
Hatcher Graduate Library, 209 Hatcher
Graduate Library   (734) 615-8610

Battle Creek: Willard Public Library,
Nonprofit and Funding Resource
Collections, 7 W. Van Buren
St.   (269) 968-3284

Detroit: Purdy/Kresge Library, Wayne
State University, 134 Purdy/Kresge
Library   (313) 577-6424

East Lansing: Michigan State
University, Funding Center, 100
Library   (517) 432-6123

Farmington Hills: Farmington
Community Library, 32737 W. 12 Mile
Rd.   (248) 553-0300

Flint: Flint Public Library, 1026 E. Kearsley
St.   (810) 232-7111

Fremont: Fremont Area District Library,
104 E. Main St.   (231) 924-3480

Grand Rapids: Grand Rapids Public
Library, Reference Dept., 111 Library
St. NE   (616) 988-5400

Houghton: Portage Lake District Library,
58 Huron St.   (906) 482-4570

Kalamazoo: Kalamazoo Public Library, 315
S. Rose St.   (269) 553-7844

Marquette: Peter White Public Library, 217
N. Front St.   (906) 226-4311

Petoskey: Petoskey Public Library, 500 E.
Mitchell St.   (231) 758-3100

Saginaw: Public Libraries of Saginaw,
Hoyt Public Library, 505 Janes
Ave.   (989) 755-0904

Scottville: West Shore Community College
Library, 3000 N. Stiles Rd.
(231) 845-6211

Traverse City: Traverse Area
District Library, 610 Woodmere
Ave.   (231) 932-8500

MINNESOTA

Brainerd: Brainerd Public Library, 416 S.
5th St.   (218) 829-5574

Duluth: Duluth Public Library, 520 W.
Superior St.   (218) 730-4200

Marshall: Southwest Minnesota State
University, University Library, 1501
State St.   (507) 537-7278

Minneapolis: Minneapolis Central Library/
Hennepin County Library, 300 Nicollet
Mall   (612) 630-6000

Rochester: Rochester Public Library, 101
2nd St. SE   (507) 285-8002

St. Paul: St. Paul Public Library, 90 W. 4th
St.   (651) 266-7000

MISSISSIPPI

Hattiesburg: Library of Hattiesburg, Petal and Forrest County, 329 Hardy St.   (601) 582-4461

Jackson: Jackson/Hinds Library System, 300 N. State St.   (601) 968-5803

MISSOURI

Columbia: Columbia/Boone County Community Partnership, 601 Business Loop 70 SW, Ste. 217C (573) 256-1890

Kansas City: Kansas City Public Library, 14 W. 10th St.   (816) 701-3400

Kirkwood: Kirkwood Public Library, 140 E. Jefferson   (314) 821-5770

Springfield: Springfield-Greene County Library, 4653 S. Campbell (417) 882-0714

St. Louis: St. Louis Public Library, 1301 Olive St.   (314) 241-2288

St. Peters: St. Charles City-County Library District, Spencer Road Branch, 427 Spencer Rd.   (636) 441-0794

MONTANA

Baker: Fallon County Library, 6 W. Fallon Ave.   (406) 778-7160

Billings: Library-Special Collections, Montana State University—Billings, 1500 University Dr.   (406) 657-2262

Bozeman: Bozeman Public Library, 220 E. Lamme   (406) 582-2402

Libby: Lincoln County Public Libraries, Libby Public Library, 220 W. 6th St.   (406) 293-2778

Missoula: Mansfield Library, The University of Montana, 32 Campus Dr. #9936   (406) 243-6800

NEBRASKA

Cambridge: Butler Memorial Library, 621 Penn St.   (308) 697-3836

Hastings: Hastings Public Library, 517 W. 4th St.   (402) 461-2346

Lincoln: University of Nebraska—Lincoln, Love Library, 13th and R Sts.   (402) 472-2526

Omaha: Omaha Public Library, Social Science Dept., 215 S. 15th St.   (402) 444-4826

NEVADA

Elko: Great Basin College Library, 1500 College Parkway   (775) 753-2222

Las Vegas: Clark County Library, 1401 E. Flamingo   (702) 507-3421

NEW HAMPSHIRE

Concord: Concord Public Library, 45 Green St.   (603) 225-8670

Plymouth: Herbert H. Lamson Library, Plymouth State University, 17 High St.   (603) 535-2258

NEW JERSEY

Elizabeth: Free Public Library of Elizabeth, 11 S. Broad St.   (908) 354-6060

Galloway: United Way of Atlantic County, 4 E. Jimmie Leeds Rd., Ste. 10   (609) 404-4483

Randolph: Learning Resource Center, County College of Morris, 214 Center Grove Rd.   (973) 328-5296

Trenton: New Jersey State Library, Funding Information Center, 185 W. State St.   (609) 278-2640

Vineland: Cumberland County College, Center for Leadership, Community and Neighborhood Development, 3322 College Dr.   (856) 691-8600

Washington: Warren County Community College, 475 Rte. 57 W. (908) 835-9222

NEW MEXICO

Albuquerque: Albuquerque/Bernalillo County Library System, 501 Copper Ave. NW   (505) 768-5141

Santa Fe: New Mexico State Library, 1209
Camino Carlos Rey   (505) 476-9702

NEW YORK
Albany: New York State Library, Cultural
Education Center, Empire State
Plaza   (518) 474-5355

Binghamton: Broome County Public
Library, 185 Court St.   (607) 778-6400

Bronx: New York Public Library, Bronx
Library Center, 310 E. Kingsbridge
Rd.   (718) 579-4244

Brooklyn: Brooklyn Public Library,
Central Library, Society, Sciences, and
Technology Division, 10 Grand Army
Plaza   (718) 230-2145

Buffalo: Buffalo and Erie County Public
Library, Business, Science, and
Technology Dept., One Lafayette
Square   (716) 858-8900

Cobleskill: SUNY Cobleskill, Jared Van
Wagenen Library, 142 Schenectady
Ave.   (518) 255-5841

Corning: Southeast Steuben County
Library, 300 Nasser Civic Center
Plaza   (607) 936-3713

Holbrook: Sachem Public Library, 150
Holbrook Rd.   (631) 588-5024

Huntington: Huntington Public Library,
338 Main St.   (631) 427-5165

Jamaica: Queens Borough Public Library,
Social Sciences Division, 89-11 Merrick
Blvd.   (718) 990-0700

Jamestown: James Prendergast Library, 509
Cherry St.   (716) 484-7135

Levittown: Levittown Public Library, One
Bluegrass Lane   (516) 731-5728

New York: New York Public Library,
Countee Cullen Branch, 104 W. 136th
St.   (212) 491-2070

Poughkeepsie: Adriance Memorial Library,
Special Services Department, 93 Market
St.   (845) 485-3445

Riverhead: Riverhead Free Library, 330
Court St.   (631) 727-3228

Rochester: Rochester Public Library,
Grants Information Center, 115 South
Ave.   (585) 428-8127

Staten Island: New York Public Library,
St. George Library Center, 5 Central
Ave.   (718) 442-8560

Syracuse: Onondaga County Public Library,
447 S. Salina St.   (315) 435-1900

Utica: Utica Public Library, 303 Genesee
St.   (315) 735-2279

White Plains: White Plains Public Library,
100 Martine Ave.   (914) 422-1480

Yonkers: Yonkers Public Library, Riverfront
Library, One Larkin Center
(914) 337-1500

NORTH CAROLINA
Asheville: Pack Memorial Library,
Community Foundation of Western
North Carolina, 67 Haywood
St.   (828) 250-4711

Brevard: Transylvania County Library, 212
S. Gaston St.   (828) 884-3151

Charlotte: Public Library of Charlotte and
Mecklenburg County, 310 N. Tryon
St.   (704) 336-2725

Durham: Durham County Public Library,
300 N. Roxboro St.   (919) 560-0100

Raleigh: Cameron Village Library, Wake
County Public Libraries, 1930 Clark
Ave.   (919) 856-6710

Wilmington: New Hanover County Public
Library, 201 Chestnut St.
(910) 798-6301

Winston-Salem: Forsyth County Public
Library, 660 W. 5th St.
(336) 703-3020

NORTH DAKOTA
Bismarck: Bismarck Public Library, 515 N.
5th St.   (701) 222-6410

Fargo: Fargo Public Library, 408 Roberts
St.   (701) 241-1472

Minot: Minot Public Library, 516 2nd Ave.
SW   (701) 852-1045

OHIO

Akron: Akron-Summit County Public Library, 60 S. High St.   (330) 643-9000

Canton: Stark County District Library, 715 Market Ave. N.   (330) 452-0665

Cincinnati: Public Library of Cincinnati and Hamilton County, Grants Resource Center, 800 Vine St.   (513) 369-6900

Columbus: Columbus Metropolitan Library, Business and Technology Dept., 96 S. Grant Ave.   (614) 645-2275

Dayton: Dayton Metro Library, Grants Information Center, 215 E. 3rd St.   (937) 463-2663

Elyria: Elyria Public Library, West River Branch, 1194 W. River Road N.   (440) 324-9827

Lima: Lima Public Library, 650 W. Market St.   (419) 228-5113

Mansfield: Mansfield/Richland County Public Library, 43 W. 3rd St.   (419) 521-3110

Marietta: Marietta College, 215 Fifth St.   (740) 376-4741

Painesville: Morley Library, 184 Phelps St.   (440) 352-3383

Piqua: Edison Community College Library, 1973 Edison Dr.   (937) 778-7950

Portsmouth: Portsmouth Public Library, 1220 Gallia St.   (740) 354-5688

Toledo: Toledo-Lucas County Public Library, Social Sciences Dept., 325 N. Michigan St.   (419) 259-5207

Twinsburg: Twinsburg Public Library, 10050 Ravenna Rd.   (330) 425-4268

Warren: Kent State University, Trumbull Campus Library, 4314 Mahoning Ave. NW   (330) 847-0571

Youngstown: Public Library of Youngstown and Mahoning County, 305 Wick Ave.   (330) 744-8636

Zanesville: Muskingum County Community Foundation, 534 Putnam Ave.   (740) 453-5192

OKLAHOMA

Oklahoma City: Dulaney Browne Library, Oklahoma City University, 2501 N. Blackwelder   (405) 208-5065

Tulsa: Tulsa City-County Library, 400 Civic Center   (918) 596-7977

OREGON

Eugene: Knight Library, University of Oregon, 1501 Kincaid   (541) 346-3053

Klamath Falls: Oregon Institute of Technology Library, 3201 Campus Dr.   (541) 885-1000

Medford: Jackson County Library Services, 205 S. Central Ave.   (541) 774-8689

Portland: Multnomah County Library, Government Documents, 801 SW 10th Ave.   (503) 988-5123

Salem: Oregon State Library, 250 Winter St. NE   (503) 378-4243

PENNSYLVANIA

Allentown: Allentown Public Library, 1210 Hamilton St.   (610) 820-2400

Bethlehem: The Paul and Harriett Mack Library, Northampton Community College, 3835 Green Pond Rd.   (610) 861-5360

Blue Bell: Montgomery County Community College, The Brendlinger Library, 340 DeKalb Pike   (215) 641-6596

Erie: Erie County Library System, 160 E. Front St.   (814) 451-6927

Harrisburg: Dauphin County Library System, East Shore Area Library, 4501 Ethel St.   (717) 652-9380

Hazleton: Hazleton Area Public Library, 55 N. Church St.   (570) 454-2961

Honesdale: Wayne County Public Library, 1406 N. Main St.   (570) 253-1220

Lancaster: Lancaster Public Library, 125 N. Duke St.   (717) 394-2651

Monaca: Beaver County Library System, One Campus Dr.   (724) 728-3737

Philadelphia: Free Library of Philadelphia,
Regional Foundation Center, 1901 Vine
St., 2nd Fl.   (215) 686-5423

Philadelphia: The Johnson-UGO
Foundation Library, Johnson Memorial
UMC Education Building, 3117
Longshore Ave.   (215) 338-5020

Phoenixville: Phoenixville Public Library,
183 Second Ave.   (610) 933-3013

Pittsburgh: Carnegie Library of Pittsburgh,
612 Smithfield St.   (412) 281-7143

Pittston: Nonprofit and Community
Assistance Center, 1151 Oak
St.   (570) 655-5581

Reading: Reading Public Library, 100 S.
5th St.   (610) 655-6355

Williamsport: James V. Brown Library, 19
E. 4th St.   (570) 326-0536

York: Martin Library, 159 E. Market
St.   (717) 846-5300

PUERTO RICO

Santurce: M.M.T. Guevara Library,
Universidad Del Sagrado
Corazón   (787) 728-1515

RHODE ISLAND

Providence: Providence Public Library, 150
Empire St.   (401) 455-8088

SOUTH CAROLINA

Anderson: Anderson County Library, 300
N. McDuffie St.   (864) 260-4500

Charleston: Charleston County Library, 68
Calhoun St.   (843) 805-6930

Columbia: South Carolina State Library,
1500 Senate St.   (803) 734-8026

Greenville: Greenville County Library
System, 25 Heritage Green
Place   (864) 242-5000

Spartanburg: Spartanburg County
Public Libraries, 151 S. Church
St.   (864) 596-3500

SOUTH DAKOTA

Madison: Dakota State University, 820 N.
Washington   (605) 256-5100

Pierre: South Dakota State Library, 800
Governors Dr.   (605) 773-3131,
(800) 423-6665

Rapid City: Rapid City Public Library, 610
Quincy St.   (605) 394-4171

TENNESSEE

Chattanooga: Center For Nonprofits,
United Way of Greater Chattanooga,
630 Market St.   (423) 752-0300

Johnson City: Johnson City Public Library,
100 W. Millard St.   (423) 434-4450

Knoxville: Knox County Public Library,
500 W. Church Ave.   (865) 215-8751

Memphis: Memphis Public Library and
Information Center, 3030 Poplar
Ave.   (901) 415-2734

Memphis: The Alliance for Nonprofit
Excellence, 606 S. Mendenhall, Ste.
108   (901) 684-6605

Nashville: Nashville Public Library, 615
Church St.   (615) 862-5800

TEXAS

Amarillo: Amarillo Area Foundation,
Grants Center, 801 S. Filmore, Ste.
700   (806) 376-4521

Austin: Hogg Foundation for Mental
Health, Regional Foundation
Library, 3001 Lake Austin Blvd., 4th
Fl.   (512) 471-5041, (888) 404-4336

Beaumont: Beaumont Public Library, 801
Pearl St.   (409) 838-6606

Corpus Christi: Corpus Christi Public
Library, Funding Information Center,
805 Comanche St.   (361) 880-7000

Dallas: Dallas Public Library,
Urban Information, 1515 Young
St.   (214) 670-1400

Edinburg: Southwest Border Nonprofit
Resource Center, 1201 W. University
Dr.   (956) 292-7566

El Paso: University of Texas at El Paso,
Community Non-Profit Grant Library,
500 W. University, Benedict Hall Room
103   (915) 747-5672

Fort Worth: Funding Information Center
of Fort Worth, 329 S. Henderson
St.   (817) 334-0228

Houston: Houston Public Library,
Bibliographic Information Center, 500
McKinney St.   (832) 393-1313

Houston: United Way of Greater Houston,
50 Waugh Dr.   (713) 685-2300

Laredo: Laredo Public Library, Nonprofit
Management and Volunteer Center,
1120 E. Calton Rd.   (956) 795-2400

Longview: Longview Public Library, 222
W. Cotton St.   (903) 237-1350

Lubbock: Lubbock Area Foundation, 1655
Main St., Ste. 202   (806) 762-8061

North Richland Hills: North Richland
Hills Public Library, 6720 NE Loop
820   (817) 427-6800

San Antonio: Nonprofit Resource Center
of Texas, Parkside Office Building, 3737
Broadway, Ste. 295   (210) 227-4333

Tyler: Nonprofit Development Center of
United Way of Tyler/Smith County,
4000 Southpark Dr.   (903) 581-6376

Waco: Waco-McLennan County Library,
1717 Austin Ave.   (254) 750-5941

Wichita Falls: Nonprofit Management
Center of Wichita Falls, 2301 Kell Blvd.,
Ste. 218   (940) 322-4961

UTAH

Moab: Grand County Public Library, 257
E. Center St.   (435) 259-5421

Salt Lake City: Salt Lake City Public
Library, 210 E. 400 S.   (801) 524-8200

Salt Lake City: Utah Nonprofits
Association, 175 S. Main St., Ste.
1210   (801) 596-1800

VERMONT

Middlebury: Ilsley Public Library, 75 Main
St.   (802) 388-4095

Montpelier: Vermont Dept. of Libraries,
Reference and Law Information Services,
109 State St.   (802) 828-3261

VIRGINIA

Abingdon: Washington County Public
Library, 205 Oak Hill St.   (276) 676-
6222

Arlington: Arlington County
Public Library, 1015 N. Quincy
St.   (703) 228-5990

Charlottesville: Center for Nonprofit
Excellence, 401 E. Market St., Exec. Ste.
26 and 27   (434) 244-3330

Fairfax: Fairfax County Public Library,
12000 Government Center Parkway,
Ste. 329   (703) 324-3100

Fredericksburg: Central Rappahannock
Regional Library, 1201 Caroline
St.   (540) 372-1144

Hampton: Hampton Public Library, 4207
Victoria Blvd.   (757) 727-1314

Hopewell: Appomattox Regional Library
System, 245 E. Cawson St.
(804) 458-0110

Norfolk: VOLUNTEER Hampton Roads,
400 W. Olney Rd., Ste. B
(757) 624-2400

Richmond: Richmond Public Library,
Business, Science and Technology, 101
E. Franklin St.   (804) 646-7223

Roanoke: Roanoke City Public Library
System, Main Library, 706 S. Jefferson
St.   (540) 853-2471

Virginia Beach: Virginia Beach Public
Library, 4100 Virginia Beach
Blvd.   (757) 385-0120

WASHINGTON

Kennewick: Mid-Columbia Library, 1620 S. Union St.   (509) 783-7878

Redmond: King County Library System, Redmond Regional Library, Nonprofit and Philanthropy Resource Center, 15990 NE 85th   (425) 885-1861

Seattle: Seattle Public Library, Fundraising Resource Center, 1000 4th Ave.   (206) 386-4636

Spokane: Spokane Public Library, Funding Information Center, 906 W. Main Ave.   (509) 444-5300

Tacoma: University of Washington Tacoma Library, 1902 Commerce St.   (253) 692-4440

WEST VIRGINIA

Charleston: Kanawha County Public Library, 123 Capitol St.   (304) 343-4646

Parkersburg: West Virginia University at Parkersburg, 300 Campus Dr.   (304) 424-8260

Shepherdstown: Shepherd University, Ruth A. Scarborough Library, 301 N. King St.   (304) 876-5420

Wheeling: Wheeling Jesuit University, Bishop Hodges Library, 316 Washington Ave.   (304) 243-2226

WISCONSIN

Madison: Memorial Library, University of Wisconsin—Madison, Grants Information Center, 728 State St., Room 262   (608) 262-3242

Milwaukee: Marquette University Raynor Memorial Library, Funding Information Center, 1355 W. Wisconsin Ave.   (414) 288-1515

Stevens Point: University of Wisconsin—Stevens Point, Library Foundation Collection, 900 Reserve St. (715) 346-2540

WYOMING

Casper: Natrona County Public Library, 307 E. Second St.   (307) 237-4935

Cheyenne: Laramie County Community College, Ludden Library, 1400 E. College Dr.   (307) 778-1205

Gillette: Campbell County Public Library, 2101 S. 4-J Rd.   (307) 687-0115

Jackson: Teton County Library, 125 Virginian Lane   (307) 733-2164

Sheridan: Sheridan County Fulmer Public Library, 335 W. Alger St. 307) 674-8585

About the Editor

Sarah Collins has worked for the Foundation Center since 1989, in various capacities, including manager of bibliographic services and director of the New York Library. Ms. Collins was co-editor of *The Foundation Center's User-Friendly Guide: A Grantseeker's Guide to Resources* (1996), and author of the online tutorial: "Orientation to Grantseeking." She also served as editor of *The Foundation Center's Guide to Winning Proposals* (2003), and as book review editor of *Philanthropy News Digest* for many years.

Ms. Collins holds a Bachelor's Degree from Grinnell College and a Master's Degree in Library Service from Columbia University. Prior to joining the Center, she held executive positions in special and public libraries.